A key resource for the whole church family

SUNDAY SORTED

BOOK 2

Rachel Summers
Eleanor King

Illustrations by Eleanor King

INCLUDES DOWNLOADABLE RESOURCES

kevin mayhew

LINK TO DOWNLOADABLE RESOURCES

http://bit.ly/2monB28

kevin mayhew

First published in Great Britain in 2019 by Kevin Mayhew Ltd
Buxhall, Stowmarket, Suffolk IP14 3BW
Tel: +44 (0) 1449 737978 Fax: +44 (0) 1449 737834
E-mail: info@kevinmayhew.com

www.kevinmayhew.com

9 8 7 6 5 4 3 2 1 0

ISBN 978 1 83858 031 5
Catalogue No. 1501625

Cover design by Rob Mortonson
© Images used under licence from Shutterstock Inc.
Illustrations by Eleanor King
Edited by Linda Ottewell
Typeset by Angela Selfe

Printed and bound in Great Britain

CONTENTS

ABOUT THE AUTHORS

Rachel Summers

Rachel lives in a vicarage in East London with her husband, their five kids, and a veritable menagerie of pets.

A teacher by trade, Rachel moved from teaching in primary schools, through doing work one-to-one with excluded teens, to retraining as a forest school practitioner. She now delivers forest school sessions to nurseries, schools, and the general public.

Sharing the magic of all things slimy and interesting, watching the seasons shift and the weather change, finding the beauty in the commonplace and insignificant, holding space for others to explore: these are some of the things which get Rachel excited.

Eleanor King

Eleanor lives by the seaside in Essex with her husband and three children, and buckets and spades on the doorstep.

She spends a lot of time running different groups in the community, both inside and outside the church, but when she is not doing this she likes to make biscuits, go walking and knit or crochet things that are not too big or complicated.

INTRODUCTION

Sunday Sorted Book 2 is a resource for the whole church family. From vicars looking for sermon inspiration, to the person preparing the intercessions, from the children's work team, to those looking to support the worship of families with young children in church, all will breathe a sigh of relief to get Sunday sorted. It ensures that everyone in church, from the youngest to the oldest, will be exploring and praying through the same themes, ideas, and scriptures. As the family of God we all have things to learn from each other and this book will enable such conversations to happen.

Each Sunday includes the following elements:

Thoughts on the Readings: This pulls Sunday's readings together, unpicking the common themes between them, and listening to how they speak into our context.

Discussion Starters: Some churches like to talk in a small group about the readings before the Sunday service. Others might use these discussion starters as part of a café church style sermon slot.

Intercessions: Offering up prayer on behalf of the worshipping church is an important job but one that often doesn't come with much support or training. The intercessions here will support you in that role, giving you confidence as you make the prayers your own.

Children's Prayer: Sometimes a shorter and simpler form of prayer is useful, either in a children's group, or in the main service to make sure prayer is more readily accessible for all.

Other Ideas!: Something to display, create, or do, that sets the scene for this Sunday and draws people of all ages into worship.

Children's Corner: Most churches have a children's corner, with books and soft toys. This provides suggestions for a simple activity to set out each Sunday, so that very young children and their parents or carers are able to join in the worship with the rest of the church community. It is also a good way of making some kind of provision for children if you are in a church where your numbers don't make a Sunday School viable, as the activities are open-ended enough for children to explore them at their own level.

All-age Talk: A talk suitable for everyone doesn't have to dumb down theological concepts or spiritual insight. These all-age talks allow everyone to understand the scriptures at a level they can understand.

Little Kids' Sunday School and **Big Kids' Sunday School:** Deliberately flexible on age grouping, these suggestions for children's activities keep things playful and explorative, as research shows that children learn best through playing. Some churches may be in the position to offer different activities for different age groups, with the younger kids' sessions including lots of gentle creative fun, and the older kids' sessions encouraging questions as much as giving answers. Other churches may find that they glance over both sessions and either run with a different one each week, or take inspiration from both to fit their group. You will know what will suit your group best.

Colouring Page: Each Sunday there is a downloadable/photocopiable colouring sheet, inspired by the readings. It is suggested that this is available in the children's corner in church, but many young people and adults also find colouring to be something that supports their faith development and aids their worship.

GOD'S WAY OF PEACE

Readings

- Isaiah 2:1-5
- Psalm 122
- Romans 13:11-14
- Matthew 24:36-44

Thoughts on the Readings

Peace is the theme today in both our Old Testament reading and in the psalm – peace between nations, peace within cities, peace within homes. The beautiful reading from Isaiah reminds us that God really will bring peace, in a real and practical way. The things that have been used to harm and destroy, the weapons of war, will be changed and transformed into tools for peaceful activities that help people instead. But God does not transform these weapons through some sort of magical shape change. It is us, as his people, who have to do this. We are the ones who have to actually take these items and repurpose them ourselves, something that may seem strange, risky and unpopular to start with.

The reading from the letter to the Romans and the Gospel reading also emphasise this. For Jesus to be near to us we need to make the choice to behave in a way that allows this to happen. To make the effort not to be offensive to others, or put ourselves in a position where we are likely to argue or upset people. We know that God's way is the way of peace – we have been told this by the prophets like Isaiah right from the beginning. So it is not a secret what we have to do to be ready for Jesus to come.

We need to work towards peace in our families, peace between friends, peace in our communities, peace in our world. This is not always easy, as the things which we do not agree on are often things which are important to us, and are part of our own values. We do not have to be all the same, but if we focus on those things that we share, and treat others with kindness and respect, we know that we are in tune with God's ways.

Discussion Starters

- **How can we keep our own values while respecting others who are different?**

Intercessions

**Lord, as we live in your light,
show us your peace.**

As we come into the light of your presence
we pray that you would be with us,
transforming us
and challenging us
to bring peace in our world.

We bring before you our church at this time
and thank you for everyone involved
in planning and leading worship,
welcoming people,
organising events
and looking after the church buildings.
We pray that you would fill them with your love and strength
and give them a vision of your wonderful kingdom.
**Lord, as we live in your light,
show us your peace.**

As we think of the world we share,
we bring before you any areas of war and conflict,
and particularly remember those places
where there has been violence, hurt and trouble
going back a long time.
We pray that somehow
those things that are used for destruction
and spreading hatred
would be recommissioned,
transformed and restored,
so that your true and lasting peace
may be found.
**Lord, as we live in your light,
show us your peace.**

We bring before you those people
whose mental or physical health
is causing them pain or distress in any way.
We pray for anyone
for whom the financial pressures
at this time of year
can seem impossible.
We also bring into your loving care
anyone separated or estranged
from family or loved ones,
and those who do not have family to care for
or who can care for them.
**Lord, as we live in your light,
show us your peace.**

We bring to mind those
who are nearing the end of their earthly life
and pray that they would feel a sense
of the welcome that is waiting for them
with you in heaven.
We also remember anyone
who has recently died, especially . . .
and those who are missed at this time of year.
As we think of them at peace
in your eternal love,
we ask that you would give comfort and rest
to their families and friends.
**Lord, as we live in your light,
show us your peace.**

As we go out into the week,
we pray that you would help us
to truly live the values of your kingdom,
and that you would show us those peaceful solutions
and the way to find reconciliation
which can only come from you.
Amen.

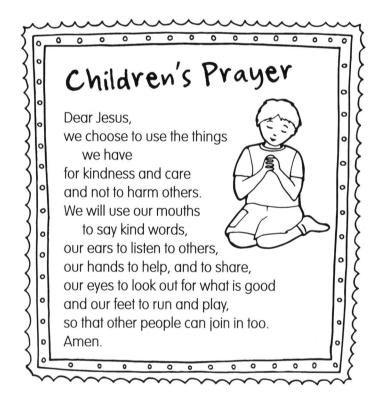

Children's Prayer

Dear Jesus,
we choose to use the things
    we have
for kindness and care
and not to harm others.
We will use our mouths
    to say kind words,
our ears to listen to others,
our hands to help, and to share,
our eyes to look out for what is good
and our feet to run and play,
so that other people can join in too.
Amen.

Other Ideas!

Display some metal gardening tools, with the words from Isaiah.

All-age Talk

Have some toy swords and daggers, and invite someone up to show how they're meant to be used. Quite frightening, you'd think they'd been brought up as a knight! So, that's how they're used for fighting, but God calls us to be people of peace. In the Bible reading today, we heard

how swords could be changed to another use. The metal was useful, there's no point in just throwing it away, but by bashing it with a hammer, people could change their weapons into tools to help them grow crops. Send your volunteer off behind a pillar, a banner, or just a held-up sheet, with a hammer. After a bit of banging, they can come back with a spade or trowel you'd secretly hidden there. Gosh, isn't that clever! Skilled metalworkers in our congregation, obviously.

Bring out some other tools of destruction to show the congregation. Here's a phone for spreading unkind gossip. Here's a copy of a newspaper, telling us to hate those who are different from ourselves. Here's a can of spray paint, for vandalising the fence with a racist comment. Here's a tub of glitter, effectively showering the world in microplastics under the guise of seasonal cheer and goodwill. If we listen to the Bible, it tells us that there are times when we should take tools of destruction and change them, give them a new use, so that they can do good.

So, what about these tools of destruction? Can we change them so they bring about goodness and growth? Sometimes it's really simple. Pass the phone to a volunteer. Do they need to take this phone off and hammer it? No, they just need to use it differently. Maybe they could phone someone who's feeling down, or use it to share positive news. Pass the newspaper to a volunteer. Maybe it is our attitude to something that needs to change. Perhaps we need to fact-check the news we read more carefully, or notice the prevailing narrative of 'them and us' and use that to spur us into action. We could fold and glue the newspaper into compostable bags to line our waste food bins, or use it as wrapping paper for a pass the parcel. Pass the can of spray paint to a volunteer. The spray paint doesn't have a mind of its own, but we do. It could maybe be used for a community project, to cheer up a dull space. Maybe it could be used to share a positive message somewhere where people need to see it, with all permissions, obviously. And what about the glitter? Pass this to a volunteer. Destructive tools can hide in plain sight, disguised as something harmlessly joyful. And yet we don't need to be complicit in adding loads more toxic microplastics into our eco-system. Eco-friendly glitter exists, but how can we use this plastic-based glitter for good? Sometimes the best way to repurpose a tool of destruction is by using it in education. This glitter is here now, so we might as well use it. And each time we use it, we can talk about how we will not be buying any more, about how important it is to be aware of everything we buy and use, and to buy and use with respect for our wonderful planet, given to us by God.

As you come across tools of destruction this week, see how you too can repurpose them to bring about God's goodness and growth.

Children's Corner

Provide a builder's mixing tray full of soil, some pebbles and stones, and some potted plants (real or pretend-fake plants, or knitted plants, or laminated pictures of plants). The children and their parents can together do a bit of gardening. Instead of trowels, forks and spades, the tools they have are toy swords and daggers, which work surprisingly well for this alternative use! They can listen out in the Isaiah reading for God's call to take the things of war and turn them to growing peace.

The colouring sheet shows a child gardening, growing flowers and fruit of peace.

Little Kids' Sunday School

Talk about all the things you can make out of playdough. Sit in a circle and play 'Pass the Playdough'. Pass around a blob of playdough, and when the music stops, the child holding the playdough can shape it into something new. Continue until everyone's had a go.

In Bible times, people would use their weapons when there was a war. But when it was peace, they would take their metal weapons, and use hammers to change them, bashing away at them until they weren't swords any more but a plough to scrape through the ground, or a hook for pruning trees. Just like in our playdough game, they changed those things of war into things of peace.

You can all pick up your pretend swords and shields in one hand, and a pretend heavy hammer in the other. Over a hot fire, you can bang and bash at your swords and shields, until you've changed them. Show each other what useful tools you've made to help things grow.

Tip out a pile of single-use plastic bottles. Here are some tools of destruction, choking our seas and rivers with plastic. Is there some way we can change these into something new, into something that will help things grow?

An adult can cut around the bottle, just under the point where it starts to slope in towards the lid. The children can carefully invert this top part (taking the lid off), and filling the bottom half with water. They can place a bulb (hyacinth or similar) at the point where the lid would have been, so that the base of the bulb is touching the water but the rest of the bulb stays dry, supported by that top part of the bottle. If these are kept in a warm place, they should flower by Christmas.

The children can decorate a label reading 'PEACE' to stick around the bottle.

Big Kids' Sunday School

Provide a big pile of Lego. Put on a timer for a few minutes for the children to create Lego swords, guns, tanks, ships, and aircraft. When the timer stops, look at the Lego constructions of destruction. Read them the reading from Isaiah. Can they guess what you're going to ask them to do next? Put the timer back on, and challenge them to use the bricks they've already used, and repurpose them into farm tools. Tidy away the other bricks, and see how fast and how creatively they can do this job.

We don't tend to use swords much these days. Most of us aren't in the army. So when the Bible tells us to turn our swords into ploughs, it doesn't feel immediately relevant. But we can all think of things that are destructive in our own lives. When kids send bullying messages on social media. When adults drop litter. When soundbites from politicians tell us who to hate.

As you all fiddle with a length of soft aluminium craft wire, crafting a sword, and then changing it from a sword to a gardening tool, talk about these destructive things, and how we can change them and use them to bring about God's peace. You can take your sword/ploughshare home to remind you of this message.

LIVING IN PEACE AND HARMONY

Readings

- Isaiah 11:1-10
- Psalm 72:1-7, 18, 19
- Romans 15:4-13
- Matthew 3:1-12

Thoughts on the Readings

As we hear in the readings for today, both the passage from Romans and from Matthew's Gospel refer back to the words of the prophet Isaiah. Wonderful words, of a wonderful King, from David's family, who would be wise, insightful and powerful. That this passage was treasured through the millennia, and is still special to us today, shows that this promise of a good and wise leader is something that we still value and yearn for. We also hear the contrast of Isaiah's words with the sad reality of what we have seen over history from various people in power. This King, Isaiah tells us, will honour the Lord, and this will show in his actions: treating the poor and needy with fairness, and not judging by appearances. The peace that this King's reign will bring is so all-encompassing that even those animals which used to be enemies are able to dwell peacefully together.

Our psalm, too, is a prayer that God will guide our earthly kings to rule in the same way that he does – to be honest and fair, to give justice to the poor (not just to give out handouts in a patronising manner), to rescue the homeless, and bring peace.

Through listening to these words we can become more aware, not just of the sort of King that God is, but of what we should look for in our own leaders. As well as this, if we have any positions of leadership ourselves, even if these are on quite a small scale, we can identify these principles and apply them to our own situation. There is a real focus on bringing peace and justice, and of empowering those who are poor and marginalised. This is not easy to do, and it is not always popular, but it is right.

The values of fairness, justice, truth and equity have endured through many generations. Paul's letter to the Romans tells us that it is God's Holy Spirit which gives us the power to be able to put these values into action, and live at peace with each other. As we come together, looking towards Jesus, we can find the strength, wisdom and understanding that we need.

Discussion Starters

- How, during this time leading up to Christmas, can we show others God's love, peace and joy? And how can we help those who come into our churches to feel a sense of belonging and acceptance?

Intercessions

**Lord, as you have rescued us,
may we share your love.**

As we come into your loving presence today,
we thank you for the way that you have rescued and saved us,
for the promise of hope that you give us
and the love, security and peace that come from knowing you.

We bring before you our church,
and pray for anyone who will be coming into our buildings
over the next few weeks.
We pray that they would find a sense of peace,
and know that they are loved and welcomed.
We pray for those who lead our worship,
and ask that you would bless those who teach us
and lead us in prayer at this time,
so that together, we may draw closer to you.
**Lord, as you have rescued us,
may we share your love.**

Lord, we thank you for our community,
and we thank you for our world.
We pray particularly for anyone
who feels isolated, lonely
or who feels they cannot find a place that they belong.
We pray for anyone who is homeless
or in insecure accommodation
and thank you for those people and organisations
that work to improve people's housing situations.
**Lord, as you have rescued us,
may we share your love.**

We bring into your loving care
anyone known to us who is finding life hard at the moment,
whether because of poor health,
poverty, family problems
or the stress caused by too much, or too little paid work.
We ask that your peace and healing would be with them,
and that we, as a church community,
would in some way be able to offer support and comfort.
We name before you today those known to us who are ill or in need, including . . .
**Lord, as you have rescued us,
may we share your love.**

We remember today
anyone who is nearing the end of their life.
We ask that your love would surround them
and pray that your peace would be near

to those who love them.
We remember those who have recently died, including . . .
and those who are missed at this time of year, including . . .
Thank you that they are able to rest in your love
in your wonderful heavenly kingdom.
Lord, as you have rescued us,
may we share your love.

As we meet people this week, Lord,
we pray that we will be able to show them your love
and that they will see
the peace and joy that come
from knowing you.
Amen.

Children's Prayer

Dear Lord,
as you care for us
we will care for others.
As you love us
we will love others.
As you listen to us
we will listen to others.
As you look after us
we will look after others.
Amen.

Other Ideas!

Create a poster with the words
'Welcome' and 'Happy Christmas'
written in different languages.

All-age Talk

We are going to visit a zoo in church today.
Invite some volunteers up to the front and
dress them up as different animals: tigers,
sheep, lions, pigs, bears, chickens. Use
whatever dressing-up kit you can find (masks/
hats/onesies) but just make sure you have
some carnivores amongst the mix.

So here's our zoo. Introduce all the animals,
and ask the congregation if there might be any problems with this zoo. The tiger is looking a
bit hungry. He's starting to look at the pig and lick his lips! Call up a zoo keeper to bring about
some order and separate the animals up into different sections to keep them all safe.

But in our reading from Isaiah today we were given a new vision of a time of peace. A time
where the peace would be so great that it would spill over into all of life. A time when the tiger

(hold its hand and bring it forward) would sit side by side with the pig (hold its hand and settle it down beside the tiger). When the chicken would sit on the bear's lap. When the lion and the sheep would play together.

In our Gospel reading we hear St John the Baptist berating the Pharisees and Sadducees coming for baptism. He tells them this isn't just about being seen to be repenting, but the kind of life you live, the fruits your life grows, that shows repentance has really happened. This vision of peace is the place we end up at when we work at forgiving, at loving, at breaking down barriers. The fruits of our life lived in God's company, following his way. It doesn't mean we can let our pet hamster out to play with our cat, but it does mean that God's peace will spill out from us, and start to change the world.

Children's Corner

Lay out toy animals as in the Isaiah reading: a wolf, a lamb, a leopard, a goat, a calf, a lion, a cow, a bear, a baby, a snake, over an upturned bowl covered in a green towel (to be 'God's holy mountain'). The children and their parents can enjoy putting together mismatches of animals, eating and playing together, as a vision of peace for the future.

The colouring sheet shows these animals playing and eating together.

Little Kids' Sunday School

Play 'Lion, lion, lamb'. One person walks round a circle, tapping each person on the head. They say, 'Lion, lion, lion . . .' until they get to someone who they tap and say, 'Lamb', who they then chase all the way around the circle and back to their space.

Some animals are not natural friends. They chase and eat each other. You can't play with your pet hamster and your pet cat at the same time. But in the Bible, we are given this beautiful picture of a world of such peace and harmony that even the animals who are natural enemies are able to live in peace.

The children can make paper plate masks of either a lion (yellow or orange crepe paper or plastic bags cut in strips and stuck around the edge) or a lamb (cotton wool balls stuck on), and walk into church holding hands in pairs, as a visual sign to the congregation of this vision of peace.

Big Kids' Sunday School

Play 'Cat and Mouse'. The children hold hands in a circle. One child is picked to be the cat and one the mouse. The children in the circle have to keep the mouse safe from the cat, who tries to get inside the circle to catch the mouse. If the cat succeeds in getting in, the children can help the mouse to escape outside the circle, and so on.

Cats chase mice. We know this is true; it's just in their nature. Tom and Jerry is a cartoon based on this fact, where the cat chases the mouse and the mouse comes up with more and more cunning ways to outwit the cat. Get someone to read the passage from Isaiah for today.

Here we have an amazing vision of peace, where even these natural enemies are able to live in harmony.

We may not be mice or cats, but how can we begin to live at peace with others, and to create a world of peace around us? Cut a string of paper dolls, with ears, so the children can decorate them as cats and mice, lions and lambs. As they colour, they can talk about ways in which they can bring about God's peace in the world, and write on some of their suggestions as promises on the paper dolls.

SIGNS OF GOD'S KINGDOM

Readings

- Isaiah 35:1-10
- Psalm 146:4-10 or
  Canticle: Magnificat
- James 5:7-10
- Matthew 11:2-11

Thoughts on the Readings

In both the reading from Isaiah today, and in the psalm, we hear about God's promise to look after and defend those who are weak and disadvantaged – the poor, the widows, the orphans and the strangers. Those who do not choose God's kind and generous ways to these people will be accountable to him. We also hear, in both these readings, how God will heal the blind, the deaf and the lame. Looking forward to the birth of Jesus, and what we know about his healing ministry, we can see that these wonderful promises are something that he brought into reality.

There are also some wonderful words about God's blessings being like rain on thirsty land, bringing life and fruitfulness where there was no hope before. This would have been such strong imagery for people living in a desert environment, but if we live in a different climate, we can think about the pictures that nature gives us where we are, telling us about the life-giving blessings of God. This is something that we can look out for this week – perhaps as we see trees which have lost their leaves for the winter, this may bring to mind the thought that the promise of God's wonderful life-giving sunshine will soon prompt little buds to form.

The reading from the letter of James, too, reminds us to think about the way that farmers wait patiently for the life-giving rains to come, so that their summer crops can grow. As we wait to see the fruition of God's good kingdom in our world, we can know that if we are looking to God, we don't need to lose heart or give up. We just need to listen to him, and draw near to him, and things will come together at the time that is right.

Our Gospel reading for today tells of Jesus' healing ministry that was truly fulfilling those ancient words that we heard in the reading from Isaiah and in the psalm. The blind could see, the lame could walk, the deaf could hear, the dead were raised to life, those with leprosy were being healed, and the poor were hearing the good news (good news both in this life – equality and justice – as well as in the next). Through this we can see that those wonderful promises from God were being brought into reality by Jesus.

Discussion Starters

- **What are we waiting for, and looking forward to – both at Christmas time and in terms of God's promises being fulfilled in our world?**

Intercessions

Healing and loving God,
we wait for you.

Lord, as we come before you,
looking forward to Christmas,
we thank you for your promise
to bring healing, peace and hope
to our thirsty world.

We bring into your loving care
our own church, and its leaders.
Look after them, and refresh them.
We also thank you for those who help
with the practical and caring jobs
that need to be done
in our church and in our community.
We thank you for our neighbouring churches
and pray that you would bless them too.
Help us to work together for your kingdom,
showing others your love and care.
Healing and loving God,
we wait for you.

Thank you for our world
and for the beauty that we see
in nature around us.
We pray for any places
where people are waiting for rain,
hoping that it will arrive
and help their crops to grow.
We thank you for reforestation
and water harvesting projects
and for those people who
are thinking of and implementing creative solutions
to help in the harshest of environments.
Healing and loving God,
we wait for you.

We bring into your loving and healing presence
anyone who is waiting to hear
about a health diagnosis
or who is waiting for treatment or assessment.
We pray that you would be with them, Lord,
and comfort them with your everlasting love
and your presence.
We pray for those known to us who are in any sort of pain
or who are unwell at this time,

21

that you would surround them with your healing
and that they would know your care.
We name before you today . . .
**Healing and loving God,
we wait for you.**

As we think of the promises of your heavenly kingdom,
we remember those who have recently died
and those who are particularly missed at this time of year, including . . .
Be near to those people who have loved them
and bring your comfort and your peace.
We also pray that your gentle presence
would be known by those
who are nearing the end of life's journey at this time.
**Healing and loving God,
we wait for you.**

Lord, as we go out of this place,
we ask that you would show us
the signs of hope around us,
so that we can wait in confidence and joy
for your kingdom.
Amen.

Children's Prayer

Dear Jesus,
we are a little bit excited about Christmas.
Actually, more than a little bit excited.
Thank you that you are there
 with us
as we look forward to
 that special time
when we celebrate
 the day
that you were born.
Amen.

Other Ideas!

If you have a Christmas cactus,
or can get hold of one, display
this along with the words from
Isaiah 35:1, 2.

All-age Talk

Prepare some road signs on large pieces of card: circles and triangles, with a red rim if you're
feeling like doing the thing properly! On one, draw a picture of an eye. On another draw a

foot. On another draw a spotty hand, and on another draw an ear. On the fifth, draw a face with crosses for eyes, and on the sixth, draw a thumbs-up.

In our reading from Isaiah we heard about a path in the desert, the Way of Holiness, where all good things would spring up. How can we find where this path is? What do we need to look for?

Well, here we have some road signs to help us find the route. When the followers of John the Baptist were sent to Jesus to find out if he was the person they were waiting for, he sent them back with this message, of way markers, road signs if you like. What do we have on our signs? Hold up the sign with an eye on it. The blind can see! The sign with a foot on it? The lame can walk! Go through all the signs in turn, remembering Jesus' words from the Gospel.

We believe that Jesus is here with us, now. And if he is, these road signs are true as much now as they ever were. Jesus and his way of holiness, that path of joy and beauty and growth through the desert, is characterised by people being healed and being made free. People who can see, not just with their eyes, but who can now see that they are loved. The lame who can now walk, not simply people throwing aside their crutches, but people given God's confidence and courage to step out in faith. People healed, not just from skin conditions, but from being ostracised in society. The deaf hearing, not just through the marvellous skill of audiologists but able to hear the voices of those silenced in society, able to hear the still, small voice of God in the clamour of the world. The dead are raised, as we see over and over again situations which look lifeless being breathed into new life through Christ. People hearing the good news: both the good news of God's love holding us throughout eternity and life everlasting, and the good news for this life too, of social justice and equality.

We need to watch for these road signs. They don't always come in the places we expect. But when we see them, we'll know we are on God's Way of Holiness, his path in the desert, and that Jesus is here.

Children's Corner

Put sand and gravel out on a tray or tuff spot. Provide a basket of extras that the children and their parents can add to the scene: silver foil to be springs of water, green plants (real ones, or pretend ones), and they can use their hands to pat down and smooth a highway through the desert, as the desert bursts forth with fresh green life and springs of water.

The colouring sheet shows this scene of a path through the desert, marked as the **'Way of holiness'**.

Little Kids' Sunday School

Play 'Who Ate the Sweet?'. One person closes their eyes, while you choose a child to go and eat a jelly sweet from a plate. The catch is that it's sitting in a pile of squirty cream, and they can't use their hands. Give them just a few seconds to eat it before getting the child to open their eyes. Can they guess who ate the sweet? Play this enough times so everyone can have a go at eating and at guessing. How on earth did everyone guess each time? The cream on the face and the chewing mouth were quite a giveaway.

John the Baptist was in prison, so he sent some of his friends to Jesus to ask if Jesus was the one they had all been waiting for. Jesus didn't answer yes, and he didn't answer no. But he reminded them of the things that had been happening, the blind being made able to see, the lame to walk, the deaf to hear. He reminded them in similar words to those a prophet called Isaiah had used long, long before. Isaiah had been telling the people how these things would show that God's kingdom had come, and here Jesus was saying, 'Look! Look at these things happening right now!' The answer was obvious. The signs were a complete giveaway.

Ice round biscuits to look like road signs, with red icing around the edge. They can give these out after church to remind everyone to watch for these signs of Jesus' kingdom.

Big Kids' Sunday School

If you can, take the group outside to a paved or concreted area and use a chalk to write on the ground. If not, write on paper stepping stones, and remind children to step across them carefully. Write the signs that Jesus talks about in the Gospel reading, one per flagstone or stepping stone, one in front of another, maybe to the side a little, so they'll form a path. Write other 'signs' on the flagstones around, but this time of things that don't point to God's kingdom: 'people are unkind', 'someone tells a lie', 'a person hurts their friend', for example. The children can try to follow the path that is the Way of Holiness, reading the signs on the ground and stepping on the ones they think show that God's kingdom is here. Can they find the path easily?

These signs are so clear and obvious that when John the Baptist sent his friends to find out if Jesus was the one they had all been waiting for, Jesus didn't even need to answer. He told them the signs and the signs told them everything they were wanting to know. You can read them this bit from the Gospel for today, if you like.

They can make some road-sign cookies today, to give to the rest of the congregation to remind them to look for these signs of God's kingdom. Roll out biscuit dough and cut it into triangles or circles. Poke a lollipop stick in the bottom before baking. If there's time, they can ice them.

GOD WITH US

Readings

- Isaiah 7:10-16
- Psalm 80:1-8, 18-20
- Romans 1:1-7
- Matthew 1:18-25

Thoughts on the Readings

The symbolic and well-known words of Isaiah are echoed in the reading from Matthew's Gospel, when the angel visits Joseph and reassures him that the young woman he is about to marry is fulfilling God's promise from long ago. The name of the baby boy will be called 'Immanuel' – 'God with us' – not just the message that God is present in a general and impersonal sense, but the real gift of God being present on earth as a human baby boy. God has shown that he will keep his promises – now and for eternity.

In many of our wonderful Christmas carols we hear the name of Jesus as 'Immanuel', and think of God coming to be present with us. As we draw near to Christmas Day, let's be ready to receive and experience God's closeness in a new way. We can also think about how the name 'Jesus' also has a special and significant meaning – 'The Lord Saves'. It is so good to know that through knowing Jesus ourselves we can find that saving, rescuing love. Sometimes the situations in our lives, in the lives of those we love, or in the world around us make us feel hopeless and afraid. Thankfully we have Jesus as a friend, to rescue us, to help us and to strengthen us, so that we can find the way ahead.

Our psalm for today also emphasises God's rescuing and saving power, linking again that character of Jesus with that of Israel's God who has been known through the generations as the one who would help them in times of trouble, and would never leave them. And as Paul explains in the letter to the Romans, God's good news has been promised from long ago, and through Jesus we have been chosen to be God's own people. Loved by him, and blessed with his peace. May we know that special sense of belonging, that we are all part of God's eternal family, chosen, rescued and loved.

Discussion Starters

- **How can we make our homes a place where others can know God's presence over Christmas?**

Intercessions

**Jesus, Immanuel,
be with us.**

As we come before you
in thankfulness for Jesus' birth,
we know that we are chosen, loved and rescued
and that you are always near.

We pray, Lord, that your presence would be with us
in our churches this Christmas,
that everyone who comes in to worship,
or to listen to the music, or to enjoy the atmosphere
will know that you are very close.
We also pray that you would bless and refresh
all those who lead us in our worship, and who help in other ways in our community.
**Jesus, Immanuel,
be with us.**

Jesus, we bring our world to you
and particularly remember Bethlehem, the place of your birth
and the areas where you lived, walked and worked.
As we remember your physical presence all those years ago,
we thank you that you are still with us, and pray
that your love and peace would spread throughout the world.
**Jesus, Immanuel,
be with us.**

We pray that your loving presence
and gentle healing
would be with all those who are unwell, in pain or in need at the moment.
We pray for anyone suffering with stress, anxiety or depression
and for those who are in long-term pain.
We also pray that you would be close to anyone
whose limited mobility
means that they feel isolated from their community.
We pray that you would make us aware
of how we can bring your love to those around us too.
We name before you today . . .
**Jesus, Immanuel,
be with us.**

We remember today
those who are nearing the end of life's journey
and are drawing close to the gate of heaven.
We pray that you would be with them in a special way,
and comfort those who love them.
We also think of those known to us who have died
and are particularly thought of at this time of year.

Thank you for the promise you have made to all of us,
that we are chosen by you, and are a part of your family.
We name before you today . . .
Jesus, Immanuel,
be with us.

Lord, as we leave this place of worship today,
we pray that we would bring your love and presence with us
to those that we meet,
so that they may know your peace.
Amen.

Children's Prayer

Jesus – you help us,
you save us, and you
rescue us,
you love us, you are
with us
and we belong to you.
Amen.

Other Ideas!

Use permanent marker pens to decorate some old baubles with the words: 'Immanuel – God is with us'. These can be used to decorate the church, and can be taken home afterwards.

All-age Talk

Write the word 'Emmanuel' in small handwriting on a piece of paper. Send someone to the back of the church, and ask if anyone can turn around and read what's on the paper. Get them to walk forward a bit, and ask again. Keep trying until someone with eagle eyesight can call out the word on the paper. This is a bit like Christmas feels, isn't it? It comes closer and closer until finally it's close enough for us to see it.

This word, Emmanuel, means God with us. As we prepare for Christmas, we think of God drawing near to us. As we draw near to Christmas, we ready ourselves for Jesus, drawing near to us. But God doesn't come to us from a distance. He's not like a tiny word written on a piece of paper, that we can't see until it's close, although it is true that in the person of Jesus, God drawing close to us, God being with us, allows us to see God more clearly.

Maybe it's more like this. Gather a clump of people and tie a length of rope around them. Make sure they're of a height, so the rope can reach around their nice safe middles and nowhere near important bits, like necks! As the rope draws closer around them, they end up drawing closer to each other. And Emmanuel, God with us, also draws us closer to those around us, just as we are drawn closer to God.

But God isn't someone or something 'out there', detached from us, from who we are and from the human condition. In the person of Jesus, of Emmanuel, he comes as one of us, a human like ourselves. Put your hand on your heart and see if you can feel it beating. Emmanuel, God with us, in the person of Jesus, has drawn near to us, closer than a piece of paper, closer than a length of rope, closer even than our own breath or heartbeat.

Children's Corner

Bring along a Nativity set figure of Joseph and of an angel, so that as the Gospel reading from Matthew is proclaimed, the children and their parents and carers can act it out. Bring along fridge magnet letters or similar to spell out 'Jesus' and 'Emmanuel', so that parents and carers can help their child to form these names and talk about what they mean.

The colouring sheet has double-sided baubles to colour (and stick together so they can be hung on Christmas trees once taken home), decorated with 'Jesus' on one side and 'God saves' on the other, and 'Emmanuel' on one side and 'God with us' on the other.

Little Kids' Sunday School

Play 'Beanbag Toss'. You can use rolled-up socks if you don't have beanbags. The first person throws a beanbag, and subsequent people try to throw their beanbag so it's as close to that first beanbag as it can be.

Christmas is getting close now, isn't it! A few weeks ago, we were a bit like this beanbag (point to a beanbag a long way away from its target), but now we're almost right on top of Christmas, like this one (point to a beanbag that's really close to the target). It's exciting to think that very soon we'll be there, and it'll be Christmas Day!

Today in church the grown-ups are hearing how Joseph had a visit from an angel in a dream, who told him not to be afraid to marry Mary, and how the baby she was pregnant with was God's own son, and would be named Emmanuel. Hang on a sec. But we know he was named Jesus! Yes, that's true, and everyone's name means something. The angel was explaining who Jesus would be, rather than what would be on his birth certificate.

Emmanuel means 'God with us'. So, unlike our clumsy attempts to get our beanbags close to the target, God himself has come, born as a human, to be one of us, to be with us. Provide some festive coloured salt dough or air-dried clay, and fridge magnet letters, so the children can print the name Emmanuel into the clay, as a Christmas decoration.

Big Kids' Sunday School

Play the 'Wind-up Fish' game. Each team has a length of string tied to a stick. At the other end of the string, at the other side of the room, is tied a paper fish. At 'go!', the first member of the team twiddles their stick round and round to reel in the fish. When the fish is caught, the next member of the team pulls the fish back to the end of the hall, and the person after that reels it in again.

Just like our frantic pulling to reel the fish closer and closer, we get frantically busy trying to get Christmas closer and closer. But with Christmas, it doesn't at all depend on how busy we are for it to arrive. Jesus will still have been born, regardless of whether we've got cards written for everyone in our class, or whether we've learned all our words for the carol service.

Read the Gospel reading for today, listening out for the name Jesus is given: Emmanuel, God with us. In Jesus, God is with us, and has drawn close to us, without any frantic action on our part.

The children can cut the letters to spell EMMANUEL out of Christmas wrapping paper, and stick them on triangles of thick paper or card, threaded on string to make Christmas bunting. They can hang it up in their homes, and when they feel like they have to manically get things ready for Christmas, they can look at it and remember that Christmas is when we remember Emmanuel, God drawing close to us.

CHRISTMAS DAY

Readings

- Isaiah 52:7-10
- Psalm 98
- Hebrews 1:1-4 (5-12)
- John 1:1-14

Thoughts on the Readings

Peace, justice, comfort, salvation and joy. These are the things which were longed for in years gone by, when Isaiah's audience listened in hope and expectation to his words. And these are the things that we also all need today. Isaiah tells us what a beautiful sight it is to see a messenger announcing these wonderful promises, sent by God – we do not need to worry or be afraid any more, because God has heard us, and will help us.

John's Gospel, too, tells us of this wonderful good news that has come through Jesus. We hear how Jesus was there right from the beginning, and is the source, with God, of all that is good. By becoming an actual human being and living on our very own planet, Jesus brings God's presence to us in a remarkable and incredible way. John tells us that through Jesus, all God's kindness and truth has come down to us. Of course, it was always there, but through living on earth Jesus brought this good and wonderful knowledge and experience of God's love right to the place where we live.

It is this experience and relationship with Jesus which is so special to us, as Christians, and at Christmas we are particularly aware of how wonderful it is that God came to live on earth with us. Jesus understands us, he knows what it is like for us to live as part of a human community, and through him we can know God's remarkable, wide-reaching and everlasting love, something we can share with those around us too.

In our reading from the letter to the Hebrews, we also hear about this surprising and amazing thing – that Jesus, from the wonderful, glorious setting of God's heaven, comes to live with us in our ordinary world. But as God values this place where we live, so we should not take our own setting for granted – God sees us as his beautiful and loved children, and his world as good, his creation is majestic – and through Jesus we can find a glimpse of this holiness around us too.

Discussion Starters

- **What do we see around us that shows us God's glory?**

Intercessions

**Light of the world,
bring us your peace.**

As we celebrate on this special day,
we give thanks that Jesus was born into a human family
on our own earth
and we pray that God's wonderful, peaceful presence
would be with us and our families today.

As we think of our church,
we thank you for those who teach us, inspire us,
lead us in our worship
and share bread and wine with us.
We remember our brothers and sisters
across the world,
celebrating Jesus' birth
with a diversity of traditions,
prayers and music.
We pray that you would bless them
and the other churches in our more local community.
**Light of the world,
bring us your peace.**

We bring into your loving care
our needy world.
All those places that desperately need
the joy and the peace that you have promised to bring.
We pray that you would give wisdom to the decision makers,
stamina to the peace makers
and help us to mobilise practical resources
where we can.
**Light of the world,
bring us your peace.**

We remember today
those whose Christmas Day
is difficult, painful, lonely or uncomfortable.
We pray that your loving presence
would bring healing and comfort,
hope and joy.
**Light of the world,
bring us your peace.**

We pray today for anyone in hospital for any reason
and also remember those women who will give birth today,
that your presence would strengthen and comfort them.

We also pray for those
who are carrying on in spite of illness or pain
and ask that the joy of Christmas
would particularly be with them at this time.
We name before you . . .
**Light of the world,
bring us your peace.**

We remember with love
those known to us who have died,
whether recently or further back in time.
Thank you that they are safely with you
in eternity,
resting in your love,
surrounded by your kindness
and filled with your joy.
We name before you today . . .
**Light of the world,
bring us your peace.**

Jesus, as we celebrate your birth today,
may our lives be filled with your presence,
your love, your hope and your joy.
Amen.

Children's Prayer

When you were born, Jesus,
you were a cuddly, wriggly,
human baby boy,
full of the love
that God gives to us all.
Thank you that you know
what it is like to be
a baby, a toddler, a child
and a grown-up.
Thank you that you
understand us
and thank you that you
love us too.
Amen.

Other Ideas!

Wrap up some slices of Christmas cake to give out. People can either take these home or give them to a neighbour or friend who may be isolated or lonely.

All-age Talk

Bring a big bunch of keys with you today. You're acting as something of an estate agent. Is there anyone out there in the market for a new house? Bring the first person up, and talk to them of the road you're walking down to find their new house. Here's a road of red brick terraced houses, and amongst the middle of them is the house for you: a red brick terraced house just like the rest. Pass them their new key.

Bring the second person up. Here's an estate of new-build houses, with square flat lawns, and winding drives. Amongst the middle of them is the house for you, just like the rest. Pass them their new key.

Bring the third person up. Here's a block of flats, you'll just take them in and press the button to go up to the middle floor. Here's your new flat, in the middle of the others, and just the same. Pass them their new key.

Bring up the fourth person. Here you are at a festival campsite, and here, in the middle of all these tents is your new tent! It doesn't actually lock, but hey, you can have a key too, anyway, so you don't feel left out!

If your local housing context doesn't fit in any of those above, feel free to tweak it so that it's relevant to those listening.

We may have an opinion about what kind of house we'd like to live in (and there aren't many people who'd rather live full time in a tent!), but the important thing about a house isn't what it looks like, but the life that happens inside it. In our Gospel reading today, we heard that God 'made his dwelling among us'. God has moved in, right inside of our context, bringing his life and love into and amongst the places we live. It can be literally translated as 'pitched his tent among us', with all that implies about closeness, immediacy, and expanding our community.

And it's not just a house amongst us that God has moved into. It's a human body. Today at Christmas we remember that God, born as Jesus, took on a human body with all our joys and sorrows. And unlike those houses where we were handed the keys earlier, God moving in isn't an outsider coming to stay for a while, but the architect, the creator, coming to live amongst his own creation, inside it.

Children's Corner

Provide a Nativity set, wrapped up piece by piece in Christmas wrapping paper. The children and their parents and carers can unwrap it, and set it up, whispering about how Jesus is sent to us as a gift so that we can see God's love in the world.

The colouring sheet has Jesus, lying in a manger, looking like a proper baby with tiny fingers and toes, and words to colour from John's Gospel:
'And the word became flesh and lived among us'.

Little Kids' Sunday School

Give the children a much-needed chance to relax with some free play. Christmas can be a hectic morning. Lay out lots of small-world play, with small-world figures and animals, blocks and bricks, sheets and scarves. They can make themselves their own little kingdom or universe.

Spend some time looking at the miniature worlds they've made. Get down low and spot all the details. Imagine you are tiny, and walking around inside. What might you do? Where might you go?

At Christmas we remember that God, our God who made the whole world, was born as Jesus, as a tiny baby. It's a bit like us, not just looking down at our tiny worlds from above, but becoming part of them, being a small-world figure just like this one. We are right to think 'wow!' about God and his amazing creation, but we can also get to know him and love him as Jesus, a human like us.

They can make a small-world baby Jesus to take home and add to their own play, by wrapping a small, oval blob of modelling clay in a square of white fabric.

Big Kids' Sunday School

Provide blankets, cushions, chairs, tables and broomsticks, so the children can construct their own indoor den.

Read them the Bible reading for today from the Gospel of John, while you sit inside their den. Draw their attention to the bit where it says he 'made his dwelling among us'. Tell them that in the original language, the words that are used are that he 'pitched his tent among us'. Here we are, inside our tent, too!

They can make a paper tent out of an isosceles triangle. Make a cut up a few centimetres at the middle of the short side, and fold these flaps out to look like the flaps of a tent. They can glue a piece of paper behind this and draw baby Jesus inside the tent, to remember that he came to live among us.

ESCAPE TO EGYPT

Readings

- Isaiah 63:7-9
- Psalm 148
- Hebrews 2:10-18
- Matthew 2:13-23

Thoughts on the Readings

Today we hear how Joseph, again, is told in three separate dreams about what he should do to keep his special little boy safe. After that previous visit by an angel in a dream who told him that Mary was going to have a baby, perhaps Joseph was less shocked to hear from God in his dreams this time. After all, Jesus' birth was pretty remarkable, with visits from the shepherds, angels and wise men.

Perhaps he was more tuned in, more open to listen to what God was going to say to him, because he knew that God had given him this very special job, to look after Mary and care for Jesus as he grew up.

As Joseph listened to and acted on God's words, and the future unfolded, it became clear why God had told him to do these things – first to escape into Egypt, and then to move to Galilee.

Sometimes it is hard to understand why circumstances seem to be leading us in a particular direction. Sometimes we are afraid of something we know, and can't work out the way ahead. All these things we can bring to God in prayer, and he will hear us. He will always give us wisdom, and will help us to find the best way forward. We won't be surprised to hear him speak, as this is what we are expecting, hoping for and listening out for. This may be through a dream, like Joseph, or through something someone says, through the necessity of particular circumstances or in another way.

As Isaiah tells us, and as we hear in the letter to the Hebrews, God has a good track record of helping, rescuing and saving his people. This may be through sending an angel from heaven to give us a message, or perhaps through another person being an 'angel' to us in our time of need. As we know, this often does not need to be anything complicated to make a big difference to us. Let's look out for where we can be angels to others too.

Discussion Starters

- **What do we, in our current community and society, need rescuing from?**

Intercessions

Lord, we know you love us,
thank you for rescuing us.

Lord, we thank you
for the blessings and gifts you have given us.
The gift of Jesus' birth
and the blessing of your presence.
Be with us now, as we come before you.

As we bring before you our church, we pray
that we would be a place of safety, and show your love,
somewhere people can find a sense of belonging
as they come to understand that they are part of your family.
We pray that you would save us
from any unkind thoughts or words,
so that your inclusive welcome is clear for everyone to see.
Lord, we know you love us,
thank you for rescuing us.

We bring to mind our needy world
and particularly think of those places
where there has been conflict over Christmas,
whether nationally, locally, in a community
or within a family.
We pray that you would bring your peace, love,
healing and understanding
into these situations.
Lord, we know you love us,
thank you for rescuing us.

Lord, we pray that your loving care and your healing
would be with those who need it most at this time:
those suffering with invisible conditions,
those waiting for a diagnosis or treatment,
those who are in pain,
and those who are quietly worried about a health condition.
We pray that you would be with them
and that they would know your saving love.
We bring before you today . . .
Lord, we know you love us,
thank you for rescuing us.

We remember at this time
anyone who is close to the end of life's journey,
whether they are aware of this or not.
We pray for those who care for them
and those people who worry about them.

Be there with your wonderful, saving presence, Lord.
We also remember with love
those who have died,
and name before you today . . .
Lord, we know you love us,
thank you for rescuing us.

Lord, as we go out from this place
we pray that your presence would be with us.
We will walk through the week with you beside us,
knowing that we can bring everything to you.
Amen.

Children's Prayer

If we're worried, sad or angry
or don't know what to do,
thank you that you've always said
that we can come to you.
You'll hold us and you'll love us,
you'll listen to us too
and then we'll know that
      we can be
friends with you.
Amen.

Other Ideas!

Have a 'sharing' noticeboard
where people can list things
that they either have spare, or that
they need. In this way we can be
angels to others.

All-age Talk

Today you'll need a comfort blanket, a teddy,
a tv remote control and a mug.

We all have times when we don't feel safe,
when things have got scary or feel out of
control. As little children we sometimes reach
out for our comfort blanket, something that
feels familiar. Maybe we were wrapped in it
as a tiny baby, or have always held it to go to
sleep. When we're a little older, a cuddle with
a favourite teddy can help. Sometimes hospitals give out teddies to sick children to give them
that comfort that they need when they feel scared.

As adults we have things we use to help us feel safe. Maybe when we're having a bad
day, we curl up in front of the telly and binge our way through our favourite box set. Perhaps

we make ourselves a nice mug of hot chocolate, and sip it slowly as the warm, sugary drink comforts us and helps us feel safe.

Often our ways to feel safe involve battening down the hatches, retreating to somewhere familiar and comfortable. Self-care is really important, and it's good to know when you need to look after yourself, and have ways to do that.

Joseph was told in a dream that he, Mary, and their baby were not safe where they were. He must have been frightened, not just for himself, but with that fear that comes when you have a young child who is dependent on you for their safety. It must have been tempting for him to retreat further into what was, after all, his home town, a familiar place, full of familiar people. And yet that's not what God tells him to do. God tells him to take Mary and the baby and to travel, to escape into Egypt, to somewhere far from home.

How can this be safe? It feels really counterintuitive to do something so risky and perilous when you're looking for safety. But in this situation, God tells them to go, and they do. And that going is what saves them. We see this kind of story over and over again in the news: families pushed to the point where to travel a long and dangerous journey is the safe option, safer than staying behind where things are familiar. Being where God told Joseph to go was the safe place, because we can trust God, and because we know that God is in that place already. As we hear of others taking their little ones on a perilous journey to safety, let us remember that this was also part of Jesus' experience. Not only is God already in the places we travel to, but God in Jesus has already been there, has walked where we walk, in the most frightening of places.

We don't need a blanket or a teddy, a box set or a mug of hot chocolate to feel safe. We can know that God loves us, cares for us, and holds us safe, no matter how frightening our situation might feel.

Children's Corner

Use your Nativity set figures of Joseph, Mary, baby Jesus, and an angel, and provide a donkey and a scrap of fabric for a bed. The children can play through the story of Joseph lying down to sleep, an angel speaking to him in his dream, and him bundling up Mary and baby Jesus and them all escaping to Egypt.

The colouring sheet has Joseph, lying asleep, with a dream-bubble of their imminent escape to Egypt.

Little Kids' Sunday School

Hide some pictures about Egypt around your meeting room: pyramids, mummies, hieroglyphics, the sphynx. Set the children off to find them all and bring them back to you, then spread them out on the floor or a table so you can all see them. Can they work out what the pictures have in common? Do they know what country they're all from? I wonder if any of them have ever been on holiday to Egypt? They might not realise how close it is to Bethlehem, where Jesus was born.

Today we're going to hear about some people taking a trip to Egypt. Joseph was busy looking after Mary and baby Jesus, making sure they were safe and happy. One night he fell asleep (you can all fall asleep), and had a dream where he was visited by an angel (dress someone up as an angel in a Nativity costume). The angel told him that baby Jesus was in danger, and that they should escape to Egypt where they would be safe. So Joseph woke up (you can yawn and stretch), got up, and packed his bags (pack your bags). He took Mary and baby Jesus and set off. Up the mountains, down the mountains, through the hot deserts and the cold nights. It was a scary journey but he did it because he knew Jesus needed to be safe. Eventually they arrived at Egypt, just as the angel had told him to do, and the family lived in safety.

Make some rice crispie cakes (by melting fairly-traded chocolate in a bowl and mixing it with rice pops), to sell after church, so that the children can send some money to a charity supporting refugees, who've had to leave their home and travel to a place of safety.

Big Kids' Sunday School

Look at newspaper articles about refugees, and try to identify the places mentioned on a world map. Does anyone know someone who's a refugee? Maybe some of the children in your group have come to this country for safety. Well, actually all of us here know someone who was a refugee. Surprised? It's Jesus.

When he was a baby, living in Bethlehem, it became clear that this wasn't a safe place for him to be. The king wanted him dead. If they'd have stayed, he would have been in real danger for his life. Luckily, God sent an angel to warn Joseph in a dream, and to tell him to take Mary and the baby and escape to Egypt. Can you find Bethlehem and Egypt on a map? Are you surprised how close they are? Imagine Joseph, Mary, and baby Jesus travelling there. It may not be that far but it's a good few hundred miles, and back in those days they didn't have trains or cars.

The children can set up a hot chocolate stall for after church, so they can raise some money to send to a charity that supports refugees. They can mix up hot chocolate powder, hot water, and milk in teapots, so they can pour them out, and provide marshmallows, squirty cream, and sprinkles. They can write some labels and posters so that the congregation members understand what they are doing and why.

GOD'S WISDOM

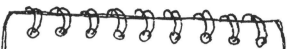

Readings

- Jeremiah 31:7-14 or
  Ecclesiasticus 24:1-12 (also called Sirach)
- Psalm 147:13-21 or
  Canticle: Wisdom of Solomon 10:15-21
- Ephesians 1:3-14
- John 1:(1-9) 10-18

Thoughts on the Readings

As we hear the reading from Ecclesiasticus and the canticle from the Book of Wisdom, the wonderful poetry paints a picture of Wisdom herself coming and dwelling with God's people, leading them out of Egypt and rescuing them by parting the Red Sea. Wisdom is also described as opening the mouths of those who cannot speak and giving voice to the youngest members of the community.

It is interesting to hear Wisdom described in female form like this, and the clear link to the vastly significant events of the rescue from Egypt clearly identifies Wisdom as one with God.

It is not something we hear that often, but is useful to us and can remind us that God is so much more than that which we can understand or imagine. Although, of course, Jesus was born as a human baby boy, and lived on earth as a human man, God is not 'just' male or female. Whatever our gender, we are created in God's wonderful and beautiful image, and there are things in all of us that reflect God's glory.

Just as we heard how Wisdom was with God the creator right from the beginning, our readings from John's Gospel and the letter to the Ephesians tell us how Christ was with God before the world was even created. As people of faith, we can know that we are part of God's family – that God's presence stretches back far before the beginning of the existence of the human race, even before our own planet existed, and will continue far into the future as well.

Once again, we are awed by the enormity and the eternity of the nature of God – particularly amazing when we have been thinking of the birth of Jesus into our world as a human baby. And this amazing God is someone we can worship, know, love – someone who will always be close to us through our lives here on earth.

It is so often God's quiet wisdom and leading that help us in our most difficult situations – whether it is knowing what to say, what to do, or through some understanding of a situation which gives us an insight into what is really going on.

Discussion Starters

- **How is wisdom different from intelligence or knowledge? Could these qualities be personified in the same way – and what does this tell us about God?**

Intercessions

**Wisdom of God,
guide us and help us.**

As we come into your eternal presence,
we ask that you would be with us,
that your wisdom would lead us
and strengthen us
and that your light would guide us.

Thank you, dear Lord,
that you were there with us and our church community
right from the start.
We pray that your Wisdom
would give us the strength we need
to reach out to our neighbours in love.
And that you would refresh us all,
in whatever way we serve you.
**Wisdom of God,
guide us and help us.**

God of eternity,
we bring you our world
with all its struggles,
but also all the things which are so special and wonderful.
We pray for the natural environment,
that we would remember to treat it with respect,
and we pray that your wisdom would guide us
in the best way to work together
to look after our earth
and all the creatures which live on it.
**Wisdom of God,
guide us and help us.**

We bring into your loving and healing presence
anyone who particularly needs your care at this time:
those who feel trapped in a particular situation
and can't see the way ahead,
anyone weighed down by stress or anxiety,
those who are weary and tired
and anyone in physical pain.
We ask that your love
would be made known to them,
so that they can know that you are always with them.
We name before you today . . .
**Wisdom of God,
guide us and help us.**

Eternal God, thank you
that you were there
long before we were
and long before the creation of the world.
Thank you, too, that your love lasts forever.
We remember today those people
who are about to enter life in eternity with you
and we also bring to mind
those who are now living in heaven,
worshipping you, together with all the angels and saints.
We particularly remember this week . . .
Wisdom of God,
guide us and help us.

As we go out into the world this week, Lord,
we pray that we would be aware of your
eternal, and enormous love
and know that you are always with us.
Amen.

Children's Prayer

Wisdom of God,
fill us.
Love of God,
strengthen us.
Light of God,
guide us.
Amen.

Other Ideas!

Show a relaxing video or find a photo of a misty landscape, to help people think about that image of Wisdom in the first reading, covering the earth like a mist.

All-age Talk

Bring along a hula hoop (the one you exercise with, not the crisp), and lay it on the floor or a table where people can see it. Ask for a volunteer. You want to count how many teddies you've got in this bag. Shake them out into the hoop, and get the volunteer to count them. If you use hymn number boards, you might like to use one to keep track of your numbers coming up; otherwise use a flip chart. So, we've got a hoopful of ten teddies.

What about children? Can they all squeeze inside the hoop? Maybe their feet can! Count them, and put the number up.

What about hymn books? (Or something else in your church that you have quite a lot of, that won't matter if it gets dropped!) Send someone to the back to carry up the leftover hymn books, and put them in the hoop, and count them. Put this number up, too.

What about letters and numbers? Can someone count how many of those will fit inside the hoop? It might take us quite a while. What about if we filled the hoop with sand? Or if we tried to count how many atoms are in all the things we've filled it up with so far?

What if we could make our hoop much bigger, so that the whole church fitted inside? Or our street? Or our town? What about if it was big enough to fit our whole country inside? Or even our planet? There would be a heck of a lot of stuff in it then! I'm not sure the numbers would fit on our hymn board any more!

But if we put everything there ever is, and ever has been, and ever will be, all within the most enormous hoop, there'll only be one everything! In our Bible readings today, we heard how in the beginning, before there was a hoop or anything in it, God was there. How all that there is, all that there ever has been and all that there ever will be, is held within God's love. And that we are able to meet this God, a God who can hold the whole universe, in the person of Jesus. Our God, who is so huge that he has filled the whole of the universe with his loving presence, was also able to squeeze himself into the person of a real live baby, so we could know him and love him.

Children's Corner

Chalk or tape an outline of a baby on the table or the floor, and provide a whole host of small objects and toys to fill it in with. As the children fill it in, whisper about how the God who is so huge that he fills the universe with his love and presence, squeezed himself into the person of a real live baby, so we could know him and love him.

The colouring sheet has the wonders of the universe, swirling around, with baby Jesus in the centre.

Little Kids' Sunday School

Have some photos of different things, from tiny (ant? tardigrade?) through middle-sized (zebra? house?) to bigger (ship? mountain?), to huge (planet earth? galaxy?). Sort these into order, chatting about them as you do so.

We've got a universe with so much variety in it. There are tiny things, and there are huge things. There are things that are really familiar to us, and some things we've never yet seen. And the God who made it all, who is bigger than all of it, who is outside all of it, did something extraordinary. At Christmas, he stepped inside his creation, being born as a tiny human baby. All this greatness and hugeness, suddenly contrasted with something small and helpless. But it is because of Jesus being born as a human, like us, that we are able to know God.

Give each child a paper equilateral triangle. They can draw or stick on as much of the universe as they can all over it. Then fold in each of the points, so it makes a much smaller triangle, and stick or draw a baby on the front. They can take this home to remind them that the God who created the expanses of the universe was born as a human in the person of Jesus, a human baby.

Big Kids' Sunday School

Spread photos of things in space taken with telescopes, and tiny things taken with atomic microscopes, and enjoy looking at them together. Can the children sort these into very large things and very small things?

Sometimes when we're looking at things at the extremes of the scale, it's hard to tell them apart. The Gospel reading for today does that kind of zooming from one extreme to another. Read them the passage from the beginning of John's Gospel. One minute we're thinking about everything that was made, about God's creation, about before the beginning of all time, and then we're shrunk right down to human size, to this huge God coming amongst us as a human person.

Follow some instructions online to make an eight-pointed transforming ninja star. You'll need eight squares of paper, and by a few simple folds, you'll be able to attach them together, and make an object that can be either a circle, or shrink down into a star. The circle can remind you of everything in creation being made and loved by God. As you shrink it down, you can remember how in Jesus, God became a human like us, stepping inside his creation, and taking on the form of a tiny baby.

THE VISIT OF THE WISE MEN

Readings

- Isaiah 60:1-6
- Psalm 72:(1-9) 10-15
- Ephesians 3:1-12
- Matthew 2:1-12

Thoughts on the Readings

As we hear in the words from the prophet Isaiah, long before the birth of Jesus, God's glory will shine on his people and even kings from far away will be drawn to this light. There will be a sense of pride within the nation, not because of some blind nationalism, but a genuine joy that God is the true King and that the nations are celebrating this together.

Sometimes in church we can feel a little apologetic for the things that we do, as a religious organisation, but then we can be surprised by the way that those who are part of the state system can start to acknowledge what we as a church community can offer. Churches can be a great help to those groups who are isolated, and often provide practical help to people who are homeless or in need of emergency food or clothes. Through tuning in to God's priorities, as described in our psalm today, such as defending the poor and helping the homeless, those people who would normally not have much to do with church can see that there is something wonderful and special about what God's love can enable his people to do. In church we can offer a different, inclusive and empowering approach, when the things that we can do to help others are done with the principle that we are all children of God. There is no 'us' and 'them' any more.

In our Gospel reading we hear of the wise men from the East who came to see Jesus. They must have been people of some status and importance, to be able to have an audience with King Herod. However, they were also people of learning, wisdom, understanding and insight. They had read the old prophecies and knew that this was something very significant that had happened in Bethlehem. Unlike King Herod, they were delighted that a new king was going to be born, one who would implement God's values. As people of God themselves, this did not make them feel threatened or jealous at all. As they listened to God, they knew that they were not to return to King Herod. They recognised the authority of God's message and obeyed this, even if it went against Herod's instructions. If we, too, tune in to God's message and values, we will also know when it is the right time to stand up to those in authority. Perhaps this might be through campaigning on a particular environmental or social issue, or getting involved in some sort of practical action.

Discussion Starters

- **How can we know when we need to stand up to those in authority?**

Intercessions

**King of heaven,
we worship you.**

As the wise men followed the star to find Jesus,
may you light our way
on our journey
as we draw near to you.

We pray, dear Lord,
for all those who lead us in our churches.
We pray that you would give them wisdom, direction
and discernment
as they listen to you.
We pray that as a church community
we would be a light in the place where we live,
so that others are drawn to you.
**King of heaven,
we worship you.**

As we think of our world,
we ask that your priorities and values
would be known in every place
without exception,
so that our world can be somewhere
that all people are valued,
and that we would work together
to fight poverty, injustice and violence.
We pray that you would give us the courage
to stand up for what is right
and that you would inspire us
with your creativity and wisdom
as we do this.
**King of heaven,
we worship you.**

We bring into your loving care
anyone travelling on a long journey at this time,
whether this is for work, visiting family
or on a holiday.
We also particularly pray for anyone
who has been forced to travel to another country
as a refugee.
We pray that you would be with them
and that they would know you, always there,
guiding them with your light and love.
We also bring into your healing presence
those people known to us who are in need at the moment, including . . .
**King of heaven,
we worship you.**

As we remember those who have gone before us
and are now in heaven with you,
we thank you for your promise
that you will never leave us
and will always be there to guide us,
wherever we go.
We pray that you would be with those
who are on the last stretch of their journey towards heaven,
and we also remember with love
those who have died, including . . .
King of heaven,
we worship you.

Thank you, Lord,
that as the wise men recognised and worshipped
the baby King, Jesus, in a very ordinary setting on earth,
we can also draw near to you
and encounter you,
just where we are.
Amen.

Children's Prayer

Dear Lord,
just like the wise men,
we'll follow your light.
Just like the wise men,
we'll do what is right.
Just like the wise men,
we'll listen to you,
getting closer to Jesus
and loving him too.
Amen.

Other Ideas!

Have a star map or globe on display, or show a picture of the night sky.

All-age Talk

Get the front of church as gloomy as you can, and set up a nice bright reading lamp. Ask for a volunteer to come and read something. As they come up, pass them a short paragraph about one of the activities supported or run by your

church. Hopefully they'll naturally step over to the light to read it but you may need to nudge them that way!

Call up another volunteer to read another paragraph about a different activity run by or supported by your church. And then a third.

There is some brilliant, life-changing stuff going on, and we should be proud of it. Sometimes as a church we can feel a little awkward or embarrassed about the stuff we do, but those outside the church, when they see it or realise it's happening, are quite often blown away by how useful it is to society. Church toddler groups, for example, are one of the major players in supporting young families in our country at the moment, and they all just happen through Christians following God's call to service, turning up, and making them happen.

And did you notice how in the gloom at the front of the church today, the readers all stepped over to the reading light to read their paragraph? They didn't have to have 'first stand in the light' as their instruction; the light drew them naturally to itself. We heard in our reading from Isaiah that 'Nations will come to your light, and kings to the brightness of your dawn.' The light is what draws people, they see it, and are attracted to it, because they know they need it.

As we seek to follow God, to live in the light ourselves, those from outside the church will see this light and be drawn to it, whether they can articulate this or not. We don't so much need to stand up and tell people to come, but it's what we do as the church, our acts of service, how we live as a people of light, that will draw them to come and meet Jesus themselves.

Children's Corner

Provide glow-in-the-dark stars, sticky tack and torches. Drape a sheet over a table, allow the children to crawl inside, and tape the stars on the underside. They can shine the torch on the stars to charge them, then lie in the dark, looking up at the stars above, as their parents and carers whisper to them the story of the coming of the wise men.

The colouring sheet shows the wise men pointing towards the star, with Bethlehem on the horizon.

Little Kids' Sunday School

Play 'Follow My Leader', and put a tinsel or glowstick crown on the leader's head. After a while, you can change the leader so that everyone gets a turn.

Today we're thinking about some wise men, sometimes we call them kings, following a light in the sky, following the star to find baby Jesus. Make your room as dark as you can, and read them by torchlight a story about the wise men from a children's Bible, shining the torch from page to page as the story goes on.

Just as we followed the light to see the story, and the wise man followed the star to find baby Jesus, so as we show God's light in the world, people will follow our light to find Jesus. The children can make badges out of star shapes cut from gold or silver coloured card, with a safety pin taped to the back, and wear them to remind themselves that they can be like the star that brought the wise men to Jesus, by showing other people God's light.

Big Kids' Sunday School

Create a really dark space, maybe under a table covered with a black cloth, or in a small room with black paper taped over the window. Give the children some fiddly tasks to do: threading a needle, tying their shoelaces, one of those puzzles where you have to get the little ball into the hole through a maze. Once they've had a try in the dark, let them see how much easier it is in the light.

We are drawn to the light when things are tricky. It is so much easier when we can see clearly. Life can be tricky, and so we are drawn towards God's light, since then we have so much more clarity to work out how to live. The wise men were drawn by a light too, following the star, to find the Light of the World, baby Jesus. Isaiah had given a prophecy about this years and years before, that 'Nations will come to your light, and kings to the brightness of your dawn.' But the light of Jesus isn't something that burnt brightly for a few short years and was then snuffed out. It's still shining brightly now, and as we live in a way that shows we know and love God, that light shines in us and in our lives too.

The children can make light-up badges to show that they are doing their best to let God's light shine in their lives, so they can act as the star did to the wise men. Use a small battery (making sure they know to be safe with batteries and not leave them anywhere a younger child might ingest them), strips of taped-down silver foil to be the wires in the circuit, an LED to light up, and a strip of silver foil that they can press down to be the switch, turning the LED on and off.

JESUS IS BAPTISED

Readings

- Isaiah 42:1-9
- Psalm 29
- Acts 10:34-43
- Matthew 3:13-17

Thoughts on the Readings

As we hear the story of Jesus' baptism, how he insisted that John should baptise him in the water just like everyone else, we see Jesus' humanity and humility shining through. What he wanted to do was to show to everyone that the close and special relationship that he had with his heavenly Father was something that was there for the rest of us humans, too. The amazing events at Jesus' baptism showed in a way that people could really see and hear, that God was present and that he could speak to us.

When we think of our own baptism, and the special times that we have drawn close to God our Father in heaven, we too can know that the gift of the Holy Spirit is just as real to us as it was to Jesus that day. And as we find that special place where we can be close to God, and as his love is revealed to us, we too can know that he calls us his sons and daughters. We are precious to him, he loves us, and when we do our best to live his way, with love and compassion, he is pleased with us.

The reading from Isaiah also tells us how pleased God is with his servant. God has given him his Spirit, so that he would bring peace, justice and reconciliation between the different countries of the world. God is not pleased with his servant for any of the reasons that people are usually given high status in our society – wealth, popularity or power – he is pleased with him because of his wisdom, his work for peace, and his gentleness. He will set prisoners free, and bring sight to the blind.

Our psalm for today describes the power in the voice of God – just as those who witnessed the voice from heaven at Jesus' baptism, so the psalmist tells us how even the wild creatures respond when God speaks.

The reading from Acts brings home the message that as God spoke those words about Jesus, he showed that he was pleased with him, So God is pleased with us, too, when we worship him and do right. It does not matter which country we come from, or which language we speak – God looks at our heart. And God sent the Holy Spirit to Jesus for a purpose – to equip him as he went about teaching and healing people. This same Holy Spirit is there for us too.

Discussion Starters

- **What seems to be the basis for people being considered valuable in our society? How is this different from God's priorities?**

Intercessions

**Holy Spirit,
bless us today.**

Lord, we come before you
thankful for the way that you take us, and love us,
just as we are.
Empower and strengthen us
so that everything we do
shows your love to those around us.

We bring into your loving care
your church, and all who lead us in our worship.
We thank you for all those who have been baptised in this place,
over the years,
and ask that they would know your presence and holiness
with them today.
We also pray for anyone in our surrounding community
who may be thinking about baptism
and ask that you would lead them on their journey of faith.
**Holy Spirit,
bless us today.**

We pray, dear Lord, for our world,
for those who hold positions of power
to be able to focus on your priorities
for the common good.
We also bring into your loving care
those who long for a new start,
who find it hard to believe
that there can be a future full of hope.
We particularly pray for those
who have had a difficult past
and for those who have been exploited by others.
**Holy Spirit,
bless us today.**

Father, we ask for your healing love
to surround anyone who is suffering at the moment –
those who are caged in by anxiety or depression,
those who are unable to take part in the activities they love
because of illness or disability
and for those who are in any kind of pain.
We pray that your voice of love
would be real and comforting to them
and we ask that you would help us
to listen out for what you would like us to do.

We bring into your healing presence . . .
Holy Spirit,
bless us today.

We remember with love
those who have died,
and thank you that they now have a home in heaven with you.
As we draw near to you in prayer
we know that heaven is close by
and we thank you for the peace that you want to give to all of us.
We name before you today . . .
Holy Spirit,
bless us today.

Lord, as we come into your presence,
we can know you as our Father.
Thank you for the way that you love us.
Amen.

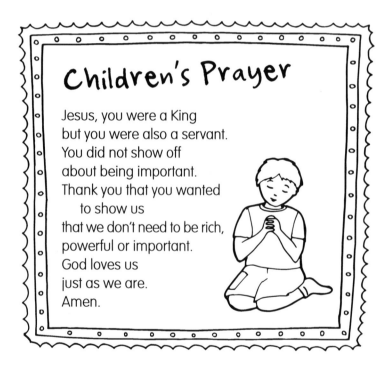

Children's Prayer

Jesus, you were a King
but you were also a servant.
You did not show off
about being important.
Thank you that you wanted
    to show us
that we don't need to be rich,
powerful or important.
God loves us
just as we are.
Amen.

Other Ideas!

Create a river scene using collage, or show a video or picture of the River Jordan for people to focus on.

All-age Talk

Bring along some things people have made for you, that make you feel fond and proud and happy. Maybe you can find a picture someone's drawn for you, a hat your friend has knitted for you, a jar of marmalade your auntie made you. Also bring along a new phone, a wallet full of cash (pretend cash if you're not feeling that rich!), and car keys.

Show everybody your new phone. Everyone should feel very pleased and proud of you for being such a success. You can tell everyone some of the stuff that makes your phone so great. Follow up by showing off your wallet full of cash, and flashing your car key. When you look at adverts, it says how everyone should be very pleased and proud of you for making such a great success of your life.

But actually we do know, really, that these things, nice as they are to have, don't make people pleased with and proud of us. Hold up your hand-drawn picture. When Solomon drew me this, I felt really pleased and happy. Not just because it's a great picture of a zombie elephant eating a banana, but because he had made it for me, and that shows the relationship we have. Put on your knitted hat, and tell everyone about the person who made it for you and how them giving you something they'd spent time on made you feel pleased and happy. You can spread some of the homemade marmalade on bread and tell them how your auntie never fails to make you a jar every year, and that makes you pleased too.

It's relationships that make us pleased and proud, in the end, isn't it? All the people we love and who love us. And when Jesus comes up from the water after being baptised, we hear a voice from heaven saying this, too: This is my son, whom I love. With him I am well pleased.

God isn't pleased with Jesus because of the success he's made of his life. He's well pleased with him because of the relationship they have; a relationship that means Jesus, as we heard in the reading from Isaiah, will bring peace, justice and reconciliation. And this is something that God says to each and every one of us, 'You are my child, whom I love. With you I am well pleased.'

Children's Corner

Provide a blue sheet, and a model of a dove, so the children can play at being baptised, and emerging to hear the voice of God: This is my beloved son, with whom I am well pleased. They can whisper about how at our baptism, God has called all of us his beloved children, and is pleased with us, as we follow him.

The colouring sheet shows a cross-section of the water of the river Jordan along the bottom half of the page, and a dove hovering above the water, alongside words reading, **'This is my Son, whom I love. With him I am well pleased'**.

Little Kids' Sunday School

There's a singing game called 'There's a Little Sandy Girl'. If you know it, by all means play it! If you don't, I can't teach you the tune just through my writing, but can give you the basic premise of the game, and that will do. Stand in a circle, and the little sandy girl (or boy) sits in the middle. You all hold hands and circle them, singing, 'There's a little sandy girl, sitting on a stone, crying, weeping, all the day alone. Rise up, sandy girl, wipe your tears away, choose the one you love the best and run the other way.' The sandy girl follows these instructions as you sing, and at the end, ducks out of the circle, and passes around the outside of the circle, until they tap the person they 'love the best', and then they race around the circle to see who reaches the vacant space first.

It's quite exciting to be chosen in this game. We all want to be the one whom they 'love the best'. Jesus headed into the desert to get baptised by his cousin John, and as he came up out of the water, those around heard a voice from heaven. It was God, saying, 'This is my Son, whom I love. With him I am well pleased.'

That's something God says to each of us. He loves us and he is pleased with us. Sometimes people give someone a ring to show they love them. We are going to make ourselves some rings today, to remind ourselves that we are loved by God. You might like to use those tiny letter beads, to allow the children to spell out 'loved', and to thread on a pipe cleaner. This ring might have to wind round their finger several times!

Big Kids' Sunday School

Play a game of 'Pearl Divers'. The 'pearls' can be ball pit balls, put in a basket at the far side of the hall. The children begin at the other side of the hall, on the 'dry land'. They have to dive into the water, swim the length of the hall, pick up a pearl, and swim back. Of course, they'll have to hold their breath all the time they are swimming as nobody can breathe under water!

It's hard holding your breath, isn't it? We need to breathe to stay alive, and breathing is impossible under water. Baptism is a symbol of drowning, of dying under the water, and being reborn as we surface into the air. Sometimes in churches it is a more symbolic drowning, with a small amount of water poured over the head; sometimes it is more literal, with the person being baptised pushed right under the water.

Jesus was baptised by his cousin John in the river Jordan. John was calling people to a baptism of repentance, to come and be baptised to show how sorry they were for the things they'd done wrong. Jesus came and asked be baptised, and John was confused, as Jesus didn't need a baptism! It should be Jesus baptising him! But John agreed, and as he walked Jesus deep into the water, and Jesus came up out of the water, there was a voice from heaven, the voice of God, saying, 'This is my Son whom I love. With him I am well pleased.'

The children can use sharpies or other waterproof pens to write, 'You are my child, whom I love. With you I am well pleased' on a plastic bottle. They can poke holes in the bottom of it with a skewer (watch out for fingers beneath), and use it in the bath, to sprinkle water on themselves and remember what God had to say to them at their baptism.

THIS IS MY SON, WHOM I LOVE WITH HIM I AM WELL PLEASED

JESUS – LIGHT OF THE WORLD

Readings

- Isaiah 49:1-7
- Psalm 40:1-12
- 1 Corinthians 1:1-9
- John 1:29-42

Thoughts on the Readings

As we hear in our reading from Isaiah, God's servant was chosen right from the very beginning. He was named, kept safe, given strength and the skills that he would need both to lead Israel and be a light for all the other nations of the world as well.

This is good news for us, as we are part of God's big story.

When John sees Jesus walking towards him, he identifies Jesus as the Lamb of God – the one who has been there, with God, right from the beginning. Even though John has grown up knowing Jesus, he did not realise the enormity of who Jesus really was until that time when they were standing in the River Jordan together, and the Holy Spirit came down on Jesus like a dove. God had prepared John for this, telling him that he would see the Holy Spirit come down and stay on 'someone'. John may have been quite surprised to find that this person was Jesus, but he was so convinced and struck by this experience that all he wanted to do was to tell others about it.

The result of this is that Andrew and Peter also come to realise that Jesus is the Messiah. Perhaps we sometimes need others to point out the wonderful truths about the things that are all around us, that perhaps we take for granted. Jesus had lived alongside these men for some time, but through John's courage and guidance, they came to see him in a different way.

It may be that there are others in our communities and families who may know something of Jesus – many people have some knowledge and respect for Jesus as a historical figure, who spent time with those that others excluded, and spoke words of peace and wisdom. Most people will know that he was put to death, and will be aware that Christians believe he came back to life. With gentleness, respect and love, we can, with God's leading, show people more about Jesus. This might be through our own actions or attitudes, helping others and choosing to forgive. We may have the opportunity to describe what our faith means to us, and how this has helped us. We might be able to think of more ways to make our church welcoming and accessible, a useful resource for the community. Or perhaps we can open up our buildings for prayer and reflection, giving others a chance to meet with God and encounter Jesus in that peaceful place. And if we are prayerful and observant, we may be surprised at how often we end up talking about Jesus with those from different backgrounds from our own, simply because they have brought up the subject.

Discussion Starters

- **What ordinary things around us speak to us of God's love? Share with each other.**

Intercessions

**Light for the nations,
bring us your saving love.**

Thank you, Lord,
that your promise of love
is for everyone on earth.
Help us to share it
through everything we say and do.

Lord, we pray that all your people
throughout the world,
however we worship you,
would all seek to follow your light.
We pray for the other churches near us
and pray that you would bless them
as they seek to draw near to you.
We also pray for understanding and respect
between people of different faiths and traditions.
**Light for the nations,
bring us your saving love.**

We pray, Lord, for the nations of the world
and thank you that your message
of peace and hope
is for us all.
We pray that you would bring peace
to anywhere that is suffering from conflict or violence
and that with your wisdom,
decision makers can start to address the root causes of this.
We also pray for areas of environmental degradation
and habitat loss,
that we could work together
to look after the world you have given us.
**Light for the nations,
bring us your saving love.**

Surround with your healing power
anyone who is unwell, in pain or discomfort,
those who are living with long-term conditions
and those who have suddenly been admitted to hospital.
We also pray that you would be with anyone
booked in for any sort of treatment this week.
We bring into your loving care . . .
**Light for the nations,
bring us your saving love.**

We think of those people
who are drawing near to the end
of their journey through life here on earth
and pray that they would be reassured of your promise
of a home in heaven with you.
We also bring to mind those who have died,
particularly those who are remembered at this time of year,
and name before you today . . .
Light for the nations,
bring us your saving love.

Jesus, Messiah,
thank you that we can know you.
Thank you that through you
we are saved and rescued
from fear and hopelessness.
Thank you that you give us hope for the future,
a family with you,
and more than enough love
to share with others.
Amen.

Children's Prayer

Jesus,
we have come to know you
and you are our friend.
Thank you that we can
help others
to be your friend too.
Amen.

Other Ideas!

Make a treasure trail for
people to follow, looking for
the arrows or the footprints. At
the end you could have a box
of biscuits or fruit to share. This
can help people to think about
leading others to Jesus.

All-age Talk

Today you'll need a glass of water, a rock, and a member of your congregation who has done something extraordinary at some point in their past (met the Queen, run a marathon, been on the telly, that kind of thing).

Hold up the glass of water, and take a sip. It is very ordinary water, just out of your tap, like we all drink and wash in and wash up in every day. Show them the rock. There are hundreds of

these on the ground. They are so ubiquitous that you don't even notice them as you walk past. Bring up Alex to the front. He looks the same as ever. Apart from his dashing good looks, you wouldn't look twice if you passed him in the street.

But did you realise that this water has been on our planet Earth for billions of years? It has been in the sea, in rivers, in lakes, and frozen in the ice ages. It has been drunk by dinosaurs, swum in by sharks, and splashed through by herds of reindeer. It has been high up in the sky as water vapour, and fallen as rain, and probably as snow as well. That makes you think a bit differently about the water in your cup, doesn't it!

And this stone was once molten lava, buried deep under the surface of the earth, until it was spewed out in a volcanic eruption. Over years and years, the rock was weathered until this stone broke off and tumbled down the mountain. It's been bumped around in rivers until it made its way to the sea. Sand settled on top of it and hardened, and the earth moved until it ended up on the top of a range of mountains. The frost and the sun and the rain weathered the rock until this stone cracked out again. It was stood on by a mammoth, and buried in the ground, until I found it in my garden this morning. Rocks are never ordinary.

And here's Alex. As ordinary as can be. Until you realise that he's done something quite extraordinary. Did you know that he . . .? Do you see him in a new light now?

John the Baptist must have grown up with Jesus. Their mums were cousins and were obviously close. Jesus must have been known to Andrew and to Simon Peter too, as they lived in the same area and mixed with the same people. But suddenly, they saw past their familiarity to see that actually Jesus was extraordinary, that here was the Messiah, here was God, walking on earth.

Sometimes the people we know, who live in our neighbourhood, or we go to work or school with, see our church building, our faith, as familiar and ordinary. The church is maybe just that building they walk past every day and barely even notice. They may know we are Christians, and that it's got something to do with Jesus, but it doesn't register with them on any deeper level. But like John to Andrew, and Andrew to Simon Peter, sometimes it is our job to help people see past the familiar to notice the extraordinary that's been in plain sight all along.

Children's Corner

Give the children some safe magnets to play with (not tiny ones they could swallow) and paperclips, so they can try and see how many paperclips one magnet can pull along. Listen out for John telling Andrew, and Andrew bringing along his brother, in the Gospel reading.

The colouring sheet shows Jesus standing with a smile on his face, and Andrew pulling the hand of his brother, Simon Peter, to bring him to meet Jesus. The writing reads, **'We can bring our friends to Jesus'**.

Little Kids' Sunday School

Run a relay race, where the first child runs up and back, then picks up the second child, holds their hand, and runs up and back, whereupon the second child picks up the third child, holds their hand, and so on, until the whole team is holding hands to run up and down.

Sometimes when you're really excited about something, you tell your friend. They might get excited too, and then tell their friend, and before you know it, there's a whole gang of you. John the Baptist had realised that his cousin Jesus was the one sent by God to save us, so he told his friend Andrew to go and find Jesus. Once Andrew had found Jesus, he got excited by him too, and went to get his brother Simon Peter, and brought him to meet Jesus too.

Make a chain of paper dolls. The children can colour the first one to be them, and colour the rest to be their friends who they want to bring to meet Jesus.

Big Kids' Sunday School

Play 'Did You Know?' Each person has to come up with three amazing facts about themselves that they think people might not know. Two of the facts are true, and one is made up. Sit in a circle and take it in turns to state your facts (and 'facts'), and then see if you can guess which facts were fake. Was the truth stranger than fiction sometimes? Haven't people done some amazing things!

Sometimes you can suddenly see someone in a whole new light. I'll never look at Alice the same way now I know that she once swung on her swing for five hours without stopping! Jesus, growing up in his community, had family and friends who had always known him. But after John had baptised him, and there'd been that voice from heaven (we heard this story last week), John suddenly saw Jesus in a new light. John realised that his cousin Jesus was actually the one they'd all been waiting for, the one who had been sent to save us all. And without missing a beat, he took this on board, and sent his friend, Andrew, to go and find Jesus. Presumably Andrew had known of Jesus for years too, but when he met him this time, he was suddenly full of excitement and began to realise who Jesus was. And he went rushing off to find his brother, Simon Peter, to bring him to Jesus too!

Lots of people in our society have heard of Jesus. They may know a little bit about him. But that is very different from meeting him. If we are able to bring them to meet him, either through something that is happening at church, or through how we live our lives, they might be able to see past the familiarity into the sudden realisation of who Jesus actually is.

The children can make themselves tickets from a strip of paper. The first ticket says 'Admit One', and the rest say 'Plus One'. They can use a pin to poke tiny holes across the 'tear line' for each ticket, so that they look (and work!) authentically. These will remind them that they've got unlimited invitations to bring other people to come to know Jesus.

WE CAN BRING OUR FRIENDS TO JESUS

JESUS CALLS HIS FIRST DISCIPLES

Readings

- Isaiah 9:1-4
- Psalm 27:1, 4-12
- 1 Corinthians 1:10-18
- Matthew 4:12-23

Thoughts on the Readings

Once John had come to the realisation that Jesus was the Messiah after seeing the remarkable events at his baptism, he led others to Jesus, and took a step back himself, allowing Jesus to begin his ministry of teaching and healing. But it was once Jesus heard that John was in prison, that the time came for him to take over telling God's message. This is described in Matthew's Gospel as a very clear message of the need for repentance and to turn back to God, because the kingdom of God was very near – the same message, consistent with John's earlier preaching.

The two cousins worked respectfully together, always listening to God's message and finding the best way to clearly communicate that to the people who eagerly came to listen, hungry to know more of God.

We heard last week how Andrew had been introduced to Jesus by John, and had visited Jesus' house, along with his brother, Peter. Today we hear how Jesus then saw these fishermen at work, casting their nets into the lake, presumably recognised them and greeted them, before calling them to follow him. Andrew and Peter immediately dropped their nets and followed Jesus – after hearing Jesus' message the first time they met, they had had time to think about it, and had come to the point where there needed to be no hesitation.

This makes us think about when we so much want our friends and family to know Jesus and that wonderful closeness and intimacy with God that we experience through our own faith. Like Peter and Andrew, they may need to be welcomed into God's house, God's family, first of all – no expectations, no pressure, just love. Then, when the time is right, and they are ready, they will be able to draw near to Jesus, and that will be something that is between them and God.

We don't know if Jesus had already had a conversation with James and John, but we are told that they, too, left their boat straight away and came to follow Jesus when he called them. Whatever the reason, their hearts, too, were ready to make that decision – perhaps because of other circumstances in their lives, the scriptures they had read, such as today's reading from Isaiah, or maybe because of John's ministry which had prepared the way.

And as we hear in the reading from 1 Corinthians, we don't need to make following Jesus complicated. Just as Jesus continued consistently proclaiming the message that John started, and John led others to Jesus, there does not need to be any conflict. We are all working together, with one aim – to know Jesus, and to help others know him too.

Discussion Starters

- How can we make our church a place where people are welcomed in, and an environment where they can meet with Jesus?

Intercessions

**As you call us,
we will follow you.**

Jesus, as you called your first disciples to follow you,
may we be ready to go where you lead us,
even if it might be something surprising
or a change of plan.
May we be open to your leading
and know your wonderful love.

We bring to you our church
and pray that you would enable us to be a place
where others are able to meet with Jesus,
somewhere that people feel welcome
and where we can show the love of God.
We pray that you would enable us
to work in partnership and cooperation
with other churches
and other people of faith,
bringing your kingdom of love
to the world.
**As you call us,
we will follow you.**

Remembering that Jesus called fishermen
as his first disciples,
we pray that we would also honour and value
the people who grow, catch and make the food that we eat,
as well as those who are in caring, practical and other roles
which may not be considered to have a high status in the world.
We pray that our priorities would align with yours
so that we come to really understand
that human value is not the same
as wealth or status,
and all people on earth
are precious to you.
**As you call us,
we will follow you.**

We pray that your healing love would surround
anyone feeling the exhaustion of anxiety,
over-work, lack of sleep or chronic pain.
We ask that you would lead them
into a place of peace and hope
in their lives,
where they can enjoy being in your company
and know your love.
We particularly remember those known to us who are in need at the moment, including . . .
As you call us,
we will follow you.

We remember with love
those people who have gone before us
to live with you in your heavenly kingdom.
We pray that you would be close
to those who miss them,
and bring a sense of peace and joy
to those who are at the end of their lives.
We name before you today . . .
As you call us,
we will follow you.

Thank you for the way
that you call us to follow you.
As we do this,
may we know your company
and companionship
through our lives.
Amen.

Children's Prayer

Jesus, we will follow you.
We want to be with you.
We want to learn from you
and we want to know
   you more.
Amen.

Other Ideas!

Have a photo of fishing boats, with
their nets and other equipment, for
people to look at.

All-age Talk

Invite some people forward to get on with a complicated but interesting task, such as following Lego instructions to make a model, playing Minecraft on a tablet, counting out dried apple rings so there are enough for everyone in church, but tell them that in a minute you'll need them to do something else. As they get on with this, talk about the things we do in our lives, how we get absorbed in them, how we get good at what we do by doing it day by day.

Andrew and Peter, James and John were fishermen, and had become better and better at fishing by doing it day in and day out. It wasn't an easy job, as they had to read the weather and the mood of the sea, the seasons and the time of day. They had to know where the fish would be swimming when, and at what depth. They had to know how to sail a boat, how to mend a boat, how to untangle nets, how to choose which fish to keep and which to throw back.

We know that Andrew and Peter had already recently had a conversation with Jesus. As they worked on their boat, they must have been mulling over the things he had said, and thinking through their response to him.

Call your volunteers over, to hold up a sign that says, 'Follow me!'. Look at that. Even though they'd just got to the interesting bit in their model, or were just about to mine some diamonds in Minecraft, they were ready to come, straight away, when I asked. And maybe that's similar to Andrew and Peter. They'd been pondering the things they'd spoken about with Jesus, and actually their response had already been made in their own minds. When Jesus called for them to 'follow me', they didn't have to think it through, to weigh it up in their minds. That had all happened as they sat mending their nets, or through the long night as they waited for the fish to swim near their boat. Their decision was already made, and they knew just what they needed to do.

Thinking through the big questions of faith means that when Jesus calls us, we are ready to respond. As we, individually and as a church, give our friends and neighbours a chance to meet with Jesus, they will be able to respond when they are ready and when Jesus calls.

Children's Corner

Use masking tape or chalk to draw the outline of a boat on the floor in the children's corner. Provide some fishing nets so the children can sit inside and fish. When their parent or carer whispers, 'Follow me!', they can practise putting down their nets and jumping straight out of the boat. They might like to get their grown-up to squeeze inside the boat, and do the 'Follow me' whisper, too.

The colouring sheet shows the disciples with their boat and net, and one with a foot on the side of the boat, climbing out ready to follow Jesus. There are also words to colour: **'Follow me!'**.

Little Kids' Sunday School

Put on some music to dance to, and supply a special hat on a table or a chair. If someone comes and puts on the hat, everyone must be ready to stop their own dancing, and follow how the hatted one is dancing. When the hat comes off, everyone can go back to their own dancing.

You were all busy dancing just now, with some brilliant moves. But you were also keeping an eye on the hat, waiting to respond to whoever put it on, and follow their moves instead.

Play through the Gospel story for today, with Andrew and Peter in their boat, and James and John in their boat, busy sorting out their nets. Along comes Jesus, who says, 'Follow me'. Andrew and Peter put down their nets and follow him. Jesus comes past James and John, and again says, 'Follow me'. They, too, put down their nets and follow Jesus.

The children can make a fishing rod out of a stick and some string, and tie a cut-out fish on the end. They can write, 'Jesus said, Follow me!' on the fish, to remind them to be ready to follow Jesus when he calls us.

Big Kids' Sunday School

Put the children in pairs, sitting back to back. Give each of them a pile of Lego and make sure each half of each pair has the same assortment of bricks. Give one child in each pair a piece of paper with something they have to make written on it, such as a car, a house or a dinosaur. The child begins to build and talks through what they're building so that the child with their back to them can copy. When they're done, see if the second child can guess what the paper said. Then you can swap and play it again with a different thing to make.

When Andrew and Peter, and James and John went to follow Jesus, it was, at least in the beginning, simple. Jesus called them, and they put down their nets and followed him. They had to follow him with their feet. It was maybe a while before they fully realised how to follow him with their hearts, minds and lives. When we follow Jesus, we don't have the luxury of using our eyes to watch where he walks, and our feet to follow him. It's more like our Lego challenge. We have to keep listening to Jesus, and making our lives, our hearts and minds match his.

Give each child eight Lego blocks. They can use a permanent marker to write a letter from 'follow me' on each block, and build them together following their partner's instructions. They can take them home to remind them to listen to Jesus, so they can follow him when he calls.

GOD GIVES US ALL WE NEED

Readings

- 1 Kings 17:8-16
- Psalm 36:5-10
- 1 Corinthians 1:18-31
- John 2:1-11

Thoughts on the Readings

Today, in all our readings, we hear the common theme of God's provision. It is when we acknowledge that we have nothing left, and are open to God's leading, humbly obeying his instructions, even if they seem a little strange, we will find that he will give us more than we could ever imagine.

This provision is always for a purpose; the widow was given enough oil and flour so that she could share with Elijah, and enable him to continue his prophetic ministry. Then, when Jesus told the servants to fill the jars with water, they had nothing to lose, as there was no wine to offer anyway. This was then transformed into something wonderful to bless those attending the wedding celebration. Our psalm, too, tells us how God provides a feast for his guests in his house, and tasty drinks that flow like a river. Then in the reading from 1 Corinthians we hear how God gives his own wisdom and power to those people who are from ordinary backgrounds – those people who do not rely on their own strength, cleverness, wealth or popularity, but who are simply ready to trust God. This is also given for a purpose – to bring people closer to God, so that they can rely on him rather than trusting in themselves, thinking that they have nothing to learn.

There is more than enough for everyone. We are told that the oil and the flour lasted a long time – it was not just a small quantity. The water jars in the Gospel reading were filled up right to the top – a great deal of wine! – and it wasn't just any sort of wine, either. The steward declared that it was the best wine he had ever tasted. Then, when we think about the wisdom and power that comes from God, this is so much more than any human strength. Those people who think they are important, and may well be considered important by thousands of people around them, do not have wisdom or power that compares in any way to that which comes from God.

If we come humbly before God, not trusting in our own strength or thinking we know best, not thinking that with our own clever formula we can 'make' our religion appeal to others, then God really can work through us. We need to leave that sense of pride behind us, and simply tune in to where God is leading us. We need to be ready to learn to listen to others, particularly those who are not considered important in the world's eyes and do not have a voice. Then God will draw near to us, and we will be able to receive from him – individually, as a church, and as a wider community.

Discussion Starters

- How can we listen more, as a church, to those who do not have a voice? Are there practical things that we can do, or ways that we can change the physical environment to make it more welcoming?

Intercessions

**Lord, we trust you,
you give us all we need.**

Lord, we thank you
that we don't have to have influential friends
or money, or power,
to be useful to you.
We just need to humbly accept
our need of you.
We do this now
as we come before you in prayer.

We bring into your loving care
our church, and all those who lead us in worship.
We thank you for them, and pray
that we would grow in your wisdom
as we trust in you.
We pray that as a church
you would help us
to listen to the voices of those
who are not considered important in the eyes of the world,
but who are precious, and chosen by you.
**Lord, we trust you,
you give us all we need.**

We pray for our world,
and particularly think of those people
whose food stores are running low,
with uncertainty about where more is coming from.
We pray for those organisations
which help to bring food and clean water
to those in need
and ask that you would open our eyes
to help where we can, too.
**Lord, we trust you,
you give us all we need.**

We bring into your loving care
anyone who is weighed down
by pain or exhaustion
and feels they have little of their own strength left.
We pray that your wonderful provision
of strength, wisdom and hope
would be with them as we bring them before you.
We name before you today, anyone known to us who is in need at this time, including . . .
Lord, we trust you,
you give us all we need.

As we bring to mind those who have entered heaven
to live with you in eternity,
where your wisdom, holiness, truth and love
fill the whole place,
we remember those who have died,
and name before you today . . .
Lord, we trust you,
you give us all we need.

Lord, be with us
as we go out into the world from this place.
May we go in your strength,
your wisdom
and your power.
Amen.

Children's Prayer

Dear Lord,
thank you for giving us
all that we need:
things to eat,
clothes to wear,
people to care for us
and a place to live.
We know that you will
   always give us
enough to help others, too,
even if it is just in a
   little way.
Thank you that you can
   use us.
Amen.

Other Ideas!

Pour some oil into a jug, some flour into a bowl, and place some flatbread or wraps next to them, perhaps with a rolling pin, so that people can think about the story of Elijah and the widow.

All-age Talk

Have a mixing bowl, some flour, and some oil. You'll need an egg cup full of flour and an egg cup full of oil, a bag of flour and a bottle of oil, and a massive sack marked 'flour' (I'm thinking of one of my chicken feed sacks, but you probably don't have chickens, so see what other large sack-like things you can find) and a huge container (a jug for baptism water, or a camping water container) marked oil.

Get out the egg cup-sized flour and oil. Tell everyone you're going to do a bit of baking, flatbread for lunch today, yum. Tip in the flour and a bit of the oil and mix it together, and squash it into a flatbread. A bit small, but it'll do for your lunch. What? You are all a bit hungry too? Well, you're in luck, because I've got a whole bag of flour here. Tip it in, and get a helper to mix in some of the oil from the bottle. We'll be able to make flatbread for all of us, I reckon. But did you hear that rumble from outside? Do you think the people living nearby and walking past would like some too? Thank goodness you brought your mega-sized flour and oil. You can make as if to tip it into the bowl, and to pour in the 'oil', and do a bit more mixing.

We heard in our Old Testament reading today about Elijah and the widow, where God was able to make just a little bit of flour and oil stretch to feed not just the three of them for one day, but the three of them for a long time, until the famine was over. God doesn't just give us a tiny eggcupful of what we need, that will scarcely be enough for just us. God provides enough for us, and for us to share, and not just in the food that we're lucky enough to have in our houses and share with others in our food bank drop-offs, but enough patience, enough courage, enough wisdom. And like with Jesus, turning the water into wine, it's not just plenty that God gives us, but plenty of the very best quality. Amazing patience. Beautiful courage. Gentle wisdom.

Children's Corner

Provide flour, oil, and water to mix into playdough. If you have small toy frying pans and plates, the children can use the playdough to squash into flatbreads. Listen out for the story of Elijah, and the widow, and God's provision of flour and oil to keep them fed.

The colouring sheet shows Elijah, the jars of oil and flour, and the widow squatting by her fire, mixing and baking bread. The writing on the sheet reads, **'God always gives us enough, and enough to share'**.

Little Kids' Sunday School

Give each child a tortilla wrap, and whisper something that they each need to nibble it into (smiley face, car, boat). On the count of three, they start nibbling until you tell them time is up. Can the other children guess what it is they've turned their tortilla wrap into?

Tell the story of Elijah and the widow. How there was a famine in the land and people were very hungry. Elijah went to the widow's house and asked for something to eat. She said she only had just enough flour and oil to make one last meal for herself and for her son, and then they would have to starve. But she shared the little she had, and found that it didn't quite run out. All the way through the famine, Elijah stayed with her, and there was always just enough flour and just enough oil to make enough bread for all three of them.

Help the children mix flour with a little oil, water and salt to a dough, squash it flat and bake it in a hot oven for 10-15minutes. As you mix and bake, you can talk about how God provided the widow with enough for herself, but also enough to share. God gives us enough too, enough food and water, enough patience and courage, enough kindness and love, and not just enough, but enough for us to share.

Big Kids' Sunday School

Try out a variety of blackcurrant squashes, from really cheap ones to really expensive ones. Can the children put them in order just from the taste? Do the expensive ones really taste better?

Retell the story of Jesus at the wedding at Cana. Explain how weddings went on for days, how it was a really big deal that the family throwing the party should be seen to be hospitable, providing plenty of everything. Imagine their embarrassment as the wine is found to have run out. Mary tells the servants to do whatever Jesus tells them to do. I wonder what the servants might have been expecting? I wonder what Mary thought was going to happen? Fill a jug with water (send someone to the sink) as you tell the bit about them filling the jars with water. Pour it out into a glass that's already got posh blackcurrant juice in the bottom. (You're not trying to do a magic trick on the children; they're not daft and have just been drinking the blackcurrant juice, but you're just creating a picture for them to help tell the story.) Tell how the steward took a sip and couldn't believe the quality of the wine.

This story isn't just about how Jesus provided plenty when there was nothing. It's also about the quality of that plenty. Like our taste testing at the start, not all wines, like not all blackcurrant juices, are created equal. God doesn't just grudgingly give us the bare minimum. He gives us plenty of the very best, and not just wine, but all the good gifts of God: love, patience, wisdom, kindness and joy.

The children can help you to make raspberry cordial to take home in little bottles or jars, and when they mix it with water, they can remember this story. Put 500g of frozen raspberries and caster sugar in a saucepan, with a few tablespoons of red wine vinegar. Heat gently until it's smushable. Sieve out the seeds, then add 300ml of water to the sieved-out seeds. Sieve them again to remove the last of the pulp and add this liquid to the raspberry liquid. Stir well and drink mixed with water, still or sparkling, and remember how Jesus turned water into enough delicious wine for everyone.

GOD ALWAYS GIVES US ENOUGH, AND ENOUGH TO SHARE

SALT AND LIGHT FOR THE WORLD

Readings

- Isaiah 58:1-9a (9b-12)
- Psalm 112:1-9 (10)
- 1 Corinthians 2:1-12 (13-16)
- Matthew 5:13-20

Thoughts on the Readings

So, did Jesus really mean that we should be obeying the laws better than the Pharisees themselves? Looking in context, and at Jesus' life and actions, we can see that he did not attach importance to obeying lists of laws which had the main purpose of causing those obeying them to feel smug. He often broke the religious laws in order to help or befriend others. However, Jesus always pointed back to the values that come from God, and reminded us that these are the most important laws of all. Everything else is just a means to that end. Love God and love each other. This is what it all boils down to.

As we read about God's wisdom in 1 Corinthians, we also hear how this is something that is different from being very good at obeying rules. Both deep and simple at the same time, God's wisdom is an understanding of that creative love that calls us all to him. As we draw near to God, and come to know him, we start to understand everything else in context. No longer do we need to be right all the time, or know all the answers. We just need to let God fill us with his Holy Spirit, and look at others and the world around us with the same love that God has for them. Then everything else will fall into place.

As we do this, we will be like salt and light for the world. As we interact with others in our everyday lives, the love and care that we can show, the sparkle from our thankful hearts and the desire to really listen to those who have sometimes been marginalised, can bring meaning to people's lives, and light up a possible way of living and being that can be more hopeful and joyful than they have known before.

Our fantastic reading from Isaiah today sums this all up. God does not want us to put on some sort of act, showing off about how holy we are. The most important things we can do are to help to bring about justice and peace for those people who are oppressed, campaign for freedom for those unjustly imprisoned, to fight inequality and poverty, free those who are abused, help the homeless, give away the clothes we do not need, and not to turn our relatives away. According to the prophet Isaiah, these things in themselves are worship.

It is a pretty comprehensive list. Many of those needs will be familiar to us. We can't do it all, but we can do something. And if we work together, in God's strength, this can add up to a lot.

Discussion Starters

- **To what extent do we see social action as worship, as described in the reading from Isaiah? What can this mean for us when we work together with other, non-religious groups which have the same aim?**

Intercessions

Heavenly Father,
may we bring your light.

Lord, as we think of you
and the problems around us,
we pray that you would help us to be
both salt and light in the world,
bringing that sparkle of love and hope
to those around us.

We pray that in our church,
as we worship, we would draw near to you
and you would refresh and strengthen us,
giving us what we need
to light up the world around us.
We pray for the projects that those in our congregation support,
both here and around the world
and pray that you would empower us
to make a difference.
Heavenly Father,
may we bring your light.

Lord, we bring to you our beautiful world
with so much treasure, and so much potential.
We bring to you the pain we feel
when we hear about war, violence and suffering
and the damage that we humans have caused
to the natural environment.
We pray that you would lead us
and give us wisdom,
as well as the courage to take action where we need to.
Heavenly Father,
may we bring your light.

We pray that you would surround with your love
and your light
anyone who is unwell today.
Whatever the reason,
however long this has gone on
and whether it is something big
or something small,
an obvious condition
or something invisible,
we know that you know and care
for everyone you have made.
Bring your peace and healing,

so that your light
may shine through them.
**Heavenly Father,
may we bring your light.**

We think of those who are nearing the end
of their lives here on earth
and pray that they would see
the beauty of heaven
and look forward to the joy
of being in your company.
We also remember anyone who has died
and particularly those who are missed at this time of year, including . . .
**Heavenly Father,
may we bring your light.**

Thank you, dear Lord,
that we don't need to be perfect
or get everything right
for your wonderful love
to shine through us.
We just need to come as we are.
Amen.

Children's Prayer

Dear Jesus,
we want our lives to
    be bright
and shining
with candles of love,
torches of patience
and fairy lights of joy.
Amen.

Other Ideas!

Have some small pieces of salted caramel, sea-salted chocolate, crisps (or all three!) for people to eat, noticing what effect the salt has on the flavour.

All-age Talk

Today you'll need a bowl of chips, a bowl of ice, and some cured meat (salami, or if you don't want to buy meat, salted butter will do). You'll need some salt as well!

We heard about salt at the beginning of our Gospel reading today. Jesus says, 'You are the salt of the earth.' What on earth might he mean by that? Let's have a think about some of the things salt can do.

Bring out your bowl of chips. Here's a tasty thing that salt can do. I've got a lovely bowl of chips here, but fried potatoes can be a bit plain by themselves. A little sprinkle of salt makes them taste delicious (sprinkle on some salt and offer them around). We need a little bit of salt in our diet to make us healthy, to make our nerves work, to balance our fluids. No wonder we crave salty foods, as it's not always easy to find in the natural environment. Our bodies have evolved to want it, so whenever it's available we eat it.

Bring out the bowl of ice. What about when we have an icy day? People put grit down on the roads and on the pavements. That grit has salt in it. Why? Have a look at this. Shake some salt into the bowl of ice and mix it around. The salt helps the ice to melt, to change states, much, much quicker and at a lower temperature than it would otherwise.

Here's something else to eat! Bring out your salami. Back in the days before there were fridges and freezers, people needed to keep food safe to eat. Some foods, like meat, get dangerous very quickly if they're not kept cold. Unless, of course, you cure them, by soaking them in a solution of salt. Germs can't survive in a high salt concentration, so the meat stays good to eat for much, much longer than it would do otherwise.

Maybe these things give us a bit of a clue about how we are called to be the salt of the earth. Like the salt on the chips, maybe we are called to help people discover the depth and flavour of their lives. Maybe we can help society to stay healthy, to stay balanced, by the way we live our lives following God.

Like the salt in the ice, maybe God is calling us to agitate for change, to be the catalyst bringing about justice and peace in our world.

Like the salt in the salami, maybe God is calling us to live in a way that protects those around us from evil and darkness, by the way that we live in the light.

Only a little salt is needed. We must not worry that we live in a society where the proportion of people identifying as Christian is declining. After all, nobody wants to eat a plate of salt, but a little salt sprinkled on a plate of chips is wonderful. God can use us, even if we are small in number, and the impact of a few Christians living a life of holiness and joy can go far beyond what you might expect.

Children's Corner

Provide a tray covered with table salt, and allow the children to draw in it using their fingers, and gently shake it to erase the picture. They can also spot how many lights they can see in the church building: candles, electric light bulbs, lamps.

The colouring sheet shows a variety of different lights to colour (torches, candles, fairy lights) and the words, **'Help us be salt & light in the world'**.

Little Kids' Sunday School

Have some little bowls of salty snacks (crisps, crackers, chunks of cheese, popcorn, rice cakes, olives), put a number 1-6 beside each, and roll a dice around the circle. Whatever number the child rolls, they can go and have a little taste of that salty snack. Be aware of allergies, and cut the olives lengthways so they aren't a choking hazard with little ones.

You might all need a drink of water as you sit and talk about salt. Jesus told his friends that they were the 'salt of the earth'. We've just eaten some salt, and it didn't taste of people! So what did Jesus mean by that? Have a think about how salt can make plain foods tastier. How it can preserve them and stop them going off. How might we be like salt in our lives as we follow Jesus?

Put some cheap table salt in a tray, and each child can use a squeezy glue pot to squeeze a design onto a piece of card. Hold the card over the tray and sprinkle on salt, a bit like glitter, until the glue pattern is full of salt. Shake off the excess, and use droppers or paintbrushes to touch liquid watercolour paint on the salt. The colour will spread out through the crystals, making a lovely picture. The children can take this home (but be careful as it'll still be a bit gloopy for a while), and it will remind them of how they can be like salt in their lives as they live God's way.

Big Kids' Sunday School

Play 'Salt, Salt, Light', by sitting in a circle, one person walking round the edge, tapping people as they go, and saying, 'Salt, salt, salt . . .' until they reach someone and tap them, saying, 'Light', whereupon that child chases them around the circle until they reach the empty space.

In our Gospel reading today, Jesus tells his disciples, 'You are the salt of the earth . . . You are the light of the world . . .' Funny things for them, and for us, to be described as. Fill a bowl with salt, and place lit tea lights amongst it. Give out post-it notes, and write down as many things you can think of about what salt and light can be used for. Does any of that make sense as far as our calling as Christians?

We are going to use some salt today. Fill a zip-lock bag with custard, cream, milk, or a combination of those! I normally go for soya options, as then you're easier with allergies and diets, but to be honest, anything works. Add in a bit of sugar and maybe some vanilla essence. Close the zip-lock bag, and put it inside another, larger, zip-lock bag. Fill this bag with ice and salt. Close this zip-lock bag, and put it all inside an insulated lunch bag or picnic bag. Throw it from one to another for about ten minutes, before taking it out. What has happened to the ice? Why has it melted so fast? That's the salt, as it speeds up the ice melting, and as it does so, the ice takes some of the heat from whatever's near it. In this case, our ice-cream mix. Take out the zip-lock bag from the middle, open it, and spoon out the ice-cream into cones or bowls. As you enjoy your ice-cream, you can think of ways in which God might be calling you to be like salt, to bring about change, like the ice into water, and the custard into ice-cream.

MAKING PEACE

Readings

- Deuteronomy 30:15-20 or Ecclesiasticus 15:15-20
- Psalm 119:1-8
- 1 Corinthians 3:1-9
- Matthew 5:21-37

Thoughts on the Readings

For practical, as well as spiritual reasons, Jesus recommends that if we have a disagreement or an argument with anyone, we should do our best to make peace with them. We will find it difficult to truly draw near to God unless we have first done this.

We humans need reminding of this. Holding a grudge or feeling resentful sometimes seems to be our default mode, and we need to make the choice to let go of this. Not only will this help our relationship with the other person, and make for a calmer, more tolerant and understanding society through our example, it will also help our relationship with God, and will enable us to find peace. Of course, this is not always easy. Some people may have hurt or upset us with their words or their actions, and we cannot always easily see a way ahead to find reconciliation. It may not always be possible to find and speak to the person, or for other reasons it may not be a good idea to speak to them face to face. But if, with God's strength, we are enabled to choose to forgive, then we can become free from those horrible feelings which were making our lives a misery anyway.

Sometimes we feel as if we do not have this choice; perhaps our feelings of hate, anger and resentment are very strong, and we might actually quite like holding on to them because it means that we are right, and the other person is wrong. But all our readings today remind us that, whatever it feels like, the choice is ours to make. The Deuteronomy reading explains how God tells us his laws – they are not difficult to find. If we listen to our conscience, we will often just know what is the right thing to do. If we choose to follow God, then we will put ourselves in a place of blessing. It is up to us. We may not have to do anything quite as dramatic as Jesus suggests in the passage from Matthew's Gospel – poking out our own eyes is a little bit over the top, by any standards – but what Jesus was trying to convey, with typical exaggeration and humour, is that we should not let anything hold us back from choosing to do what is right, even if it means letting go of something we like doing very much.

Our reading from 1 Corinthians gives a similar message. Jealousy and arguments show that people are not living in a spiritual way. This is normal for people in the world, but with God, we do not have to live like this. We need to find a way to work together with others, to treat each other with respect, and care for each other, even if we disagree. So often, when we do this, we then find that the disagreements were not as big, or as difficult to resolve, as we thought they were.

Discussion Starters

- **What makes it possible for us to forgive others and make peace? Is it a certain attitude, a choice, having something positive to focus on, or something else?**

Intercessions

**Lord, as we choose to live your way,
we find we are closer to you.**

Lord, we thank you
that you are always ready
to listen to us,
that you understand our situations
and that you care for us.

We bring to you in thankfulness
those who lead our churches;
those who help us to draw near to you
through prayer and worship.
May we come to know your healing
so that we are enabled
to make peace with others
through an attitude of respectfulness
and reconciliation.
**Lord, as we choose to live your way,
we find we are closer to you.**

We pray for our world,
particularly any situations
where choices based on selfishness,
fear or insecurity
have led to suffering, pain and destruction.
We pray that your nurturing love
would bring healing
and that our actions
would help to create
a place of peace.
**Lord, as we choose to live your way,
we find we are closer to you.**

We bring into your loving care
anyone who has been treated badly by others,
whether deliberately, or by lack of thought.
We particularly pray for anyone
who is holding on to past pain
and cannot see the way ahead.
Bring your freedom, and your healing,
so that they may know that they are held gently by you
and loved unconditionally.
We bring before you anyone in need or pain at the moment, including . . .
Lord, as we choose to live your way,
we find we are closer to you.

Thank you for the welcome into heaven that you give
to those people who have passed from this world into the next,
a place where pain and resentment will melt away in your presence.
We pray for those people who are on that journey at the moment,
and ask that you would be with them, and the people who care about them.
We also remember today those who are now in heaven with you, including . . .
Lord, as we choose to live your way,
we find we are closer to you.

Lord, we make a choice
for love, for kindness
and for forgiveness.
Thank you for the strength and encouragement
you give us,
as we live for you.
Amen.

Children's Prayer

Dear Lord,
we choose to live your way.
We choose to forgive.
We choose to be thankful.
We choose to give.
We choose to be friendly.
We choose to share,
bringing your love
and showing your care.
Amen.

Other Ideas!

Have some images of
peace makers (e.g. people
from different religions and
backgrounds working together)
displayed on a screen or in
a collage.

All-age Talk

Find a volunteer and give them the offertory plate, or whatever you use to collect gifts in your church. Let everyone see there are some notes in there, and a good handful of coins as well. Invite them to go and lay this wonderful gift for God on the altar, or a table at the front of church.

Oh sorry. Stop there a moment. You'll need to carry this too. Pass them some huge shopping bags full of awkward shapes (I find big cereal boxes hard to carry, and maybe some bottles of pop to weigh them down). Pass them a giant teddy, and a saucepan, and a coat. It doesn't have to be these things, but you get my drift. You're wanting them laden down with bags and not just bags, so that it's really difficult to carry all of these as well as manoeuvre the offertory plate to the right place.

Having a bit of difficulty, are we? Does anyone have any ideas? Hopefully someone will suggest that they could put all the other stuff down!

Jesus tells us that if we have a gift for God, no matter how wonderful the thing is that we're offering, money, or our time, or our talents, we need to first go and make peace with our neighbours. Holding on to anger and resentment makes us actually unable to offer our gift to God. Jesus suggests we put our gift down (help the volunteer to do this) and go and sort things out with those who we are feeling angry with. The volunteer can go and find some people to go and pass all their bags and things to. We need to stop clutching on to our righteous feelings of anger and frustration, and make our peace with others. There are times when the situation is such that we can't go and make peace. Maybe the other party is not in a position where they're able to meet us, or we might need to protect ourselves from another confrontation, but we need to look at what we are carrying, and make a decision not to drag it around with us. Once we are liberated, and have made our peace, we are able to pick up our gift easily (the volunteer can do this now) and offer it to God, who will gratefully receive it and turn it into something that no doubt blesses us too.

Children's Corner

Set up a variety of teddies and small world figures, facing away from each other in pairs or small groups, as if they've been having an argument. The children and their parents and carers can spend some time helping them to listen to God's laws and to make peace with one another.

The colouring sheet shows people from different backgrounds working together to create peace. The writing says, **'Make peace'**.

Little Kids' Sunday School

Play some music. The children can dance around the room. When the music stops, they have to find someone and go and shake their hand. Can they keep track of everyone they've shaken hands with, and make sure they shake hands with everyone?

We sometimes do shaking hands at church, don't we? We call it the Peace. It's not just a bit of the service where, after arriving and singing a bit we randomly decide to wander about and say 'Hello, how are you doing?' to everyone. But it's actually responding to some good advice from Jesus. In our Gospel reading today, Jesus says that if you are coming to bring an offering to God (it might be money, but it might be your time, or the things you're good at), you need to have made peace with those around you first.

Cut out giant hands from those foam washing-up cloths, or just pieces of cardboard, and attach one to a stick. The children can have a go at the handshake game from before, but high five each other with their Mega Hands instead. If you go back into church in time for the Peace, maybe they'd like to Mega High Five everyone in church, so that the rest of the congregation really notice that the Peace is happening!

Big Kids' Sunday School

Do a little bit of role playing being annoying and getting annoyed. Children can take it in turns to be doing something (drawing a picture, maybe, or making a model from Lego) when the other child comes and knocks them, or spoils the picture, or breaks the model. Emphasise that we are just playing around with this, nobody is really doing it on purpose, and be prepared to cut it short, and swap around partners if someone is getting genuinely upset.

That feeling of anger, of frustration, bubbles up inside us easily, doesn't it? Even when we're just playing around, and we know we're playing around, people being annoying is still, well, annoying! Mention the Peace in church. Do the children know which bit of the service you're talking about? Why might that be in there? It's not just an excuse for a wander and a chat, but actually following some great advice from Jesus. He tells us that if we're coming to bring an offering to God, an offering of money, maybe, or our time or our talents, we need first to go and make peace with those around us. God will give us the courage and strength to do that, but until we're a community of peace, there's not much more we can do, and we won't be able to be a force for good in the world.

Nobody is saying this is easy. Those feelings of anger and frustration are very real, and often appear with good reason. But dragging them around with us takes up a lot of energy. If we are able to put them down, we can walk freely into the future, into God's future for us, as we offer our money and time and talents to God's glory, and he takes them and uses them in amazing ways we have yet to imagine.

Provide some coloured paper for them to rip up into the letters PEACE. As they rip, they can talk about times they've felt angry, cross and frustrated. As they stick the letters down, they can talk about times they've turned around this ripping anger and created peace.

GOD'S RULE OF LOVE

Readings

- Leviticus 19:1-2, 9-18
- Psalm 119:33-40
- 1 Corinthians 3:10-11, 16-23
- Matthew 5:38-48

Thoughts on the Readings

God's laws are useful for us, practical and sensible, and help us to care for those around us who are in need. Sometimes when we read about the particular laws in the Old Testament, they can seem dated and strange – indeed, they were written a really long time ago. But the passage we have today to read from Leviticus has a lot of common sense advice. Like now, there must have been some people who would not have done these things without it being the law – things like leaving some grapes and grain around the edge of your field for the poor in your community. It is also God's law not to make fun of a deaf person or cause a blind person to stumble – some things which have only relatively recently come into our own laws today. It is good to think that things like food hygiene laws, making our buildings accessible, providing safe places to cross the road with bumps in the floor for blind people to feel the edge of the pavement with their feet, and legislation against hate crime all fits together with those laws given by God thousands of years ago. These modern laws may not have been put in place by people who had a knowledge of the Old Testament, but perhaps it shows us how God can be at work in all the people he loves and has created, if they want to do what is right.

Our psalm for today also tells of the goodness of God's laws – they are not harsh or unreasonable, but will help us live in the right way, close to God. Through knowing that we are making good, generous and kind choices, like our good, kind and generous God, we will not need to worry about any unkind things that anyone says about us.

Jesus, in our reading from Matthew's Gospel, talks about how God's laws should not be used to limit our kindness and compassion, through thinking that by obeying them we have done enough. The idea of taking an eye for an eye and a tooth for a tooth was never intended as some right to a certain amount of revenge, but rather was to limit the amount of retaliation and punishment that might be meted out. Jesus says that we should instead forgive others and show that radically different attitude that comes from God's compassion. We should love our enemies, not hate them – not an easy thing to do, but a practical and freeing step that we can take to release ourselves from living tied up by resentment and pain. We have the opportunity to make the choice to love our enemies, and we may have to choose this again every day, but with Jesus beside us this will become easier the more we do it.

Jesus' words do not go against God's law, but really clarify it and help us understand the principles behind it. If we make the choice to act in a loving way, then this will be good both for us, and for others around us.

Discussion Starters

- As a church, what do we communicate about our understanding of God's laws – is it as something that shows love? Are there other things we could do to share with the poorest, and welcome those with disabilities into our buildings?

Intercessions

Lord, we treasure your law,
show us the way of love.

Thank you, Lord,
that you show us the right, good
and compassionate way to live.
Be with us as we choose
to follow you.

We give thanks for our church leaders
and anyone who helps to lead us closer to you.
We pray that together,
we would understand your law of love
and that you would show us
how this can help us to make a difference
to others around us.
Lord, we treasure your law,
show us the way of love.

We bring into your care
our world
and particularly think of places
where either civil or religious laws
are interpreted in a way
which causes suffering and exclusion.
We pray that those in authority
would experience a revelation of your love
and an understanding that following rules
is different to holiness.
Lord, we treasure your law,
show us the way of love.

Lord, we bring into your loving care
anyone whose physical or mental health
has been affected by poverty or exclusion.
We pray that their voices would be heard
by those who can make a difference.
We also ask that your healing arms
would surround anyone suffering today, including . . .
Lord, we treasure your law,
show us the way of love.

We thank you that in heaven
you will welcome us into a place
filled with your love,
where there will be no more pain or problems.
We think of those people who are on that journey
to be with you today
and we also remember with love
those who have gone before us, including . . .
Lord, we treasure your law,
show us the way of love.

May we hold your law of love in our hearts
as we go out from this place,
a law that brings us freedom
and brings our world peace.
Amen.

Children's Prayer

Jesus,
instead of hating
we will choose love.
Instead of taking
we will choose giving
and instead of hurting
we will choose helping.
Amen.

Other Ideas!

Put out a large piece of paper (make it look old by rubbing a wet teabag over it if you like) and write at the top, 'Good Laws'. People can then add on any good laws which help those who are sometimes left out and treated badly.

All-age Talk

Bring along a powerful torch, or make a large sunshine out of card painted yellow, and get a volunteer to hold it.

Have you ever heard the phrase, 'The sun shines on the righteous'? Can we have some volunteers up here to do some righteous things, so the sun can shine on them? Maybe they

can mime helping an old person across a road, comforting someone who's sad, putting the recycling in the right bin, holding hands and playing happily together. The 'sun' can shine on them, and we can all look at the lovely things they're doing. How wonderful.

Can we get some nastier people up here please? Maybe someone can mime having a tantrum, stealing a handbag, ignoring someone who is asking for help. What do we think the sun should do now? Should the sun shine on these people too?

Well, we all know what the sun does. It shines on all of us. The 'sun' can shine on everyone up at the front. It brings light and life to our whole planet. Almost every species is reliant on the sun for life, for food, for warmth, for safety. The sun shines on the nice people walking down the street, and it shines on the bad people doing bad things. It doesn't switch off when a nasty person comes out of their house, and switch on again when a nice person needs it.

Did you notice the whole quote from Jesus in the Gospel? Jesus knows that the sun doesn't switch off and on. That's the whole point he's making. 'The sun shines on the righteous and the unrighteous.' Why should we love our enemies? Because this is precisely what God does. He sends the sunshine and the rain to everyone, whether they love him or not, whether they follow him or not. God's love is big enough to cover everyone. God's rule of love is the rule we need to follow.

Children's Corner

Set up a toy farm, and display a list of rules: all the animals need lots of space, cows need to be able to eat grass, sheep must be fed hay in the winter, ducks must be given a pond to swim on, chickens need a safe house to sleep in. The children can set the farm up so that they follow all the rules. They can whisper with their parents and carers about what useful things good rules can be, and what good rules we follow in our own lives.

The colouring sheet shows some of God's rules in pictures, to colour in.

Little Kids' Sunday School

Set up some rules for the children to follow, e.g. to jump when they hear you clap, to lie down when you stamp your feet, to skip when you wave your arms, to march when you tap your knees, to sit down when you click your fingers, to make sure that they're always in their own space, to move carefully when they're near obstacles, to help others remember and follow the rules.

Games are more fun when we all know the rules. When rules are good rules, they keep us all safe and happy. Maybe the children know of some good rules from home or school, and would like to share these.

God has given his people rules to live by, too, to keep his people safe and happy. In the book of Leviticus in the Bible, written a really, really long time ago, there are rules about leaving some grain around the edge of the field so that the poor people can find food to eat. There are rules about not making fun of a deaf person or causing a blind person to stumble. There are rules about keeping food safe to eat. These are all good rules, and we follow rules similar to these even today. Jesus takes these rules a step forward. It's not enough to simply follow the rules, but we need to make sure we are living them. And if we are filled with God's love ourselves, God's rule of love will spill out into how we treat others. God's love is our rule to live by.

Today you can work together on creating some rules for your Sunday School group to use, week by week. Think them through together, checking that they fit against God's rule of love, and write them up on a large piece of paper or a blackboard, and display them for you all to see each week.

Big Kids' Sunday School

Play a game of 'Dragons Eggs'. Put the children in teams, and a bowl of 'dragon's eggs' in the centre of the room. The eggs can be beanbags or ball pit balls, or something similar. Each team of children also has a bowl to be their own team nest. When you shout, 'Go!' each team can send someone into the middle to collect an egg. The rules are they can only carry one egg at a time, and only one runner can collect an egg at a time. Once all the eggs from the centre have been collected, they can raid each other's nests (and can't stop another team from taking one of their eggs). When you shout 'Stop!' count up how many eggs each team has, and declare a winner.

In this game there were some rules, and we all followed them. It doesn't stop us feeling frustrated that the rules don't go further, though, when someone comes and takes the egg we've only just acquired! The Bible reading they're having in church today comes from the Old Testament and has lots of good rules for how people should live. But in the Gospel reading, Jesus takes these and goes one step further. Following rules, even to the letter, isn't enough. We need to have the courage, God's courage, to follow God's rule of love wherever it takes us. Jesus says, 'The sun shines on the righteous and the unrighteous.' God shows love to everyone, whether they love him and follow him or not, and if we are following God, this is what we need to do, too.

Use circles of card (you can get this from your recycling bin) to weave sunshines. Draw a circle a few centimetres in diameter in the centre, and a circle a few centimetres from the edge, and draw straight lines between the two so it looks like a wagon wheel. With a sharp knife (on another stack of card to protect your floor) cut along these straight lines. Cut a weaving 'needle' out of a small rectangle of card, and punch a hole in the end to tie on some wool, ribbon, or long strips of old coloured plastic bag. Weave round and round to create a circle for the centre of the sun, and then weave round, leaving a space between every other woven bit, so that it looks like the rays of the sun. They can take these home and remember that God's sun shines on everyone, and we need to have the courage to shine God's love on everyone too.

Care for each other

Share what you have

Take time to rest and pray

DON'T WORRY

Readings

- Genesis 1:1 – 2:3
- Psalm 136 or
  Psalm 136:1-9, 23-26
- Romans 8:18-25
- Matthew 6:25-34

Thoughts on the Readings

As we hear Jesus' words in the Gospel of Matthew, about not worrying, it is sometimes hard to really put this into action in our own lives. Our anxiety as a society increases the more we perceive inequality around us. Those on the lowest incomes are genuinely concerned about where the next meal is coming from, while the most privileged are fearful that what they have accumulated may be taken away.

Worrying about what we are going to eat, drink or wear can paradoxically become more of an issue the more we have, rather than the less we have. Those people who have the most money to spend are also often anxious about wearing the right clothes, serving the right drinks, and eating the best or most healthy foods. Of course, it is good to look after our own health, but we need to keep this in proportion, and not let concern about our own diet and health become an obsession in itself.

Jesus tells us not to worry about these things. If we take a moment and look at what we already have, often we will find that there is more than enough for our needs. Jesus reminds us of the beautiful flowers that just naturally grow with amazing colours – they don't have to buy anything! And the birds don't have to go to work. They are fed by God. Perhaps we can learn from what we see around us – to see the beauty in what is already there, and to appreciate what we already have.

The wonderful story of creation from the first chapter of Genesis tells us of God's creativity and provision. None of this happened because a human being caused it, or because they wanted the plants or animals to be this way or that way, more like this or less like that. Everything has come about because of God, and all that he has created fits together as a whole. We are part of that universe. God feeds the birds in the sky, the animals and the fish, and provides for us too. Perhaps this ancient story of God's inclusive and generous love can inspire us today to see ourselves as part of God's creation. The good things that he gives are there for us, but they are also just as much there for the other creatures and plants that we share our planet with.

The psalm for today also echoes this idea, praising God for his wonderful creation and thanking him for the way that he provides for every living thing.

Our reading from the book of Romans gives us some encouragement which can help us today, when we see so much destruction and lack of care for the world around us. It really can feel that nature is groaning like a woman about to give birth. We wonder if she can take any more. But we are reassured by Paul's words that the Holy Spirit will help us when we don't know what to pray. It can be hard to know where to start when faced with the problems that we see around us in the world. But if we come before God, and let his Holy Spirit fill us, we don't need to be afraid. We will never be separated from God's love and as we pray, we will draw near to him.

Discussion Starters

- Locally, what can we be thankful for in God's creation? This can be anything, large or small.

Intercessions

**Lord, for the way you provide for us,
we thank you.**

As we come before you, Lord, in prayer,
we thank you for the way that
in your presence
we do not need to worry about anything;
you give us all we need.

We bring before you our church
and all its needs and challenges,
whatever these may be.
We thank you that we can trust you
to give us what we need
and that sometimes the answer we are looking for
is nearer than we think.
**Lord, for the way you provide for us,
we thank you.**

Thinking of our world, we know
that there are many people
who are genuinely concerned
about where their next meal is coming from,
while others are wrapped up in anxiety
about whether they are going to be seen as 'good enough',
although they have plenty.
We pray that we would all come to an understanding
that we are part of your family
and part of your creation
and that your wonderful provision
is there to share so that everyone's needs are met.
**Lord, for the way you provide for us,
we thank you.**

We bring into your loving care
those who feel that they do not know
the way ahead

and those who are in despair.
We pray that your wonderful Holy Spirit
would cover them, help them,
lead them and strengthen them.
We also pray for those who are suffering
or who are in pain at this time,
and pray that you would give them
everything that they need.
We name before you today . . .
**Lord, for the way you provide for us,
we thank you.**

We prayerfully bring into your presence
anyone who is nearing the end of their life's journey
and pray that they would know
that you are very close to them.
We also remember those people
who are now worshipping you in heaven,
at peace, and free of pain.
This week we particularly think of . . .
**Lord, for the way you provide for us,
we thank you.**

Lord, we thank you
that whatever concerns us, big or small,
we can bring it before you.
This week, if we find ourselves
starting to worry
we will choose to turn to your loving presence
and trust in you.
Amen.

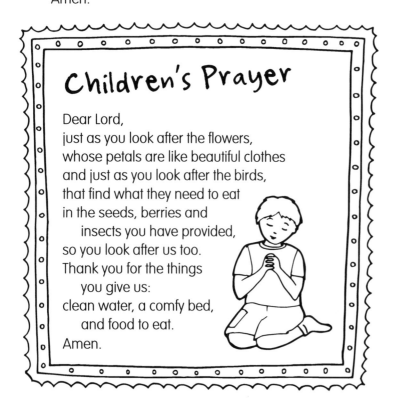

Children's Prayer

Dear Lord,
just as you look after the flowers,
whose petals are like beautiful clothes
and just as you look after the birds,
that find what they need to eat
in the seeds, berries and
    insects you have provided,
so you look after us too.
Thank you for the things
    you give us:
clean water, a comfy bed,
    and food to eat.
Amen.

Other Ideas!

Show a picture of a flower meadow, with the words from today's Gospel (Matthew 6:27-30).

All-age Talk

Have a packet of wildflower seed, and a pack of bird seed to hand for today's talk.

You've brought some things along today to help with rewilding the space around the church building. Shake the packet of wildflower seeds, and tip some out onto the hands of a few volunteers. As they head outside the building to scatter them, they can show the tiny seeds to others as they go past. Read from the packet the different kinds of flowers that will be growing, and imagine together how the church might look surrounded by the blue of cornflowers, the red of poppies, and the yellow of cowslips.

Shake and open up the pack of bird seed, and tip some into the hands of a few volunteers who can head off outside the building to scatter the bird seed where it can be pecked up by hungry birds. Talk about the birds you've seen around your building, that might fly down for a bite to eat.

Worrying comes easily to us humans. We worry about what to wear, but flowers don't, they just look stunning exactly as they are. We worry about what to eat, but birds don't, they just peck away at the food God has provided for them, in the seeds, nuts, berries and insects already abundant in nature. We worry because we feel we should be in control. We should be in control of what we wear, and what we eat, of what we do, of who we hang out with. Even in what way our poor old planet should be recovering from the worst of our species' excesses.

But maybe we need to take a leaf (pun intended) from the flowers and the birds. Not just in the ways we worry about clothes and food, but in a much broader sense. Sometimes our worrying gets in the way of things happening gently, perfectly, in their own good time. Just look at the countryside around Chernobyl, for example. It has rewilded beautifully and richly, simply because it's been left to get on with things. Doing nothing, like the flowers and the birds do, gets a bad press sometimes. And yet sometimes it's in the fallow space, the expectant space, of 'doing nothing' that God is able to work. Maybe we should worry less about the doing, and more about simply just holding the space to let things be.

Children's Corner

Provide a selection of wild flowers and grasses, so the children can enjoy making flower arrangements in strong vases. It's a bit early in the year, but there's always something growing! They can listen out for when Jesus talks about flowers in the Gospel reading, about how they don't have to worry about what to wear because they grow beautifully, just the way God intends for them. And how we don't have to worry either, because God has promised to care for us too.

The colouring sheet shows a wild flower meadow with birds flying overhead. The passage from the Gospel reading is written on the sheet so they can have it read to them as they colour.

Little Kids' Sunday School

Print out photos of wild flowers (you can find these online, on the Woodland Trust's Nature Detectives website, or on Grow Wild), two copies of each photo. Place them photo side down on the floor or a table to play a large game of Pelmanism, turning over two sheets to see if the flowers match. If they match, that child can keep them. It's a little tricky with wild flowers, as they'll have to look more closely than just looking at their colour.

Jesus used wild flowers to teach people not to worry. Look at these flowers, he said. They don't worry about what clothes they have to wear, and yet they always look beautiful. He talked about the birds too. They don't worry about getting food, they just eat the seeds and nuts that God gives them. Try being more like these flowers, like these birds, said Jesus. They know that God will give them what they need, and God will give you what you need too.

Get some of those cardboard cut-out figures you can buy in kids' art suppliers or even in a high street shop, but if you can't buy them, make them by cutting a simple person out of card. Stick a strip of double-sided carpet tape down the middle, and they can peel off the paper covering of this, and decorate the person's clothes using plants. You might have some plants outside your church building, but if not, maybe you could buy some bunches of flowers that are on sale as they've got to the end of their shelf life. As they decorate their people with beautiful clothes, they can talk about all the ways that God gives us what we need.

Big Kids' Sunday School

Give the children a pile of old newspapers and masking tape to create clothes for a fashion show. You can play some music as they strut their stuff on the catwalk. Clothes are useful, they keep us warm and it's fun to show off our style. But clothes, like lots of things, can also lead to worry. Are these clothes cool enough? What will people think if we're wearing them? We worry about food too: is this healthy? Is this an embarrassing food choice? And we have other things that worry us, and crowd into our minds.

When Jesus was walking around, teaching people and healing them, he would have passed many wild flowers on his way. Travelling by foot brings you close to the nature around you. Jesus was obviously struck by the variety and beauty of the flowers, and he used them to help people understand about how God gives us what we need, so we don't need to worry. Look at the flowers, Jesus said. They don't worry about finding the right things to wear, and yet they always look amazing. They are amazing just the way they grow. And that's the same as us, isn't it? We don't need to worry about what impact we're making, what impression we're making, because as long as we're growing, rooted strongly in God's love, we will be able to be wholly and completely ourselves, and it is who we are that is beautiful, as far as God's concerned.

Mix up some mud and roll it into balls. Roll the balls in wildflower seed, and the children can give these out to the congregation after church, so they can take them home, and throw them into a patch of waste ground, and maybe in the summer there'll be lots of reminders of this teaching from Jesus on all their routes to church.

Don't worry about what to eat or what to wear - your Heavenly Father feeds the birds and gives the flowers beautiful clothes to wear. How much more will he look after you!

SEEING GOD'S GLORY

Readings

- Exodus 24:12-18
- Psalm 2 or Psalm 99
- 2 Peter 1:16-21
- Matthew 17:1-9

Thoughts on the Readings

Peter's experience on the mountain with Jesus was something that stayed with him, and gave him the confidence to tell others about Jesus. Seeing those holy prophets, Moses and Elijah, in person, must have been pretty amazing, and Peter writes that this made him even more certain that what the prophets said was true. He had heard the voice of God himself speaking from the cloud, and had seen God's glory shining around them all.

Moses, too, encountered God when he climbed Mount Sinai. We hear that Moses made arrangements for while he was away – presumably he had no idea how long God would ask him to stay up that mountain. Moses knew what the people were like and left Aaron and Hur to deal with any arguments. (We can imagine that this was usually Moses' job, and perhaps he was pleased to have a bit of a break from it!) As the cloud covered the mountain and Moses sat, waiting for God's next instruction for six whole days, just gazing on the brightness of God's glory, we may wonder what was going through his mind. It was only after this, on the seventh day, that God asked Moses to come into the cloud.

Moses and Joshua had climbed the mountain in order to meet with God, to draw near to God and to hear what he had to say. It is not easy climbing a mountain – there are steep and rocky parts, and the weather can change quite suddenly. It isn't quick either – you have to allow enough time for the climb, and it's important to prepare for that sort of trip, bringing with you all the things you need. This deliberate intention to meet with God, an expectation that there is no shortcut or instant fix but that it may take a bit of time and effort, is something that we can learn from.

But the experience at the top of the mountain was worth it. Both Peter and Moses were given messages by God to give to the people, and so this encounter was something that could bless many other people. They were also transformed personally through experiencing God's light and glory, something that they could then take to others.

Discussion Starters

- **Share any special places you have been where you have been struck by the beauty of creation or felt particularly close to God.**

Intercessions

**As we come into your presence,
may we see your glory.**

Holy God,
we want to draw near to you,
we want to know you
and we want to experience
your glory and your love.
We pray that you would be close to us now.

We bring before you our church
and thank you for the worship
that takes place here, week after week.
We pray that it would be a place
where your glory would be known
and where your light can shine
into the communities around us.
**As we come into your presence,
may we see your glory.**

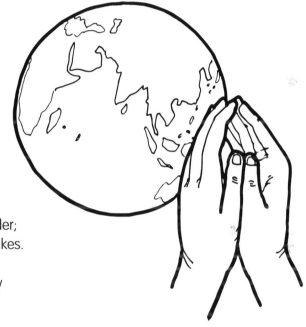

We bring to mind our world
and thank you for those beautiful places
created by you
which inspire in us a sense of awe and wonder;
coastlines, mountains, deserts, forests and lakes.
We pray for the organisations
which work to protect areas of natural beauty
in spite of many challenges
and we ask that you would help us
to take action to protect these places too.
**As we come into your presence,
may we see your glory.**

We know that there are many people around us
who feel that there is a lot of darkness in their lives,
who may be feeling isolated, misunderstood,
anxious, sad or in pain.
We pray that you would enable us
to lead them into your loving and healing presence
through our words and actions,
so that they may know something
of your glory, light and love.
We name before you today . . .
**As we come into your presence,
may we see your glory.**

We remember with love
those people who have now passed
from this life into the next
and who can now gaze on your glory
and rest in your love
for eternity.
We think of those who have recently died,
and those who are missed at this time of year
and pray that your presence would be close
to their family and friends.
We remember today . . .
**As we come into your presence,
may we see your glory.**

Precious and Holy God,
may your light shine through us,
so that others may see your glory
and be drawn to you.
Amen.

Children's Prayer

Dear God,
we love the things you have made.
When the sea crashes and splashes
we see that you have made something
fun, lively and powerful.
When we feel the warmth of your sun
we know your care and your strength.
And when we look up at the
    bright, twinkling stars
and the round,
    yellow moon
we know that your love
is bigger than we
    can ever imagine.
Amen.

Other Ideas!

Create a collage using pictures of
mountains and other spectacular
and beautiful places.

All-age Talk

Invite your volunteer up today. They are going to be climbing a mountain! They can take off their shoes and put on walking boots. Pass them a climbing pole and a backpack with a waterproof coat in, and give them a nice fat looped rope to hold.

They can set off (on the spot) at a nice brisk walk. Can they see the mountain looming up ahead? They've got lots of energy after eating their porridge for breakfast. Setting off for a spiritual experience, with the intention of meeting God, can feel like this as we begin, can't it? We are full of enthusiasm and excitement.

The path is getting steeper now. Get your volunteer to make a bit more heavy weather of their climbing (on the spot). Sometimes they have to scramble from rock to rock. They might bump their knee or stub their toe. And sometimes that's a bit like us. We set off to have a spiritual experience with God, and find that it can be unexpectedly difficult. The path that looked so smooth from a distance is much harder going as we encounter it. Although, sometimes, when we trip we notice tiny wild flowers growing in the crevasses in the rock as we go. Glimpses of glory to come, maybe.

The weather might change. Storm clouds have gathered and are about to break. Get your volunteer to reach into their backpack and put on their waterproof coat. It's hard to see their way ahead. But because they prepared, and brought with them the things they needed, they can keep on going. They have a map, and a compass, and a coat to keep them dry. We have the Bible, our church community, our friends of faith, and all of these can help to protect and guide us as our journey gets difficult.

And finally, they reach the top. They can stand and gaze in wonder at the beautiful view stretching out before them on every side. Like Moses, like Peter, they are caught up in God's glory all around them. And no doubt, like Moses and Peter, it will change how they live. If you want to catch them after church for coffee, I'm sure they'll tell you how brilliant the experience was. They'll tell you that the climb was difficult but that the view was so awesome, so awe-inspiring, that it was totally worth it. That this glimpse of glory has put everything into perspective. And this glory is something all of us can catch a glimpse of, whether we are mountain climbers or not. God's glory is all around us. We just have to make a decision to see it.

Children's Corner

Provide a basket full of different sized and shaped stones and pebbles, for the children to build into a mountain. A small world figure can climb up the mountain, like Moses, like Peter, and meet with God in the splendour and grandeur of the place.

The colouring sheet shows a mountain scene, with the words, **'God's amazing creation can help us to meet him'**.

Little Kids' Sunday School

Collect some amazing and beautiful natural objects for the children to enjoy exploring, e.g. skulls, feathers, flowers, leaves, bark. Give them magnifying glasses and maybe a hand-held microscope and enjoy being wowed by God's creation.

Tell them the story of Moses, going up the mountain to meet with God, and of Peter, going up the mountain and seeing Jesus in all his heavenly glory. You can act it out, walking up the mountain bit by bit, as it gets steeper and steeper, and as you stand puffed out on the top you can gaze down at the world around you. Like Moses and Peter, you are also able to see God's glory all around you. And once you've noticed God's glory once, it's easier to see it everywhere. We got in practice earlier, didn't we?

Use paper plates and cut out the middle so they make a little window. Cover this with a square of sticky-backed plastic, and then stick on natural objects. Leaves work well, and petals and feathers if you can find any. Cover with another layer of sticky-backed plastic, like a sandwich. The children can take these home and hang them on their window so the light shines through, as they remember to notice the shining light of God's glory everywhere, throughout his whole creation, even in the most ordinary places.

Big Kids' Sunday School

Place enough chairs for everyone, facing the centre, apart from the person who is standing in the middle. They say a statement: 'Over the mountain everyone who's wearing purple/ likes eating blue cheese/has ever weed in the swimming pool.' Anyone who fits that category stands up, and crosses 'the mountain' aka the space in the middle, to sit on another chair. The person from the centre tries to find a space to fit inside, and whoever's left comes up with another statement. If you have a parachute for parachute games, you can trap a bubble of air inside to make a mountain to clamber over.

It's interesting that this game is called 'Over the Mountain'. If we are climbing a mountain with other people, it is certain that we will know more about them after climbing over the mountain than we did before we started. It's as we walk and talk, and tackle difficult things, that we grow close to people. There are two stories about mountains in the Bible readings today: Moses climbing up the mountain to meet with God, and Peter ascending the mountain to see Jesus in his glory. You can precis or retell one or both of these, but it's interesting for them to hear both, or at least know of the existence of both.

In a small jam-jar, they can use grey or green modelling clay to form a mountain on the inside of the lid. Add water, a little baby oil, and some eco glitter. Once the lid has been screwed on, you can shake the jar to see the glory that surrounded Moses and Peter when they were at their mountain top.

GOD'S AMAZING CREATION CAN HELP US TO MEET HIM

JESUS IS TEMPTED IN THE DESERT

Readings

- Genesis 2:15-17; 3:1-7
- Psalm 32
- Romans 5:12-19
- Matthew 4:1-11

Thoughts on the Readings

Not trusting that God really does have our best interests at heart leads to wrong choices – his laws are for our own good and wellbeing, and that of others. In the reading from Genesis, the snake implies that he knows better than God, and plants the idea that God is trying to withhold something good from Adam and Eve. This attitude led Adam and Eve to act against God's laws and choose to eat the fruit that they had specifically been told not to have. They thought they knew better than God, and perhaps that is often the root of sin. We may think up reasons and excuses why we should act the way we want, although deep down we probably know that this is not right.

Thankfully, when we realise that we are starting to do this, there is a way to put it right. Today's psalm reminds us that until we confess our sins they will weigh us down and make us feel weary. The best thing we can do is to confess them to God, who loves us so much and will give us a new start.

In the Gospel reading we hear how the voice of the devil tells Jesus that he should rely on his own power and use that to satisfy his needs. Perhaps he was also trying to unsettle the exhausted and hungry Jesus by sowing seeds of doubt in his mind – suggesting miracles that he should be able to do, but just somehow didn't sound right. Perhaps we also feel this pressure from those who question our faith – 'Surely your God should have prevented that person from dying? Surely if your God was real that earthquake would not have happened?' This sort of thinking is understandable, but would require a world in which the laws of nature were constantly being overturned, and does not understand the eternal nature and enormity of God's everlasting love and the heavenly home that he has for us.

When tempting Jesus, the devil also pretends that he has more to give than he really does – 'all the kingdoms of the world' – if Jesus agrees to worship him. These, of course, were not his to give. It was all a lie. Sometimes a deal looks too good to be true, and it usually is. It can be tempting to follow the ways of the world, so that we can achieve our goals (and these may well be good goals). But we need to be really careful about this, and make sure that everything we do is infused with God's true values, and led by his love.

In this last temptation, the devil goes too far. Jesus tells him in no uncertain terms to get lost, and he leaves Jesus alone at last. Often situations may go on for a while, and then something happens where it just becomes clear that what is going on is not ok. That is when we need to be strong, speak out and take action. God will give us strength to do this.

In our reading from the letter to the Romans, we hear how in a way, God's gift of kindness through Jesus was an antidote to Adam's sin. We humans all have the ability to make wrong and selfish choices, but through Jesus we can be given the strength and vision to do what is right and act in a way that brings glory to God. We don't need to be afraid to bring our sins before God – he is kind and compassionate, and will always be ready to forgive us.

Discussion Starters

- **As we bring our sins before God, we feel a sense of love, peace and oneness with him. How can we communicate the difficult topic of sin with those outside the church, who may have had negative experiences of feeling excluded, made to feel guilty or judged by religious organisations in the past?**

Intercessions

**Lord, may we speak with grace
and act with love.**

Father, we know
that it isn't always easy to make the right choices.
We pray that as we come before you
we would tune into your way of love.

Lord, we bring before you our church
and pray that you would fill it with your love and grace
so that it can be a place of welcome
where people do not feel judged or excluded
but where we can all come in honesty, just as we are
and meet with you.
We pray that as we do this
you would lift our burdens
and strengthen us to live
in your way of love.
**Lord, may we speak with grace
and act with love.**

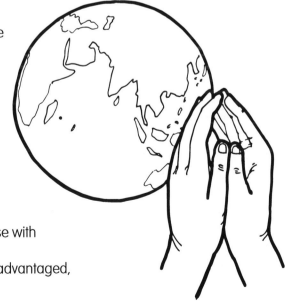

Lord, we know that in our world
there are many choices to be made.
We see situations where the decisions made by those with
political, economic, cultural or religious power
have made life worse for those who are already disadvantaged,
and there are also positive examples
of when things have got better.

We pray that you would help us to take action
and to speak out where needed
so that we can use our influence for good.
**Lord, may we speak with grace
and act with love.**

We bring into your loving care
anyone who is thinking about a difficult decision at this time
and pray for those who are being pressured to act
in an unethical or unkind way.
We pray that you would strengthen them with your love
and empower them with your wisdom.
We also bring to you those who are in any kind of need,
whether they are in pain, exhausted or lonely.
We pray that you would be with them
and surround them with your loving care.
We name before you today . . .
**Lord, may we speak with grace
and act with love.**

Thank you for the promise
of a home in heaven with you.
We remember today those known to us
who are now at peace in your eternal kingdom,
worshipping you with all the angels and saints.
This week we particularly remember . . .
**Lord, may we speak with grace
and act with love.**

As we go out from this place
may we be strengthened with your love
and inspired with your wisdom,
as we grow more like you.
Amen.

Children's Prayer

Dear Lord,
when it's hard to know
what's the right thing to do,
we know we just need
to turn to you.
You'll help us to act
with kindness and love,
so that others will know
your grace from above.
Amen.

Other Ideas!

Give people the opportunity to make a cross out of a couple of sticks, with wool wound around them to hold it together. This can be carried as a reminder of God's love and wisdom.

All-age Talk

Bring along a large stone, a crown and a magic wand.

Hold up the large stone, and remind everyone of what the devil tempted Jesus with first. That's right, Jesus had been fasting. He was really hungry; he needed to eat. The devil tempted him by saying why not use his power to turn this stone into bread, to get the thing he needed using his own power. That can be something we are tempted by, too. We think that we can do things by ourselves. It's something often celebrated in our society, the idea of the 'self-made man'. We are tempted to use our power, our money, our status, to get us what we want, forgetting that all good things come from God, and it is God who always gives us what we need. Obviously our weekly shopping won't come delivered by angels, but if we shop full of gratitude that we are able to get what we need through God's grace, rather than congratulating ourselves for our own cleverness, we will be following the example of Jesus.

Hold up the crown, and remind everyone of what the devil tempted Jesus with next. All the kingdoms of the world! That's a lot of kingdoms. Sounds like a tempting offer. But all is not always as it seems, just as in those emails you get, offering you untold wealth if only you respond with your account details. The kingdoms of the world were not the devil's to give. Sometimes a path to success, even success growing our church, getting more people to come on a Sunday morning maybe, can look tempting and easy. We need to check carefully the small print. We need to see who is offering what, and if they can really follow through. We need to measure it up against the values of God's kingdom and check that it fits.

Hold up the magic wand. The devil tempts Jesus with an easy way to show that he is the Son of God. A way that is so scripturally sound that all who would saw it would instantly be convinced. An act of such supernatural power that nobody could be in any doubt. **If** you are the Son of God, the devil says. **If**. Sometimes we feel that as Christians we shouldn't be beset by doubts. We shouldn't struggle with temptations. **If** we were truly following God, we hear a whisper in our hearts, **if** we were truly saved, we wouldn't doubt, and be tempted and fail and have to try again. We should take comfort in this Gospel story. Jesus himself was tempted, and as we gird our loins to travel through the wilderness of Lent, we can trust that the God who gave strength and courage to Jesus, is here to give strength and courage to us too.

Children's Corner

Bring along a toy snake, so that the children and their parents/carers can use it to whisper 'temptations' to the church teddies, and then help the church teddies to say no.

The colouring sheet shows three scenes of Jesus being tempted, with the words written showing his answers.

Little Kids' Sunday School

Play a game of 'Snake Says'. It's a bit like Simon Says, but the other way round. If Snake says 'Pat your head', you don't!

It's quite hard stopping yourself doing something if someone tells you to. Even in this game when you know that you've got to listen out for Snake's voice, there are times we all slip up. How much harder is it in real life, when someone tells us to do something, and it might be wrong? We have to make sure we listen harder to the message of God's rule of living in a loving way, than the voices all around us. Tell them the story of Adam and Eve, and the temptation from the snake. Eve had heard God's instruction not to eat from the tree, but the instruction 'eat!' from the snake somehow shouted louder in her ears. Adam had heard God's instruction not to eat from the tree, but the instruction 'eat!' from Eve overwhelmed it. We all know deep down what is right and what is wrong. But we can get muddled by the messages all around us, of our friends telling us to do something mean, of the clothes in the shops telling us that we mustn't try to be clever if we're girls, of the toys in pink and blue telling us that boys shouldn't be gentle and caring. Those messages are wrong.

Chop up paper straws to make big beads, and thread them onto a pipe-cleaner. Each child will need at least 11. They can draw the head of a snake at the end, and one letter on each bead, to spell out: 'Is it right?' When they hear an instruction from their friends, from society, from those around them, they can remember the snake, and check out whether the instruction fits with God's rule of love.

Big Kids' Sunday School

Bring along a large collection of big stones that you've found outdoors. Stones with some character are going to be more interesting than a bag you've bought from the garden centre. The children can pick one up each, and spend a moment getting to know it really well. Put all the stones back in the centre, and jumble them up. Can each child find their own stone again? What do their stones remind them of?

After Jesus' baptism, he had gone off into the desert to pray and listen to God. He was fasting, so hadn't eaten or drunk for days. He must have felt really hungry. It's no surprise that when the devil visited him, he tempted him first with a stone. To a hungry person, a round stone would remind them strongly of a round loaf of bread. 'Why not use your power to turn this stone into bread?' tempted the devil. When Jesus rebuked him, the devil tried again. 'Look at all the kingdoms of the world! I can give them all to you, if you'll just bow down and worship me.' But the kingdoms of the world weren't the devil's to give; they all belong to God. The devil tried a third time: 'If you are the Son of God, do something so spectacular and supernatural that everyone will know that's who you are.' But the path Jesus was set on wasn't a game for playing party tricks to impress people. Jesus replied, again by quoting from the Scriptures: 'You shall not put your God to the test.' And then the devil left Jesus and angels came to look after him.

As we begin our time of preparation for Easter, our time of Lent, we will face challenges and temptations. It's good to know that Jesus did too. Each child can choose one of the stones, and paint on it those things we need that we can trust God to provide. We can trust God to give us what we need; we don't need to be tempted to grasp at more with our own power.

YOU MUST BE BORN AGAIN

Readings
- Genesis 12:1-4a
- Psalm 121
- Romans 4:1-5, 13-17
- John 3:1-17

Thoughts on the Readings

In both our reading from Genesis and today's psalm, we hear about God's wonderful promise of blessing and protection. This is not limited to one time, or one place; God guaranteed Abraham and us that wherever we go, he will be with us.

As Paul tells us in the letter to the Romans, God did not give Abraham this promise and blessing because he had done anything clever or amazing. Even if he had, he could not show off to God about it anyway. It was because of Abraham's faith – his close, trusting and loving relationship with the God who created the universe.

Sometimes those around us find it hard to understand why we believe what we do. It may be suggested that we are worshipping something that is made up, or believing in an ideology created by a powerful organisation wanting to control us. Or perhaps it is implied that our beliefs are just wishful thinking.

We know that our faith is more than this. It is a real, warm and ever-evolving personal relationship with God. That experience is something we could never make up. It is as real to us as the relationships we have with our friends and family. As we worship God, we draw close to him and experience a sense of love, peace, belonging and acceptance. Perhaps if we describe our faith in terms of our personal experience this may mean more to others than any quantity of intellectual reasoning.

This was the experience of Abraham, Paul and so many others through the course of history, including the saints we may have heard of, and the ordinary saintly people who we may not have heard of. We are not on our own.

This is why Jesus tells Nicodemus that he needs to be born by the Spirit. It is God's Holy Spirit, dwelling within us, who can enable us to know that wonderful closeness to the creator of the universe. Without that, we are just relying on dry rules and instructions.

When we find some space to be with God, in prayer, worship or wonder, we can experience that sense of closeness and love for ourselves. Those outside the church may also sense the presence of the Holy Spirit, although they may use different words to describe it, perhaps talking about the atmosphere of the place or a sense of welcome and love. This can be a starting point to help us communicate about our faith, too.

Discussion Starters

- **How do those outside the church describe and experience what we would know as the presence of the Holy Spirit? And how can we create an environment where this is able to happen?**

Intercessions

Holy Spirit,
fill us with your love.

Lord, we thank you
for those who came before us
who trusted in your promises
and whose faith inspires us.

We bring before you our church
and give thanks for all those, through the years,
who have helped us in our faith
through their words
and their example.
We give thanks for the faith of those
who wrote our hymns,
who translated our scriptures
and who spoke about God's care for us.
Holy Spirit,
fill us with your love.

We pray for those places in our world
where your love is badly needed
and where ideological or religious differences
have led to conflict or violence.
We pray that the presence of your Holy Spirit
would be known,
bringing peace, understanding and hope.
Holy Spirit,
fill us with your love.

We bring into your kind and caring presence
anyone who is searching for peace at this time
and those who feel alone.

Help us, as a church, to be a place
where your Holy Spirit's healing presence
can be felt and found
by those who are searching for it.
We also bring before you
anyone who is suffering at the moment, including . . .
Holy Spirit,
fill us with your love.

As we remember with love
those who have entered your heavenly kingdom,
we know that through your presence with us
heaven is nearer than we think.
We pray for those people
who are on the last stage of life's journey
and ask that they would know and experience
your company at this time.
This week we particularly remember . . .
Holy Spirit,
fill us with your love.

Lord, we thank you
for the way that you are near to us
wherever we go.
We pray that through our week
we would know you close
as we walk with you.
Amen.

Children's Prayer

Lord, inside my heart
there is a special place
where I know your love
like a nugget of golden
treasure.
I know you will never
leave me
and you will always
look after me,
wherever I go.
Amen.

Other Ideas!

Use a large canvas or piece of
card to write the words from
John 3:16 inside a heart shape.
Draw other hearts around this
as an outline, and ask people to
choose different coloured pens
to help fill in the layers. Keep
doing this until the whole page
is covered.

All-age Talk

Today you'll need something very tasty, something that feels amazing (one of those squishy toys, something with really soft fake fur, or those sequins that rub two ways), and headphones playing some amazing music. Write some long, poetic, advertising description for each.

Invite a volunteer up to come and taste this amazing food. Make sure it's something the volunteer is able to eat. Get them to read out the description. It sounds amazing. You can show them the food. Maybe they'd like to smell it. Now ask them to sit down and as they begin to walk off, looking a bit confused and a bit disappointed, invite them back. No, of course, they need to actually eat the food to find out what it's really like. Let them try it, and share their enthusiastic opinion.

Invite another volunteer up to come and stroke this fantastic object. Get them to read out the description. Wow, what an object! Let them look at it. Maybe shake it gently by their ear, in case they can hear the sequins shiver, or the fur wafting gently in the breeze. Now ask them to sit down and as they begin to walk off, looking a bit confused and disappointed, invite them back. No, of course, they need to actually feel the object to find out what it's really like. Let them stroke it, and share with the congregation how amazing it feels.

Invite a third volunteer up to come and listen to some marvellous music through these headphones. Get them to read out the description. That music sounds out of this world! They can feel the headphones, and the music device. Now ask them to sit down and you know what's coming next! Put the headphones on them, and they can share how brilliant the music is.

Jesus told Nicodemus that he needed to be born again, born in the spirit. It was not enough to just hear about Jesus. It was not enough to know the stories from the scriptures, or to know what other people said about God's love in their life. It was not enough to know the rules and to follow them. Nicodemus needed that relationship with God actually living inside him, that closeness of the Holy Spirit in his life. And that relationship, that closeness is what we all need.

Children's Corner

Provide heart-shaped baking tins/cupcake cases/ chocolate boxes, full of 'treasure' for the children to enjoy opening and sorting and putting back. God's love is like this treasure in our hearts.

The colouring sheet shows a heart shape full of treasure, with **'God's love is like a treasure in my heart'** as the writing to colour in.

Little Kids' Sunday School

Play baby races, crawling up to a rattle, giving it a shake, and then crawling back. You can add in some 'goo goo ga ga's for extra baby fun!

Babies are cute and funny, noisy and exhausting! Some of the children here may sometimes wish they could go back to being babies again, when they don't have to tidy their toys or walk to school, and someone carries them around and is kind to them all day long!

A man called Nicodemus came to see Jesus, sneaking through the darkness, so that his friends wouldn't know that he'd gone. He came to speak with Jesus, to try to understand the things that Jesus was saying and doing. He knew that Jesus must have been sent by God. Jesus told him that to truly see the kingdom of God, he must be born again. Born again?! Nicodemus was confused. How can a grown-up be born again? Fit back inside their mummy's tummy? Become a baby all over again? Jesus explained that this is how you get born as a human person. He was talking about being born in the Holy Spirit, being filled with the Holy Spirit so that you have a closeness with God.

The children can be given two pieces of fabric and a blunt needle. They can sew the pieces together up the spine to make a soft book, of the type that babies often play with. They can write 'How to truly see the kingdom of God' on the front, and one word per page of 'You must be born again'.

Big Kids' Sunday School

In a darkened room, or using blindfolds, set up an obstacle course for the children to make their way across. Have some adults on hand to keep them safe!

In our story today we hear of someone who came creeping through the streets at night. Nicodemus, a Pharisee, a member of the ruling council, had been watching Jesus, listening to what he said, and seeing what he did. He was interested and wanted to know more, but didn't want those he lived amongst and worked with to know he was going to see Jesus. He decided to come under the cover of darkness, to speak with Jesus. Jesus told him that to really see the kingdom of God, he must be born again. Born again?! What a strange thing for Jesus to say. Could he really climb back inside his mother and become a baby all over again? But that wasn't what Jesus meant. He meant being born of the Holy Spirit, instead, beginning his life as a baby Christian, with God's Holy Spirit living inside him and guiding him, drawing him closer to his heavenly Father.

Give each child a square flannel, and help them follow instructions to fold the flannel into a tiny nappy. You can give each child a safety pin to hold them together, and tie on a parcel label reading 'You must be born again'. As they fold the nappies, they can think about how being born as a baby Christian, no matter how old we are, is a bit similar to being a baby. How we have to trust that we'll be cared for. How we sometimes make mistakes but keep trying because that's how we learn. How we want the simple things that keep us alive, rather than worrying about complicated stuff.

GOD'S LIVING WATER

Readings

- Exodus 17:1-7
- Psalm 95
- Romans 5:1-11
- John 4:5-42

Thoughts on the Readings

Imagine how hard it must have been for Moses, leading that huge group of people through the desert, trying to do his best to listen to and obey God. How they had ended up camping somewhere without water, we do not know. We might imagine that someone young, fit and mobile would usually go ahead to check that the place they were heading to was suitable for a mixed group of people including the very young, very old, disabled and pregnant to stay in for some time. Perhaps someone had checked and reported back that there was water, which later dried up – perhaps they had started out together and had not managed to travel as far as they had hoped. Whatever the case, Moses was in trouble. As the leader, the buck stopped with him.

His first reaction, characteristically, was to call out to God. He felt comfortable enough in his relationship with God to express his frustration about the people he was looking after, who were now starting to threaten violence towards him.

God answers first of all with a practical suggestion. Moses is to surround himself with some of the other leaders, something which would make him less isolated and safer. Next, they were to go ahead of the people, so that they were separate from the rowdy crowd, hopefully giving them all a bit of a chance to calm down. After that, God told Moses to strike the rock at Mount Sinai with the famous walking stick which he had used to part the River Nile – a visual reminder to anyone looking that the authority of God was with Moses. Perhaps, as Moses carried this along, he would have also felt his confidence growing that God, again, was going to do something amazing.

As Moses, guided by God, struck the rock in faith, the water poured out for the people to drink. Yet again, their faithful God had provided for their needs in the most unlikely places.

Today's psalm picks up on this story of God's provision for us, and how he cares for us like the sheep in his own pasture. This is a reminder to us not to complain and test God like when the Israelites were in the desert – although things may not always make sense to us at the time, we really can trust God to be with us and care for us.

In our Gospel reading we have another story about water. This time, Jesus uses the setting of a well to engage the Samaritan woman in a conversation which then leads to him being able to tell her about the life-giving water that only he can give. Jesus didn't mind that other people were making comments and staring at him for going over to the well and starting to chat with a woman – a Samaritan woman at that! Jesus just knew that the most important thing was to show his Father's love. Perhaps this is sometimes the case for us, too. To step out in faith and make contact with others who are different from us may take some courage and be out of our comfort zone, but we may well find that we have a closer connection than we think and that actually we have more in common than we thought. Interestingly, this Samaritan woman had been wondering about when the Messiah would come, and when she asks Jesus about it, he tells her that it is him. The Messiah is speaking to her right now! Jesus often leaves people to work out who he is, but in this setting he is pleased to tell the woman and her friends quite clearly. He must have felt that it was the right time and the place to do this, and we are told at the end of the reading that many Samaritans came to faith because of this.

Sometimes, where we are, we need to listen to God so that we can know how best to lead others to him. Sometimes we need to listen to others tell us about their lives and experiences, sometimes we need to show God's love in practical ways, and sometimes it is the right time and place to speak directly about Jesus and the good news that he brings to us all. This might be in a place we are expecting, or we may be surprised. We might not be waiting in a queue to get water from a well, but there may be other places where we are waiting, and others are there, ready to listen. We just need to be open to God, and sensitive to the needs of those around us.

Discussion Starters

- **Who do we meet when we are 'waiting at the well'? Our equivalent might be in the queue at the supermarket, in the café or in the school playground. How can we show God's love and help people to come and meet with Jesus?**

Intercessions

**As we wait,
may we meet with you.**

Lord, we come before you
and thank you for the water of life that you give us –
refreshing us, sustaining us
and quenching our thirst for you.
May we receive this from you today.

We bring into your loving care
all those who lead our church,
locally, nationally and around the world.
We pray that you would refresh them
with your living water
and that we would all be ready
to come and receive this wonderful gift from you.
**As we wait,
may we meet with you.**

We pray for those areas in our world
where water is in short supply,
for people in refugee camps
and those who have to travel long distances
to collect the water they need.
We also pray for a greater sense of responsibility
among those in places where there is plenty
to treat water with respect and care,
so that our water sources are kept free of pollution
and our precious drinking water
is not wasted.
As we wait,
may we meet with you.

We bring into your loving and healing care
those groups who are marginalised
or who feel they are treated as less valuable than others.
We particularly pray for those who feel
that they do not have a voice, and are not listened to.
We pray that, as a church, we would be a place
where people's voices can be heard
in a supportive and caring environment,
where we can show your love.
We bring to you anyone who is unwell at the moment,
especially those whose conditions are little understood.
We name before you today . . .
As we wait,
may we meet with you.

As we remember those who are on the last stage of life's journey,
we pray that they would know your love and care,
like sheep in your own pasture.
We also bring to mind those who are now
at rest in heaven with you,
and ask that you would care for and comfort
those who miss them.
We name before you . . .
As we wait,
may we meet with you.

Heavenly Father,
we pray that as you have filled us, sustained us and refreshed us
we would be ready to bring your love and good news
to the people we meet as we go through our week.
Amen.

Children's Prayer

Lord, when we are thirsty
you give us water.
When we are tired
you give us rest.
And when we feel alone
you are always there to be
our friend.
Amen.

Other Ideas!

Set up a solar water fountain, if you have one, to trickle over some stones. Alternatively, provide a jug of water and a pile of stones or rocks in a tray for people to pour the water over. Leave a Bible open at the page with today's Exodus reading on it.

All-age Talk

You need a clear container and a large jug of water for your talk today, and maybe a towel to lay them on in case of spillages!

Show the clear container. It is empty. It is dry inside. Maybe this is how the woman at the well felt. She was there collecting water in the middle of the day, a time when nobody else was there. Maybe she wanted to be alone, maybe she couldn't bear to be around the rest of the village with all their staring and gossiping.

Pour in a little water. She let down her bucket into the well and drew some water. Drink the water in the container. But the problem is that pretty soon her water would be used up. Some things can feel like they fill our emptiness, such as getting new things, being really busy, drinking too much, but the problem is that the result doesn't last. Soon we are empty again, just like this container.

But today is different. There's a man sitting by the well, and this man chooses to talk to the woman. Maybe he doesn't know her history, or he wouldn't. He asks for a drink of water. She tries to explain the situation to him. Maybe he's just a bit daft. He's a Jew. She's a Samaritan. His kind don't mix with people like hers. Pour a little water into the container. Sometimes reaching out beyond our comfort zone, reaching out to people who are a little less like us, and treating them as if they too are children of God, is a bit like the start of filling up an empty container with life-giving water. Even before Jesus has done anything, the act of him being there, talking, is trickling some life into her.

Jesus goes on to say that if she knew who he was, she'd have asked him for water. 'What water?' she says. 'The well is too deep and you don't even have a bucket!' But Jesus says, 'Anyone who drinks the water I give will never be thirsty again. It'll be like a spring of water inside them, welling up to eternal life.' Pour a bit more water into the container. The woman's interest was piqued. She didn't quite understand but she was interested. And being interested is in itself a life-giving thing. As you want to find out more, life begins to bubble up inside of you.

Jesus speaks and shows he knows her own messy and difficult situation. But he doesn't speak in a way that is full of judgement, just stating facts. Pour a little more water into the container. Being understood and loved as we are in all our own mess and problems is life-giving.

The woman begins to talk and discuss theology. How she had the courage, we don't know, but maybe looking at the container, we can see that she is fuller than she had been at the beginning. And Jesus, surprisingly, most amazingly, doesn't hide behind his status. He doesn't shut her down, as someone who is not learned enough, not from the right social background, the wrong gender, to be trusted to think and to wonder around ideas. He talks with her as if she has every right to think about things. Pour some more water into the container. How often do we pre-approve people before we'll talk with them about the things of God? Are there people that we dismiss as being the wrong type to have that conversation with?

She speaks out: 'I know when the Messiah comes, he will come and explain this all to us.' Jesus replies, 'I am he.' Pour some more water into the container until it spills right over the edge as you're talking. As the woman is filled to overflowing with Jesus' living water, it begins to spill out of her life. She runs back to the others in her village, the ones she was trying not to have to speak to, and pours out to them what she has heard and felt. When we are so full of God's love, when we begin to overflow with it, that's when amazing change happens for everyone.

Children's Corner

Provide a deep-sided container, set on a couple of old towels, with a couple of centimetres of water inside, and various scoops and water toys. As the children play with the water, they can listen out for water being mentioned in the Bible readings, and pour it whenever they hear it.

The colouring sheet shows Moses striking the rock, and water gushing out. The Bible verse is on the sheet so the children can look this up to read it later.

Little Kids' Sunday School

Put on some music and do some very energetic dancing. Maybe you can take it in turns to lead the dancing and everyone copy you. Once you're all hot and puffed out, turn the music off, sit down, and drink some lovely fresh water.

We all get thirsty every day. It's easy for us to find something to drink. We just need to walk to the tap, and turn it on, to get fresh clean water that's good for us to drink. Back in the time of Jesus, it was a bit more complicated. Each day, someone (the women, because it was their job) had to walk to the well with a big jar. They'd have to send down a bucket and splash! it would fill with water at the bottom. They would heave it up, and pour it into their jar. When their jar was full, they would have to carry it all the way home, a hot and heavy job.

Jesus spoke to a woman by the well. He said that anyone who drinks the water he gives will never be thirsty again. It'll be like they have a spring of fresh water, bubbling up inside of them. After getting hot and thirsty we enjoyed our drink, didn't we? But later on, we will get thirsty again. The woman was very interested, as it was hard work to keep collecting water. Imagine if she didn't have to do it any more!

But Jesus didn't mean this water, that you drink. He meant the way we get thirsty for goodness and love. When we know Jesus and are filled with the Holy Spirit, it is like we have a spring of goodness and love bubbling up inside us, and it never runs out.

Use glass paint pens to draw on small glasses or see-through plastic cups, all the ways that Jesus refreshes us. When we use our glasses to drink water, we can remember that God's love is always bubbling up inside us.

Big Kids' Sunday School

Create an obstacle course around your meeting room or outside, finishing at a tap. Give each child a really large water container, like the ones you have when you're camping. They have to carry the water container to the tap, fill it, then get it back to the start again. It's amazing quite how heavy water can be!

For the woman in the Gospel reading today, this was a massive part of her life. Carrying her water jars to the well, filling them, and struggling home again under their weight. Watching every single drop of water she used, knowing how much effort went in to getting it. And this is a reality for millions of people today, mostly girls and young women, who spend much of every day walking to the well, filling their water containers, and walking home again. Never mind the exhaustion of this never-ending task, it also eats into their precious time to play and to learn.

Jesus, when he meets her at the well, tells her of the living water he can give her, which will never run out, but will be like a spring bubbling up inside her. He has the courage and the courtesy to treat her as a person with a mind, talking about things of faith with her, a woman and a Samaritan of all people! That spring of God's love, peace and joy can bubble up in all of us, and as it does so it spills over into the world around us.

We are blessed with many good things, and out of that we are able to be generous, and pass on some of this goodness to others. Prepare some posters and labels for water jars and jugs, so that the congregation can come and watch you on your water obstacle course once again. But this time, you can share what you've learned about girls and young women collecting water from wells, just as this woman did in the Gospel story. You can help the congregation to give generously to a charity such as Water Aid, so that girls and young women will be freed from this daily drudgery, and released to play, and to learn. To explore big ideas, like the woman at the well, which will go on to give new life into their whole communities.

Exodus 17:6

MOTHERING SUNDAY

Readings

- Exodus 2:1-10 or 1 Samuel 1:20-28
- Psalm 34:11-20 or Psalm 127:1-4
- 2 Corinthians 1:3-7 or
  Colossians 3:12-17
- Luke 2:33-35 or John 19:25-27

Thoughts on the Readings

Today our choice of readings has stories of all different types of families. The Egyptian princess, helped by her young ladies in waiting, who lifted baby Moses out of the water and adopted him. Moses' birth mother, living in politically turbulent times, who loved him with all her heart and did her best to keep him safe, even if this meant letting him grow up within another family. In her other role, as wet-nurse to Moses, her true identity and status hidden, she took on the vital but often undervalued job of caring for a baby who officially belonged to another woman.

The prayerful Hannah longed for a child for so many years, and when her little son Samuel was born, a miraculous gift from God, she did not forget her promise to dedicate him to the Lord. She kept him close to her until he had finished breastfeeding – we don't exactly know how long this was, but he was certainly old enough to be of some help to Eli in the temple. Together, the young Samuel and the old and holy Eli seek God together, working in God's temple as another, different sort of family.

In our choice of Gospel readings we hear Mary's story, first when Jesus is brought to the temple and after blessing her, Simeon warns Mary of the suffering that is to come to her, the suffering that is only there because of the deep love she feels for her son. In the other Gospel reading we hear about Mary at the other end of Jesus' life, when he is hanging on the cross, and those words of Simeon's must have echoed in Mary's ears. As Jesus gives John to Mary as her son, and gives her to John as his mother, we see this ongoing need to be part of a family, beyond the ages of 0-18. John then takes Mary into his own home to live with him – another sort of family.

The reading from Colossians really sums up how these very different types of families can all work. It is because of love. Through God's love, and the way that he holds us with care and has chosen us, we can then do the things which help love to thrive in our own family situations. God knows it is not always easy or straightforward; he understands that sometimes we will need to forgive others, and sometimes we will do things that need forgiveness too. Through that peace which comes from Christ we will be able to 'put up with each other', as it says in the reading. Being close to God puts everything in perspective – those annoying little things that others do or don't do, are not actually nearly as important as they seem. It is good on Mothering Sunday that we can really focus on being thankful for the kind and caring things that others have done for us, and we are thankful too, for the way that God understands and nurtures us as well.

Discussion Starters

- **How can we show that all different shapes and sizes of family are welcome within our church community? Is our publicity inclusive, or do our events favour particular types of families?**

Intercessions

**Lord, as you have nurtured and loved us,
may we love others.**

Lord, as we come before you in prayer,
may we know your caring love
and understand that you value us
just as we are.

We bring before you our church family,
made up of all different sorts of people.
Thank you for the relationships and care
between the different generations
within our community.
We pray that we would be a place of welcome
to those who either live on their own
or with others
as we come together to know you more.
**Lord, as you have nurtured and loved us,
may we love others.**

As we pray for our world,
we particularly think of those families
who have been torn apart by conflict and violence;
refugees who have been separated
from their mothers, grandmothers and aunties
and the family members who miss them.
We also pray for the situations where
family relationships have broken down
for any reason
and pray that you would bring your healing and peace.
**Lord, as you have nurtured and loved us,
may we love others.**

We bring into your presence
all women who are giving birth at this time,
throughout the world.
We also pray for those who are pregnant,
particularly those who have additional health conditions
or are living in challenging circumstances.
We pray for those women who have just given birth
and ask that you would be with them
at this wonderful, exhausting and joyful time.
We also name before you those who are in need, including . . .
Lord, as you have nurtured and loved us,
may we love others.

As we remember with love
those who have entered heaven to live with you,
we think of our unbroken line of female ancestors,
without whom we would not exist.
We thank you for these women, through history
who have carried, fed and cared for their children.
We also name before you today
anyone who is particularly remembered at this time of year, including . . .
Lord, as you have nurtured and loved us,
may we love others.

As we give thanks
for those who have cared for us
we also are so grateful
for the way you look after us too.
May we know this love with us
as we leave this place today.
Amen.

Children's Prayer

Dear Lord,
thank you for the people
who listen to us,
who read to us,
who play with us,
and who look after us.
Thank you for the way
you love us too.
Amen.

Other Ideas!

Ask people to bring in some photos of their own mums, grandmothers and great-grandmothers who have now died. These can be placed in a beautiful display, surrounded by flowers and plants.

All-age Talk

Tape some lining paper to a frame (maybe one of those freestanding clothes rails) and cut out the shape of a dad, a mum, and a child. Make sure these are about the right kind of size to fit the family you've got in mind as your volunteers today.

Today it's Mothering Sunday, and we're celebrating mums, and the role they play as part of our families. Invite your volunteer family to the front. Here's a lovely family, here's the mum, and the dad, and the child, and look, they fit perfectly through our family-shaped hole. And that is great, you can see how they love each other and look after each other. Like a little picture of what we as the church should be like.

And what about some of the families from our Bible readings today? Invite up two women, a little girl, and a baby. Here's baby Moses, his big sister, his birth mum, and the princess who adopted him. Shall we try them out for size in our family-shaped hole? Invite them to step through, encouraging them to go through at the same time. Oops, the paper is starting to rip a bit. Oh well, never mind.

What about Hannah? Invite up two women, a man, a little boy, and an old man. Here's Hannah and her husband, her husband's other wife, her little boy Samuel, and Eli, the old priest at the temple, who looked after Samuel once Samuel went to live there and help him. Invite them to step through all together. The paper might be starting to complain a bit!

And what about Mary? Invite up an older woman and an adult man. Here's Mary, who at the foot of the cross was given Jesus' friend John as her new son, to be her new family. Invite them to step through the paper.

These families don't exactly fit the hole. And that's what God does, time and time again. He rips up our preconceptions of how things ought to look. (You can rip the paper here.) We are right in seeing family as a little picture for how we as the church should be, but families come in all kinds of shapes and sizes. Some are small, some are large, some include a bunch of other people we are not related to by blood but are part of our family through the love and care we share together. Just like these Bible families, in fact. Next time we see a family that is different from our own, we can try not to see how it doesn't fit in that family-shaped hole, but to see the ways in which it reflects how we should be living, as God's family on earth.

Children's Corner

Provide modelling clay, straws, sticks, and beads (remind parents and carers to be aware of choking risk) so that the children can create a family to look after each other. They can chat about how families come in all different shapes and sizes, whisper about who is in their family, and how they show their love together.

The colouring sheet shows a wide variety of families loving and caring for each other. The writing says, **'All families are part of God's family of love'**.

Little Kids' Sunday School

Have a pile of clothes, from tiny baby clothes, right up to teenage clothes. Get the children to put them in order. To make it trickier, you can blindfold them, and see if they can do it just by touch!

Tell the story of Hannah, longing for a baby, longing to be a mother. How she visited the temple, and made God a promise that if she had a child, when he was old enough, she would offer him to the temple, to live in God's service. And she did get pregnant and have a child, baby Samuel. After all the years of wishing, he must have felt like such a blessing. And, as he grew older, and eventually old enough, she brought him along to the temple, and gave him to Eli the priest to be his helper. But her loving and caring didn't stop then. She may not have been with him every day, but she sewed him a tunic every year, a little bit bigger every time.

The children can cut out tiny t-shirt shapes out of an old t-shirt. They can fold a length of card concertina style so it has two folds/three faces. They can stick their tiniest t-shirt on the front, a medium sized t-shirt in the middle, and a large t-shirt at the end. They can write 'Thank you for looking after me as I grow bigger and bigger', and give it to their mum, or someone else who cares for them.

Big Kids' Sunday School

Bring along a few small, medium, and large t-shirts. Put the children in teams ready for a relay race, and place the small ones just in front of the children, the medium-sized ones halfway, and the large ones at the end. On 'go', the child runs to the small t-shirt, squeezes into it, runs to the medium t-shirt, takes off the small one and puts on the medium one, runs to the large t-shirt, takes off the medium t-shirt and puts on the large one. They run to the end, and back to where they left the medium t-shirt. They take off the large one, put it down, pick up the medium one, run to where they left the small one, put down the medium one, pick up the small one, run to where the small one should be, and put it down. Then the next child goes. (Phew! You still with me?!)

Hannah really wanted to be a mum. Her friends had all had children. Her husband's other wife (they did things differently in those days!) had children. And yet she still didn't. When she went to the temple, she made God a promise. If she had a child, she would dedicate him to God's service at the temple when he was old enough. And sure enough, she got pregnant, and was soon happy as a mother of baby Samuel. Samuel grew, and grew, and when he was old enough, she took him along to the temple, where he lived as the helper to Eli the priest. Each year she would sew him a new tunic, each one a little bit bigger than the last, as he grew (a bit like our t-shirts in our game at the beginning).

Bring along some old t-shirts, maybe ones bought from charity shops, and have a look at some ideas online for upcycling t-shirts. Have some large fabric scissors available, and the children can upcycle themselves each a new t-shirt. Whenever they wear it, they can think of Hannah sewing a new tunic for her little son. Even though she didn't get to see him every day, she could still show him her love. The children can remember all those who show them love, and of God's love that underpins it all.

ALL FAMILIES ARE PART OF GOD'S FAMILY OF LOVE

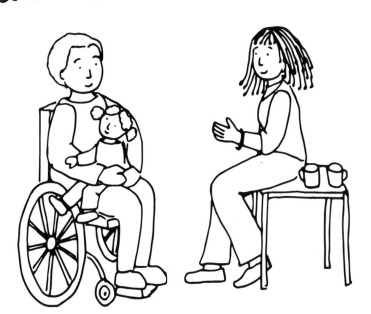

GOD'S BREATH OF LIFE

Readings

- Ezekiel 37:1-14
- Psalm 130
- Romans 8:6-11
- John 11:1-45

Thoughts on the Readings

As Ezekiel watches, in amazement, God bringing life to the bones that were dry and dead, we too are given a powerful picture of the overarching love, healing power and restorative nature of God. Those bones were past it. No one would have ever thought that they would ever be any use to anyone. If you were looking for a healthy and fit group of individuals to form an effective army, you certainly wouldn't be looking here.

Yet in spite of this, even while Ezekiel is still in the middle of speaking out God's promises to the bones on the ground (he must have wondered whether it was even worth saying anything to them if they could not hear him!), they start to come together, forming bodies again, and being covered with skin and muscles. Then, as the wind blows over the bodies, life fills them and they stand up together.

God tells Ezekiel that this is a picture of what he can do for his people. They may feel like there is no hope left, and sometimes we too, can feel burnt out, exhausted and we can't see the way ahead. We may spend time and energy trying to 'make' our churches grow and be successful, but God's message is something quite different.

We need to be bold, like Ezekiel, to speak out God's good promises of hope, even if it seems like there is not anyone there to listen. It may well be that people are more ready to hear the words of God's wisdom than we think. We need to trust that it is God who brings life – not us. Sometimes, like Ezekiel, the things which God leads us into doing may seem pointless or strange. We need to be ready to be surprised at what God will do.

Our Gospel reading for today also tells of someone who was dead being brought back to life – Jesus' good friend, Lazarus. Again, this was someone who was well and truly dead, and had been in the tomb for four days. No one could possibly think that he could come back to life after this. Both Mary, Martha and many of the rest of the crowd believed that Jesus would have been able to prevent Lazarus from dying, but to bring him back from the dead was something else altogether.

Jesus stood by Lazarus' tomb, and simply prayed to his Father in heaven. Nothing complicated, nothing showy, nothing difficult and nothing dramatic. This was enough. Lazarus came walking out of the tomb, draped in strips of burial cloth. It must have been a bit of a shock.

Because of what Jesus did, many people came to have faith in him. Jesus had said that he would bring eternal life to everyone. Although Lazarus would have eventually ended his earthly life in the normal way, we imagine probably as an old man, Jesus used this sign as a way of showing people that he really did have power over death. It was not something to be afraid of any more.

Discussion Starters

• How can we make space to allow God to breathe new life into us, our churches and our communities?

Intercessions

**Renewing and refreshing God,
give us new life.**

Lord, we come before you as we are,
knowing our need of you
and ready to receive from you.

We bring before you our church,
and thank you for the way
we can meet with you here.
We pray for a new experience
of your presence, power and love,
and pray that we would be open
to wherever you would lead us.
**Renewing and refreshing God,
give us new life.**

As we think of our world,
we know that there are places and situations
where it seems as if there is no hope,
where things are getting worse instead of better
and the values of your kingdom
seem far away.
We bring these things into your holy presence, and pray
that your healing and hope
would bring peace, wholeness and reconciliation.
**Renewing and refreshing God,
give us new life.**

Jesus, we know that you brought healing
to so many people during your time on earth.
We pray that your healing presence would be
with those who are suffering at this time,
particularly those whose mobility is restricted,
those who find it difficult to communicate,
and those whose poor vision, or limited hearing
makes daily life difficult.
We pray that your compassionate love
would bring comfort and hope,

and we pray that you would help us, too,
to be a healing, inclusive and accessible community
in your name.
We name before you those known to us, including . . .
Renewing and refreshing God,
give us new life.

We remember with respect and love
those who now enjoy eternal life in heaven with you,
forever in your presence, and in your loving care.
We also think of those who are nearing the end
of life's journey,
and pray that they would be comforted
by the knowledge of the wonderful welcome
that awaits them in heaven.
We name before you those people who we particularly think of this week, including . . .
Renewing and refreshing God,
give us new life.

Lord, may your hope fill us
and may your love guide us
as we live our lives
in you.
Amen.

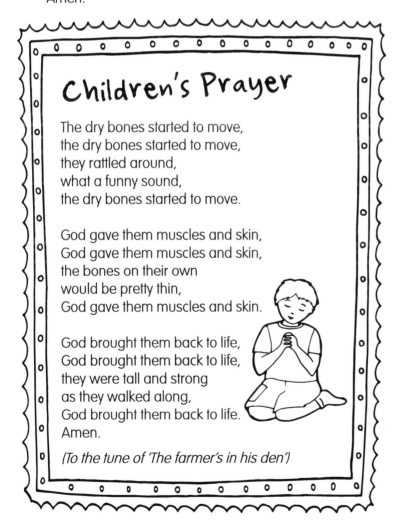

Children's Prayer

The dry bones started to move,
the dry bones started to move,
they rattled around,
what a funny sound,
the dry bones started to move.

God gave them muscles and skin,
God gave them muscles and skin,
the bones on their own
would be pretty thin,
God gave them muscles and skin.

God brought them back to life,
God brought them back to life,
they were tall and strong
as they walked along,
God brought them back to life.
Amen.

(To the tune of 'The farmer's in his den')

Other Ideas!

Play a recording of 'Dem bones', a negro spiritual song, and talk about the significance of Ezekiel's prophecy in this situation.

All-age Talk

Invite a volunteer up to the front, along with some helpers. Here is Lazarus, Jesus' very good friend. Whenever Jesus was in the area, he would go and visit Lazarus and his sisters, and stay with them, eating and talking until late into the night. But, while Jesus was away elsewhere, Lazarus got sick. A message was sent to Jesus, but Jesus didn't come. Lazarus got so sick, that he died. His family were so sad. But they wrapped him in graveclothes, and put him in the tomb.

Pass a toilet roll or two to your helpers. As 'dead' Lazarus stands there (a nice stiff corpse!) they can wrap him up like a mummy.

A few days later, Jesus arrived at their house. The Bible says that he wept. Lazarus was, after all, his very good friend. Jesus asked to be taken to the place they had laid his body. Jesus asked them to roll the stone away. 'But he's been dead for days! It will stink!' they argued. But they rolled the stone away anyway.

Jesus called into the tomb, 'Lazarus, come out!' And, coming through the gloom, came his friend Lazarus! Not a stinking, smelly zombie but his friend, real and alive! They unwrapped his graveclothes (you can help your 'Lazarus' out of theirs), and Lazarus and Jesus embraced and went off to eat and talk together, just like they always did.

When we are stuck in a place or a situation that feels like death, when we can't see any possibility for life or growth, and we feel trapped and bound up, Jesus calls us all. His voice is strong enough to reach right into our lives at their most despairing, and call us back to life.

Children's Corner

Provide a tub full of big sticks collected from gardens and parks. The children can lie down as their parents and carers shape their outline using sticks, and fill in their bones. They can listen as the bones in the Old Testament reading are brought back to life as Ezekiel prophesies.

The colouring sheet shows Ezekiel prophesying over the valley of dry bones. The writing reads, **'God brings life where we least expect it'**.

Little Kids' Sunday School

In teams, provide each team with a toilet roll, and they can mummify up someone in their team, who then has to run a race. Give out points for winning the race, and also for their mummification skills.

Retell the story of Lazarus, using the children as actors in their own story. When Lazarus dies and is laid in the tomb, you can use another toilet roll to wrap the child up and tuck them in a tomb-like space, maybe the space under a table. When Jesus calls, 'Lazarus, come out!', the child can emerge from under the table, and get unwrapped by the rest.

The children can wrap old toilet roll tubes in thin strips of kitchen towel, leaving a little space at the top to glue two googly eyes, making a model of Lazarus. They can take this home to remind them of how Jesus is able to call us, even when things seem dead and hopeless.

Big Kids' Sunday School

Bring along lots of pots of plants, plants that look rather sorry for themselves. (There are plenty of these in my house, but if you are better at looking after plants than me, it won't take many days for a bunch of baby spider plants to start drooping if you 'forget' to water them.) If budget permits, buy a few 'resurrection plants', those ones from South America that dry up into a ball, and once soaked in water, grow green and lush again within 24 hours.

Have a grand watering session, looking at how floppy the plants look, how pale their leaves are, how dry their soil is. The plants may need several waters to allow the wetness to soak into the soil.

Look up the Gospel reading for today in a child-friendly Bible translation. If you have a stop-motion animation app, the children can create a Lego Bible story version, using strips of loo roll to wrap around a Lego figure, to be Lazarus in the tomb.

They can write situations that feel dead or impossible on little pieces of paper, roll them up, and push these into the soil of their plant. They can take their plant home, and as they watch it come back to life, they can remember how God is able to call us out of even the most dead, the most impossible situations, and when he calls, amazing things happen.

God brings life where we least expect it

PALM SUNDAY

Readings

Liturgy of the Palms
- Matthew 21:1-11
- Psalm 118:1-2, 19-29

Liturgy of the Passion
- Isaiah 50:4-9a
- Psalm 31:9-16
- Philippians 2:5-11
- Matthew 26:14 – 27:66 or Matthew 27:11-54

Thoughts on the Readings

Jesus looked an unlikely hero, riding on a borrowed donkey, with a saddle made from spare clothes. This made a real visual contrast with the efforts of the Roman rich and famous, for whom money was no object, travelling in expensive carriages with a huge entourage. The people loved it. Here was someone who was like them, who in the ordinariness of life could show them that there was something to celebrate. And the way that people honoured this was using what was around them too – by waving the branches from the surrounding palm trees, and placing their cloaks on the floor to form a sort of DIY red carpet. Those who welcomed Jesus into Jerusalem would have been familiar with the words of the psalm which we hear today, with the image of joyful crowds marching with palm branches towards the altar. They knew who Jesus was, and were able to tell the people from the city who asked what was going on – he was the 'Son of David', the 'One who comes in the name of the Lord', the one they had all been waiting for.

As we move on, the mood changes. Jesus' attitude when accused by Pilate is reflected in the readings from Isaiah and Psalm 31. Though rejected, misunderstood, ill-treated and tortured by the people around him, he chooses still to put his trust in God and to know his protection, trusting him to bring justice at the time that is right.

After the crowd cheering 'Hosanna' as Jesus entered Jerusalem, the atmosphere turns nasty as the crowd are convinced by the chief priests to call for Barabbas to be freed, and for Jesus to be killed. Whether any of the people in the crowd from the entry into Jerusalem were also there as Pilate sentenced Jesus, we do not know. However, it must have felt an uncomfortable and frightening time for those who had supported and cheered for Jesus not long before.

As Jesus is tortured and mocked it could not be more of a contrast with the atmosphere of celebration as he rode the donkey, not long before. Any claim to be the Messiah was rubbished, and through their taunting, the soldiers implied that anything Jesus had said before was simply made up and ridiculous. As the account of Jesus' crucifixion and death continues, we hear the words of those around him rejecting him and criticising him, even while he is in great physical pain. Passers-by, soldiers and religious leaders all had something hurtful and destructive to say to Jesus.

It is not until after Jesus' death, when the earth shook, and the curtain in the temple is torn in two, that we start to hear the voices of the officer and the guards, shocked and frightened, acknowledging that Jesus must really have been God's Son. We also hear about the many women – presumably quite a crowd – who had come to help Jesus, standing at a distance, looking at the cross. And we notice the kindness and generosity of Joseph of Arimathea, who was presumably relatively wealthy and of some status, and offered his own tomb for Jesus to be buried in. This would have made it very clear that he was one of Jesus' supporters, not an easy or safe thing to be at this time.

As we begin Holy Week, and reflect on Jesus' journey to the cross, it is a time when we can think about how we can encourage those people who are going through a difficult time, and to speak with kind words to those who are suffering. There may also be a way in which we can support those who are discriminated against, imprisoned or tortured because of their political or religious beliefs, their nationality or ethnic origin, their gender identity or for speaking out against those in power.

And as we look towards Easter, we know that even in the middle of this suffering and pain, God has promised a future full of hope and joy, with life that will last forever.

Discussion Starters

- Does Jesus' example of riding a donkey into Jerusalem challenge or inspire the way we reach out to others as a church?

Intercessions

**Jesus, our gentle King,
make us like you.**

Lord, thank you for the example
that you gave us
when you rode a donkey into Jerusalem.
A humble mode of transport
for a king.

We bring before you our church
and pray that you would open our eyes
to use the resources already around us
to reach out to others with your love.
We pray that you would keep us
from trying to compete
with the wealthy and powerful organisations

in our world
and help us to show another, kinder
and gentler way of life.
Jesus, our gentle King,
make us like you.

We pray for our world
and particularly remember
people suffering under oppressive political regimes
and those who are imprisoned or tortured
because of their beliefs, or because of who they are.
We pray that you would strengthen those
working to bring peace, justice and freedom,
so that your kingdom may come.
Jesus, our gentle King,
make us like you.

We bring into your loving care
those who are living with a disability or long-term condition.
We also pray that your kindness and encouragement would surround anyone
who cares for children with additional needs
and those who look after relatives with dementia.
We pray that you would strengthen them and encourage them
and that those around would be supportive and loving.
We name before you anyone who has asked for our prayers, including . . .
Jesus, our gentle King,
make us like you.

As we remember those who have died,
we thank you for your promise of
a home in heaven with you,
where suffering and pain
will be no more.
We particularly think of those
who are missed at this time of year, including . . .
Jesus, our gentle King,
make us like you.

As we go through this week
with our eyes looking towards your resurrection,
may we draw nearer to you
and understand more
of your wonderful love.
Amen.

Children's Prayer

Jesus, you rode a gentle donkey
with long, soft ears
and warm breath,
plodding along,
giving you time
to talk and smile with people
along the way into Jerusalem.
May we find time
to be kind and gentle,
to listen and smile with people,
showing your love too.
Amen.

Other Ideas!

If you have a Palm Sunday procession outside the church, this could be the chance to give out palm crosses to passers-by and neighbours, perhaps along with a hot cross bun.

All-age Talk

Provide some placards, as you might see at a political demonstration, made of rectangles of card mounted on a stick. You might be able to find a megaphone and some whistles or a vuvuzela, too.

We live in a country where thankfully we have freedom of speech. We see footage of people demonstrating on the news; sometimes some of us have been those very people. It must have felt like a demo, as Jesus entered Jerusalem, with thronging crowds of people, loudly expressing their dissatisfaction with the status quo by calling 'Save us! Hosanna! Save us now!' A joyous demonstration, calling for change, and naming the way that change should come. And sometimes this is how we are called to live as Christians, speaking out loudly when things are wrong, naming the way that change should come. You can call some people to the front to demonstrate a demonstration (!), waving their placards, and blowing their whistles.

There are other ways to speak truth to power, though. As Jesus hangs, dying, on the cross, he is watched by a group of women, who are there, supporting him. Sometimes we are called simply to turn up, to express solidarity with those who are suffering, not at this point offering our solutions but simply to be with them in their time of distress. Being visible around those who are in pain makes them know they are not alone, and also acts as a signal that their suffering, that their pain, has been noticed. Call some women to the front, to quietly stand in a group.

And what about the doers, like Joseph of Arimathea? A wealthy man, he comes forward and offers his own family tomb for the body of Jesus. An offer that was more likely to make him enemies than friends, an offer that would annoy and irritate those in power. Sometimes we are called to speak out, not by something we say, but simply by our actions. Actions can speak for themselves. As we get on with doing the things of God, things that may be annoying or frustrating for those in power, we send a strong message of how things need to change. Bring someone to the front with a bag or box of groceries, labelled Food Bank.

And what about Jesus, riding into Jerusalem on a donkey? Sometimes it's how we do things that matters. Riding on a donkey, humble and gentle, turning people's expectations on their head. A new way of doing things, where power isn't about exploitation and control, but of gentleness and compassion. As we grow closer and closer to God, we begin to show this in our lives, and the whole world will get infected with this peace.

Children's Corner

Bury these objects within a tray of rice: a plastic toy donkey, a palm cross, a wooden cross, a stone, a square of towel, a candle. The children can use paintbrushes to uncover the objects and listen out for where they might fit in, in the two Gospel readings for today.

The colouring sheet shows Jesus on a donkey, smiling at people in the crowd.

Little Kids' Sunday School

Play some donkey races. Provide a couple of hobby horses, and put the children into teams to race up and back on the hobby horse as a relay race.

Invite one of your 'donkeys' up to come and tell the story about how they were tethered up outside their owner's house, when along came a man, and borrowed them for an important job. They were a little bit nervous about where they were going, but soon they met a man who made them feel safe and happy. He stroked their long ears and they knew he was a friend. More than a friend, they got the feeling that he was the most important man they'd ever met. They started to feel excited about what it was they were going to do. The man's friends threw a blanket over their back, and the kind man climbed on for a ride. What a surprise. A man like this should be riding a big impressive horse, not a little donkey like them. The man leaned forward to whisper in their ear: 'This isn't the first time I've ridden on a donkey!' (Do you remember some other times Jesus might have ridden on a donkey? Maybe when he was in Mary's tummy on the way to Bethlehem? Maybe when he was in Mary's arms as they escaped to Egypt?) The donkey stepped forward proudly along the street, twitching his ears as he heard the crowds around them, shouting 'Hosanna! Hosanna!'. People were pulling branches off the trees to wave like flags and throwing their cloaks down on the ground to make a beautiful path. The donkey walked along, carrying Jesus into Jerusalem. He felt like he was carrying a king.

The children can use some old socks and strong long sticks to make their own hobby horse donkeys. Stuff the sock with old scraps/stuffing, and tie it on the end of the stick. Glue on eyes and they can practise riding their donkey like Jesus.

Big Kids' Sunday School

Play 'Donkey Ears'. Sit in a circle, and one person is the donkey. They put both hands up to their head to be long, twitching donkey ears. The person to their right puts up their left hand, and the person to their left puts up their right hand, so the donkey is flanked by two half-donkeys. The donkey twitches for a bit, and then 'throws' their donkey ears at someone else in the circle. That person puts up both their donkey ears, and the half-donkeys beside them put up one ear. If you want to start getting people out, they can be out if they put up the wrong donkey ear. If someone is out, it gets more complicated, working out who you are next to.

Donkeys are quite sweet and comical animals. Their fur is soft. Nobody could say they were graceful. Their long ears are very expressive. And yet donkeys are tough. They work in difficult situations, working hard, working long hours. They are strong and tenacious and sure-footed. Donkeys are not about status. But they get stuff done.

When Jesus was entering Jerusalem, to the shouts of the crowd, and as they waved their branches as flags and threw their cloaks on the ground in a gesture of submission to a king, he did not choose to ride on a fine horse, towering above the crowd. He didn't ride on a war horse, something that would befit a king. He chose a donkey, a symbol of the ordinary working person, an animal that would plod him along at walking and talking speed, at head height, so he would be part of the crowd, rather than lofty and detached above it.

Cut the shape of a donkey's hoof out of several layers of thick card, or out of a large sponge, the type you use to clean cars. Attach this to a piece of card, and tie it on to your shoe. Step in some paint, and walk along a length of lining paper to make donkey footprints. We often talk about following in the footsteps of Jesus. What would it look like if we followed in these footsteps? What would we do, that would be like Jesus choosing a donkey to ride on, to Jerusalem?

EASTER DAY

Readings

- Acts 10:34-43 or Jeremiah 31:1-6
- Psalm 118:1-2, 14-24
- Colossians 3:1-4 or Acts 10:34-43
- John 20:1-18 or Matthew 28:1-10

Thoughts on the Readings

Some of the faithful women who were there with Jesus as he was put to death on the cross are the first to see him in our reading today, and to speak to him once he had come back to life. They must have been frightened, as the situation was very tense and not only had they lost a close friend and teacher, but they were also in danger from having been associated with him.

However, Mary Magdalene and her friends go to see Jesus' tomb early in the morning, just before daybreak. Perhaps they had not slept very much, thinking about the events of the last few days, and afraid that something similar might happen to other people they cared about.

In the quiet dawn light of the early morning, with only a few people there, there was another earthquake (after the one on Good Friday when Jesus died). God's angel came down from heaven and rolled the heavy stone out of the way of the entrance to the tomb. We can imagine that the vivid description of the angel, looking as bright as lightning, with wings as white as snow, as well as the guards dropping down in a dead faint, was excitedly told by these women to others, and that is how we now can picture this dramatic event.

The angel, characteristically, first told the women not to be afraid. Angels seem to know that humans can be a bit frightened when they see them, and like to reassure them before telling them the rest of the message. Jesus was alive! He was on his way to Galilee, and the women were to tell the disciples that, and make their way to go and meet him.

When Jesus suddenly appears in person and greets them, the women are amazed and delighted, falling to the ground and holding onto his feet, probably not wanting to let him go again. In Matthew's Gospel we hear Jesus' words of reassurance, not to be afraid, that he will appear in Galilee, while John describes how Jesus tells Mary not to hold on to him – perhaps in the light of hearing the reading from Matthew we can imagine that this is said in a way which brings reassurance, comfort and confidence for the future.

The women presumably got on pretty well with Jesus' disciples, and went to tell them the wonderful, incredible news about the angel, the empty tomb, and meeting their friend Jesus who had now come back to life. Through the recent days of pain, sadness and hopelessness these faithful friends of Jesus had stayed with him, not worrying what other people said or thought.

What does this mean for us? We have already been raised to life with Christ, Paul tells us in his letter to the Colossians. It is in response to this, and not in order to gain it, that we can look to Jesus and live in a way which reflects his glory, treating others around us with respect, generosity and love.

Discussion Starters

- **As many people around us celebrate spring rather than the religious festival of Easter, what can we too learn from God's message of new life which is all around us? And is there a way we can share this with others?**

Intercessions

**Risen Christ,
may we live in you.**

On this wonderful morning
we thank you
for your victory of life over death
and the promise of hope
you bring to all of creation.

Lord, thank you for the joy of Easter
that we can share with you
and our fellow Christians, both here and around the world.
As we celebrate with them,
may you fill our churches
with peace, light and hope,
so that we can bring your new life
to everyone around us.
**Risen Christ,
may we live in you.**

We thank you that your love is more than enough
to transform any situation
and ask today
that your healing power
would bring peace to areas of conflict
and compassion where there is hate.
We pray for those who trust only
in possessions or wealth,
that they would know
the true treasure of friendship with you.
**Risen Christ,
may we live in you.**

We bring into your healing presence
those who are in need,
particularly anyone who has lost hope,
not knowing the way ahead.
Fill them with an understanding
of the new life you bring
and the joy that comes
from being with you.
We also pray for those who are unwell,
who are exhausted and in pain
and pray that you would comfort and heal them.
We name before you today . . .
Risen Christ,
may we live in you.

As we celebrate your victory
of life over death,
we remember those who are on the last stage of life's journey,
soon to know the joy of heaven with you.
We also remember those who have died,
and pray for those who miss them here on earth.
May we know the closeness of heaven
as we draw near to you.
We remember with love . . .
Risen Christ,
may we live in you.

May the joy of heaven
and new life in Christ
fill us and strengthen us,
today and always.
Amen.

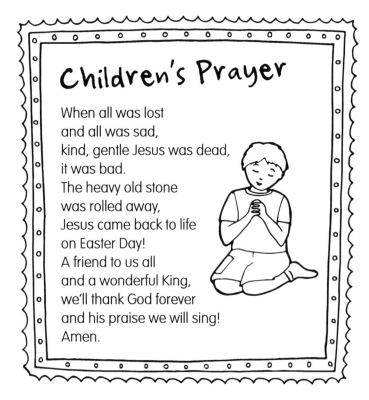

Children's Prayer

When all was lost
and all was sad,
kind, gentle Jesus was dead,
it was bad.
The heavy old stone
was rolled away,
Jesus came back to life
on Easter Day!
A friend to us all
and a wonderful King,
we'll thank God forever
and his praise we will sing!
Amen.

Other Ideas!

Make a cross out of a couple of
sticks, tied together, and attach
paper or real flowers all over it.
This can be put outside church as
a reminder of the joy and new life
that God brings, at Easter and all
through the year.

All-age Talk

Bring a pedal bike to church today.

Ask the congregation for a show of hands: How many people here can ride a bike? How many people here have fallen off a bike when they were learning? My goodness, it's pretty much the same number of people! Invite someone who fell off a bike when they were learning to ride to come up and have a go on your bike.

When they fell off the bike, did they hurt themselves? Sometimes when you're learning you get the odd tumble, bruise or scrape, don't you? It can feel a bit humiliating or upsetting. It can feel a bit scary. Some people might give up, and never ride a bike again. But this person didn't, did you? When you were learning to ride a bike, and falling off it, you climbed back on and tried again. Going back to a place of hurt, where you've been sad, where things have felt awful, that shows real bravery and commitment. And the good thing about that is that you can now do this! Get them to cycle up and down your church.

Those women, Jesus' friends and followers, had been through the most unimaginably tragic few days. They'd seen Jesus, who they loved, killed in the most awful way. They'd seen his body taken down from the cross, and laid in the tomb.

They must have been tempted to hide away, like the other disciples. Revisiting somewhere that has caused you pain takes a huge amount of courage. Going back to the scene of a tragedy is hard. And yet these women somehow found the strength they needed. Early in the morning, maybe before they lost their nerve, they retraced their steps to the very place they had experienced such loss before. But this time, it was different. Jesus was not dead and in the tomb, but alive and in front of them! Their courage in revisiting this place of death and despair resulted in them experiencing joy! And yes, there was joy when the other disciples eventually met with the resurrected Jesus, of course there was. But how special to get there first, to see him and touch him on that first Easter morning.

Those women can be our inspiration. When we are faced with a situation that feels full of death and despair, maybe we can find the courage to visit it again, and this time find Jesus there waiting for us, risen from the tomb.

Children's Corner

Lay out a blanket with toy chicks, lambs and rabbits on it. If you have other baby animals, you can add these, alongside some plant pots where the plants are just beginning to grow, and maybe a container of pussy willow. The children and their parents and carers can enjoy stroking and caring for the baby animals, and investigating the baby plants, as they talk about new life at springtime and at Easter.

The colouring sheet shows Jesus by the empty tomb, with signs of new life in the picture for the children to spot and colour.

Little Kids' Sunday School

Play 'What's the Time, Mr Wolf?' Get Mr Wolf to stand at one end of the hall, while everyone else faces 'him'. They chant, 'What's the time, Mr Wolf?' and he answers, 'Six o'clock' or 'Three o'clock' or whatever. The children take that number of steps forward. If Mr Wolf says, 'Dinner time!' he chases the children back to the beginning, and the child who's tagged becomes the next Mr Wolf.

What time did you wake up this morning? Who woke up first in your house? Was it the kids or the grown-ups? Our Bible story this morning is about some adults who woke up really early in the morning. Jesus' friends, some women who had been following him, who had been there when he was on the cross, and had seen his body when he was buried. That had been on the Friday. Through Saturday, the Sabbath, they had to rest, but now it was early Sunday morning, and they were up and about. They crept along quietly, through the dawn, as the day was waking up. But when they arrived at Jesus' tomb, he wasn't there! They saw angels who told them that Jesus wasn't dead, he was alive and then Jesus was there, alive, and in person. What an amazing surprise!

Use yellow paint to make a handprint on a paper plate. This will be your sunrise. Stick on a green hill in front, and a cross on the top of the hill. The children can use this to remember the women, who woke early, and went and found the risen Jesus.

Big Kids' Sunday School

Do egg and spoon races using Easter eggs, and talk about how eggs are a sign of new life, something that looks dead, and a new life comes pecking its way out of it.

We're going to do some cooking today to help us remember the story of Easter. Turn your oven on hot, and get everyone to wash their hands.

You'll need marshmallows, a tin of ready-made croissant mix, melted butter, a bowl of sugar and cinnamon, and a bun tin.

Give each child a marshmallow. This is the body of Jesus, taken down from the cross on Good Friday. Dip the marshmallow in the melted butter and the cinnamon and sugar. This is what normally happened to a body before it was buried. It was anointed with sweet-smelling spices and oils as a mark of respect, but this didn't happen with Jesus, his burial was all in too much of a rush before sundown at the start of Sabbath. This is what the women, arriving early in the morning, were planning to do, a couple of days late. Wrap the marshmallow up inside a triangle of croissant mix, making sure there aren't any holes, and dip this dough ball in melted butter and the cinnamon and sugar mix. This is like the body being wrapped in graveclothes. Pop it in a hole in the bun tin, and bake them all in a hot oven for 10-15 minutes. The oven is like the tomb.

When you open the oven again, give the buns a few minutes to cool slightly, then eat them hot. As you break them open, discover what has happened to the body inside! It is gone! Just like the women arriving early to anoint Jesus' body, who discovered that instead of a body resting in a tomb, there was an empty space, angels, and Jesus, very much alive. If every child makes two each, they can eat one together and give one away, giving them a chance to share the story of Easter.

JESUS APPEARS TO THE DISCIPLES

Readings
- Acts 2:14a, 22-32
- Psalm 16
- 1 Peter 1:3-9
- John 20:19-31

Thoughts on the Readings

When we look at today's psalm, together with the reading from Acts, which highlights David's words in the light of Jesus' death and resurrection, we can see one of the many instances where Old Testament prophecy is fulfilled. Indeed, as Peter speaks to the crowd about this, he describes David as a prophet – there are different layers of meaning to his words in the psalm, both for the people at the time, for those early followers of Jesus, and for us now.

This can help us understand how that miracle of Jesus' resurrection can really make a difference to us today. God's promise to keep us safe, to lead us through the darkest night, and to always be near to us is the same promise that stayed with Jesus through his suffering on the cross, and brought him through the other side to new life.

As we hear the words of Peter's letter this also helps us think about the strength that faith in God can bring. Things may be hard, and we may go through tough times, but God will always be with us. We do not need to be afraid because Jesus' resurrection has brought hope and life even to the most difficult situations, and we can know God's love in the most unlikely circumstances.

The disciples in today's Gospel reading were in a dangerous and fearful situation; they had locked themselves in a room because they knew that the Jewish authorities would be after them, for having been associated with Jesus. Even meeting together could put themselves and their families in danger. But Jesus appeared there with them, locked doors clearly not being a barrier for someone who had risen from the dead. He greeted them, and showed them the wounds from his crucifixion. It is interesting that these wounds, in Jesus' resurrection body, were not 'gone', although they no longer were debilitating or painful. The suffering that he went through was not something to be forgotten, in relief, after the whole thing was over. This was all part of the love of God, and it reminds us that even in our pain, we are not forgotten, and Jesus understands.

And what does Jesus mean by saying that those who have faith in him without seeing him are the ones who are really blessed? We may feel we would have loved to know Jesus as he walked on earth, and it seems strange that he should say this about us. But now that Jesus has come back to life, we can know him with us all the time, every moment of every day, and he loves us to come and spend time with him. We too, can know that peace, wisdom and strength that comes through eternal life with Jesus – something that has already begun and that we can already experience.

Discussion Starters

- We may be lucky enough not to have
to hide away when meeting together
because of our faith, but so often we
meet inside a building and our worship
is not visible. Thinking about the outside of our church,
what is there that shows others about our faith, and
about God's love? Is there anything else that could
be added or changed?

Intercessions

Risen Jesus,
may we know your presence.

Lord, we thank you
that you are with us here
as we come together to worship you,
and thank you for the joy and peace
that come from knowing you.

We pray for our church
and thank you for those people
who lead us in our worship,
who help us to pray
and who read and explain the Scriptures to us.
As we learn and grow together,
may we be a welcoming community
where others are drawn to your love.
Risen Jesus,
may we know your presence.

As we think of our world,
we particularly pray
for places where people are afraid
to gather together for worship
and where they are discriminated against
for their peaceful religious beliefs and practices.
We pray that your presence
would be with them, encouraging them,
and that there would be a greater understanding and respect
for the different thoughtful and prayerful
traditions and beliefs in our world.
Risen Jesus,
may we know your presence.

We bring into your loving and healing presence
anyone who is in pain,
including those who are recovering
from physical and mental wounds
caused by conflict, torture and violence.
We pray that you would bring healing
and a hope for the future.
We also pray for those known to us
who are in need, including . . .
Risen Jesus,
may we know your presence.

As we remember with love
those who have died,
we thank you for the promise
of eternal life with you.
It is so wonderful to know
that your heavenly kingdom is near,
where you bring freedom and peace.
We name before you today . . .
Risen Jesus,
may we know your presence.

Confident in the promise
of your eternal life,
may we keep our eyes on your heavenly kingdom,
bringing your love to everyone we meet.
Amen.

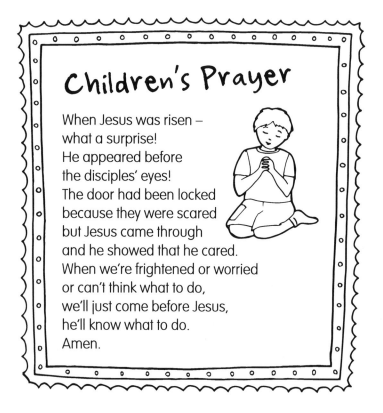

Children's Prayer

When Jesus was risen –
what a surprise!
He appeared before
the disciples' eyes!
The door had been locked
because they were scared
but Jesus came through
and he showed that he cared.
When we're frightened or worried
or can't think what to do,
we'll just come before Jesus,
he'll know what to do.
Amen.

Other Ideas!

Have a crucifix out where people
are able to look at it and touch the
wounds on Jesus' hands and feet,
remembering Thomas' experience.

All-age Talk

Today you'll need a pair of dark glasses, a clipboard, a diary, a chocolate bar, and an overflowing laundry basket.

When we are scared or sad or overwhelmed, we all have our own coping strategies. Some of us find it really hard to do our daily routines (bring out the laundry basket and pass it to a volunteer). The worse we feel, the worse things get around us, and the worse they get, the worse we feel! Such a vicious circle, and it's so hard to get yourself out of the cycle of self-blame.

Some of us turn to obsessions, maybe obsessions around food, eating it, not eating it, eating only the things we see as 'good'. Maybe clothes, making sure we are always dressed in what we feel is the 'right' way. Maybe thoughts in our minds that we pull out like our favourite comfy sweater, and we walk down the same well-trodden tracks. Pass the volunteer a chocolate bar.

Some of us deal with these feelings by being careful to do everything we are meant to do in the right way. We worry about all our items on our own checklist, and even the items we feel other people should have on theirs. Pass the volunteer the clipboard.

Sometimes we cope by getting ourselves busy. Getting ourselves busier and busier, filling every moment with activity, in case we should stop and those feelings of sadness and fear should come crashing back in on us. Pass the volunteer the diary.

Some of us cope by shutting the world out. We may retreat deep inside ourselves, keeping our feelings safely away inside us. We may retreat from relationships, unwilling to risk hurting or being hurt. Like the disciples in the Gospel reading, we may retreat inside our homes, away from society. Pass the volunteer the dark glasses.

When Jesus came to the disciples, his friends, hidden away, feeling sad and scared, locked inside a room, he didn't come and tell them to buck their ideas up. He didn't come and say, 'For goodness' sake, get out and enjoy yourselves!' He didn't roll his eyes at them and make them feel judged and guilty and wanting.

He came simply to be with them. And to be with them in his body that still retained its wounds. He didn't come as a glorious figure of impossible perfection, but as someone they loved, who had suffered unimaginable things, and was yet still filled to overflowing with life and with love. And Jesus still comes to simply be with us now, in all our places of fear and sadness, to fill us with his courage and his peace by his very presence.

Children's Corner

Provide some crucifixes for the children to explore and wonder at, crucifixes where Jesus is hanging on the cross. They can talk about and touch his wounds, and listen out for when Thomas, too, does this, in the Gospel reading.

The colouring sheet shows Jesus appearing in the upper room, among his disciples, his wounds plain to see, yet strong and very much alive. The Gospel reading reference is included so they can re-read this together later.

Little Kids' Sunday School

Bring along a selection of really well-worn and patched-up cuddly toys. It's great if you know the story behind them, and even better if some of them belong to you. Play some music as you pass them round, and when the music stops, the children holding the teddies get to give them a cuddle. After a few rounds, talk about the teddies and why they look the way they do. How they have holes, and places that have been patched, and bits where the fur has worn smooth. Basically, how life and love has happened to them.

Tell the story of the disciples, hiding away in a locked room after Jesus' death. Some of the women had said they'd seen Jesus alive! Later, some of the men had said they'd seen Jesus alive, too. But the disciples were still scared and unsure. Scared enough to make sure they'd locked themselves in to stay safe. And then, who should appear right there in the room with them, but Jesus! Even though it was locked, Jesus was there. And Jesus, fully alive again, but his body still bearing the scars of his crucifixion, of his death. Just like our teddies, it's the broken bits that prove how really alive something is. His resurrection hadn't made his wounds disappear. They were there, as part of his body, a body that was fully alive.

Give the children a tea light candle each, and put it in a small glass or glass jar. Cut out a chain of paper doll people, and attach them around the outside. These can be the disciples, in their locked room. When you light the candle, that is Jesus, appearing there in the middle of them all.

Big Kids' Sunday School

Lock up two bikes with a variety of bike locks (ones that need a key). Put the children in two teams, and give each team a pile of keys, some of which are the ones they need for the locks, and some which are extras just to make things difficult! They can see which team can cycle away 'their' bike first, either making them run up in a relay with one key per person to try, or all of them just trying to get their bike unlocked.

We use locks to keep things safe. We lock up the things that are important to us to stop bad people taking them. We lock up our house when we go out to stop people breaking in. When Jesus' disciples were afraid and sad after Jesus had died, they locked themselves into a room. They wanted to be together, but were frightened that what had happened to Jesus might happen to them. To keep safe, they locked themselves up.

And yet, despite all the locks, suddenly there was someone else standing in the room amongst them. They realised that it was Jesus! Jesus was there, more alive than they'd ever seen anyone before. And it wasn't a Jesus, sanitised through death, but a Jesus still bearing the scars of his crucifixion.

The children can make a key ring for the key from one of those tiny locks. The key ring can be as simple as a ribbon tied through the top of the key, with a card label attached, reading 'When you are scared . . .' Write on a piece of cardboard, 'Jesus is already here with you'. Fold the cardboard over, and make a hole through both pieces, so that when you push the lock through, the cardboard will stay closed. The children can keep this to remind them that when they are locked away inside themselves out of fear, Jesus isn't kept out, and is with them.

John 20:19-31

ON THE ROAD TO EMMAUS

Readings
- Acts 2:14a, 36-41
- Psalm 116:1-3, 10-17
- 1 Peter 1:17-23
- Luke 24:13-35

Thoughts on the Readings

It may seem strange that the two disciples on the way to Emmaus did not recognise Jesus at all as they walked and talked together – we may wonder why they did not take a closer look at his face, or why they did not recognise his voice. However, they were not at all expecting to meet Jesus on their journey – as far as they were concerned, he had died three days before, and although they had heard about the women finding the empty tomb, in this era where news was spread by word of mouth, they were not aware of anyone seeing Jesus in person.

They were sad and downcast, probably looking at the floor or the road ahead as they walked along, and did not notice Jesus' familiar face. Even if they had, it was out of context, and Jesus was not the same now he had been through death and out the other side. We may remember some television programmes where a company boss puts on a disguise in order to work alongside their employees, to see what it is like for them. It is fascinating to see that they are never recognised until the end of the programme, when their true identity is revealed. Even though their face was the same, and their voice was the same, the clothes and context were different, and the workers did not expect to see them in this way.

As Jesus spoke to the two disciples about the scriptures, and how the prophets explained what would happen to the Messiah, their hearts were prepared through their understanding and knowledge. It was only after this, when sitting down together to eat, that they suddenly became aware that this thoughtful, wise stranger was actually their friend Jesus. As he broke the bread and shared it, this connection and relationship brought the disciples a sudden understanding of all that had been said before.

This can be true, too, of our own faith and relationship with God. We can read the Bible and hear others explain it to us, but as well as this we need to be ready and open to be led into God's presence, to know his love and kindness, and to experience this as a relationship with him. As humans we are all on a journey to know and encounter God. As we seek him together, may we help others to know him too.

God's promise of hope, freedom from sins, eternal life and the offer to be part of his family is something that is open to everyone. As we choose to treat others with the same love that has been shown to us, we will also grow closer to God.

Discussion Starters

- **Have any surprising places or situations enabled us to know more about God during our own journey?**

Intercessions

**As we journey through life,
walk with us, Lord.**

As we come before you in prayer
and draw near to your presence,
we pray that we would know you with us
and experience your love.

Lord, we thank you
for the people who have introduced us to you,
and for those who have helped us to understand
more about your wonderful love and promises.
We pray, that in our churches
you would continue to surprise us
with your presence,
that we can really know your company
on the way through our lives.
**As we journey through life,
walk with us, Lord.**

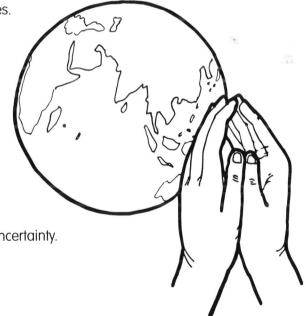

We pray for our world
and remember those situations
where people are longing and waiting
for an end to conflict, violence, danger and uncertainty.
We also pray for those places
where there is distrust, tension and fear
between different groups
and we pray for your peace.
**As we journey through life,
walk with us, Lord.**

We bring into your loving and healing presence
those who are at a stage of life's journey
which is painful, exhausting or sad,
whether through illness or other circumstances.

We pray that they would know you with them
and be comforted with the joy that comes from you.
Today we particularly pray for . . .
**As we journey through life,
walk with us, Lord.**

We remember with love
those who are near the end of their lives
and those who have recently stepped into
the glory of your heaven.
We also think of those people
who are missed at this time of year.
We name before you today . . .
**As we journey through life,
Walk with us, Lord.**

As we travel through this week,
may we know your presence with us,
informing our thoughts,
inspiring our words
and encouraging us in our actions.
Amen.

Children's Prayer

As we walk
we'll walk with Jesus,
as we talk
we'll talk with Jesus,
as we eat
we'll eat with Jesus.
Thank you for being
    with us, Jesus.
Amen.

Other Ideas!

Create a trail to follow around
the church, with signposts to
'Emmaus'. At the end, there can
be some bread to share.

All-age Talk

Have some masks of different famous people and invite up some volunteers.

Set two volunteers off playing a game of catch. Put a mask on a third and send them to
join in.

Set another two volunteers at a table, polishing silver, or washing up mugs. Put a mask on
a third and send them to join in.

Set another two volunteers off dusting the church. Put a mask on the third and send them to join in.

We have two people in our Gospel reading today, doing something very everyday and ordinary. They were walking. Walking from one town to another. They were walking from Jerusalem to Emmaus, and as they walked they talked, just as you or I might. And then like our volunteers today, they were joined by a third person.

Ask the volunteers if they know who it is (the mask not the identity of the wearer!) who has come alongside them as they've been working or playing.

It's a bit easier when it's a mask, isn't it? Sometimes when you see someone where you least expect to see them, like the Queen doing the washing up, or the Prime Minister playing catch, your brain doesn't really register that it's them. It assumes that it can't be them, here, in this situation. We don't know exactly how that happened for the people walking to Emmaus. It might be that because they were expecting Jesus to stay dead, they didn't recognise him when they saw him very much alive. It might be that his resurrection body looked different to the body that they knew. But for whatever reason, Jesus came alongside them, as they walked and as they talked, and he joined in.

It wasn't until he blessed and broke the bread that they recognised him. We need to keep our eyes open to recognise Jesus when we see him. We'll notice Jesus is there because we'll see the things he does, his trademark signs of love in action. We may sometimes find it hard to recognise him, as Jesus doesn't always come in the places and the people we expect, but when we see loving happening, that's Jesus, right there.

Children's Corner

Provide some flatbread (tortilla wraps or pitta bread) so that the children can hold it up and break it, and share it. They can listen out for when Jesus does the same in the Gospel reading, breaking and sharing the bread, and how it was at this point that his friends knew it was him.

The colouring sheet shows Jesus sitting at the table at Emmaus with his friends, holding up the bread to break it, and their surprise as they recognise him.

Little Kids' Sunday School

Play a game of 'Port/Starboard' but using Jerusalem/Emmaus, tying up your sandals (bend down to tie sandals), finding a friend (find a partner and put arms round each other), breaking bread (pretend to hold bread up and break it), looking for home (hand shading eyes from sun). Name one end of the room Jerusalem, and the other Emmaus. As you call out instructions, the children have to follow them. You can get them really running around if you're clever!

In our story from the Gospel today, we hear of two people travelling from Jerusalem to Emmaus. Get yourselves ready to start walking by tying up your sandals and picking up your walking sticks. As you start to walk, begin to talk about the events of the last week (that's Holy Week to us), and the rumours you've heard that Jesus' body isn't in the tomb any more. As you are talking, you mention how someone else came to walk along with these two people, Jesus' friends. As he walked alongside them, he explained all the things that had been happening. Look! You were all so busy talking as we walked that we've arrived already! Here we are at Emmaus. Let's invite him in for something to eat. We pass him the bread so he can say grace for us, give thanks to God for the food, and look! he's holding the bread up and blessing it and we suddenly realise who it is! It's Jesus!

Cut out two circular holes at the base of a rectangle of card, on the short edge. The children can draw on a head and arms and torso, and poke their fingers through the holes to be the legs. As they make their card person walk, they can remember how Jesus walked along beside his friends, and he walks with us now.

Big Kids' Sunday School

Bring along some scarves so the children can tie their ankles to run three-legged races, or to complete an obstacle course three-legged.

The Gospel story has two followers of Jesus walking along together, on the road from Jerusalem to Emmaus. As they walked, talking of the things that had happened over the past week, the happenings of what we know of as Holy Week, and these rumours that Jesus' body was no longer in the grave, they were joined by a third person. A bit like how your legs, from two people, were joined and became three! This third person spoke with them, asking what they were talking about. And as they walked and talked, this person explained to them all that had happened, referring to the scriptures. They invited him to join them to eat, and as he blessed and broke the bread, they suddenly recognised him. It was Jesus!

Use thick cardboard from packing boxes, and draw round everyone's feet, their left and their right. Cut these feet out, and tape over a strip of thinner card to turn them into sandals. Write 'Jesus walks with us' on each one.

JESUS, OUR GOOD SHEPHERD

Readings

- Acts 2:42-47
- Psalm 23
- 1 Peter 2:19-25
- John 10:1-10

Thoughts on the Readings

As surprising and as counter-cultural then as it is now, the early followers of Jesus sold their possessions and property, and gave the money to whoever needed it. They shared everything they had, and met together in the temple to worship, and in each other's houses to share food and break bread together. It was those simple things of spending time together, drawing near to God in worship, and sharing ordinary food that gave them the most joy. Any luxuries or any items they owned which conveyed status were no longer of interest to them. All that they could think about, and what united them, was the good news in Jesus that they all shared. A message of freedom, of hope, of love, of belonging and of a home in heaven.

This was what then drew others to join them. They were not putting on elaborate events. They did not have a publicity machine. They were not even offering an easy answer to life's problems. But it was that genuine love, showed through these radical actions that demonstrated to others that here was something different, something of value, and a way of living that was really worth it.

We hear in today's Gospel reading about Jesus being the gate for the sheep, the safe and reliable way into the security of the sheep pen. If we keep looking towards Jesus, we will not be distracted by those who would lead us the wrong way, into a place which may seem nice for us but is actually going to do us no good. Jesus will always look after us.

In our psalm for today, too, we hear the well-known words of Psalm 23, reassuring and comforting us with promises of God's provision, refreshment and protection.

Those early Christians got it right. They prioritised spending time worshipping God, and sharing with each other. No one was excluded. They were always welcoming to new members of the group. Through putting all of their lives in the right place, they were able to make sure that they did not lose sight of God's true values. Through this they found joy, strength and peace.

Discussion Starters

- **What can we learn from those early followers of Jesus, when we think about their approach to worship, friendship and inclusion?**

Intercessions

**Good Shepherd,
lead us.**

Lord, we thank you
that you care for us
and that you will lead us to a place
of rest and refreshment
when we follow you.

We pray for our church
and ask that you would lead us together
in your ways,
so that we can help others
to know your wonderful promises too.
May our church be a place
filled with all the good things
that come from you.
**Good Shepherd,
lead us.**

We bring to you our world
and particularly think of the places
where extremes of wealth and poverty
exist side by side.
We pray that the example of your people
in sharing their possessions
would inspire action for a fairer world.
We also pray for a release from materialism
and the constant search for more possessions,
so that the resources we have,
which we do not need,
can be used to make life better for others.
**Good Shepherd,
lead us.**

We bring to your loving care
all those who feel excluded,
or who long to be accepted.
We particularly pray for those
who feel isolated because of their own illness or disability,
or that of a family member
and we pray that you would help us
to be a welcoming community
as we share and eat together.
**Good Shepherd,
lead us.**

As we thank you for the promise
of freedom from sadness and pain
and a home in heaven with you,
we remember those known to us who have died,
and their families and friends.
We bring before you today . . .
Good Shepherd,
lead us.

We know that you love us
and that you will never leave us.
Thank you for being beside us,
leading us, guiding us and loving us
through all our lives
and everything we do.
Amen.

Children's Prayer

Jesus, thank you
that you are like a good
and kind shepherd
and we are your sheep.
You are always with us,
you care for us
and you keep us safe.
Amen.

Other Ideas!

Create a landscape with some toy
sheep using a green sheet, towel,
piece of carpet or pretend grass,
and place an open Bible next to it
with the words from Psalm 23.

All-age Talk

Ask for some helpers to help you move some
chairs or cushions into a circle. You're making
a sheepfold, a pen for some sheep to live
in. They need somewhere safe to protect
them from all the wolves roaming around the
church at night time. Make sure you leave a
gap for the door, so they can get in and out.

You need some more helpers now. Ones
who are good at 'baaahing'. Herd these little
sheep into the sheepfold. Any ideas how

we can stop these cheeky sheep running straight back out again? A chair or a cushion as a gate? That's an idea. Move one over. There. We can leave them overnight and get someone to let them out again in the morning.

But Jesus said, 'I am the gate.' How can he be a gate? Gates just sit there and don't do anything, do they?

What about if we remove the chair or the cushion, and find a nice shepherd to come and sleep in the doorway instead. Find a volunteer and settle them down in the doorway as a human gate.

When the sheep wake up (they can start to 'baaah' again) the shepherd can let them all out, giving each one a little pat. When they need to come back in, the shepherd can herd them back in, giving each one a little pat.

If one of the sheep is a bit poorly, the shepherd will know straight away. The sheep will grow tame and feel secure around the shepherd, as he'll have contact with them every morning and every evening. Their gate is now a relationship, rather than just a piece of wood or stone. And this relationship with Jesus, our gate, is what keeps us safe and knowing that we are loved, keeps us wanting to listen to his voice and follow him.

Children's Corner

Lay out a green towel, and provide some toy sheep (or cotton wool balls) and some sticks or stones to make the sheep pen. The children can herd the sheep into the pen, then use their hand across the entrance to stop them getting out and the wolf getting in. When it's time for the sheep to head back out to pasture, they can open up their hand, and as the sheep go past, they can give them each a little pat, just like the shepherds in Jesus' time who lay across the doorway, and checked the health of the sheep on their way in and on their way out.

The colouring sheet shows sheep in a stone sheep pen, with a shepherd half-sitting, half-lying protectively across the entrance. The writing, **'Jesus says, I am the gate'** can be coloured in.

Little Kids' Sunday School

Pull some cushions or chairs into the shape of a round sheepfold, leaving a space as the door. The 'sheep' chant, 'What's the time, Mr Shepherd?' 'Mr Shepherd' answers, 'Time to graze on the green grass', 'Time to drink from the stream', 'Time to jump in the field', 'Time to lie down and chew the cud', and the children do all these things. When 'Mr Shepherd' answers 'Bedtime', the 'sheep' run back into the sheepfold to go to sleep.

In Jesus' time, this was what sheep did all day! They ate, they drank, they played, they lay down in the fields and chewed the cud, and when it was bedtime, they trotted back to the sheepfold to sleep safely inside. The shepherd looked after them in the day, and then when night-time came, the shepherd lay down in the doorway of their sheepfold to sleep. The shepherd kept them safe both day and night. Jesus said, 'I am the gate.' Jesus is like that shepherd, lying down in the doorway of the sheepfold, keeping us all safe, day and night.

Bring along a bag of old white school socks and some cotton wool. The children can use the socks to make sheep sock puppets. Use double-sided tape to attach some cotton wool to the top of the sheep's head. Use a permanent marker to draw on eyes, a nose and a mouth. Their sock puppet sheep can act out playing all day, and sheltering all night, while their owner looks after them and keeps them safe.

Big Kids' Sunday School

Cut sheep shapes out of white tissue paper and create a sheep pen out of cushions. Scatter the 'sheep' around the room, and get the children to flap newspapers to herd them into the sheepfold. Hopefully it'll be as crazy and chaotic as a real field of sheep.

Jesus talked a lot about sheep. It was something he would have seen a lot of, and something that would have been immediately understandable for his audience. Today's sheep story is at first glance a slightly strange one. 'I am the gate', says Jesus. The gate? How can a person be a gate?

Well, actually, quite easily. His listeners would have known about sheep, about where sheep were kept overnight while the wolves were around. A sheepfold was built out of stones, a bit like our sheepfold built out of cushions, and the sheep were protected inside. The shepherd would go to sleep lying down in the entrance, so that as the sheep came in and as the sheep went out, they would all pass by him. They'd build up a close relationship through this daily contact, and the shepherd would know them all intimately and notice as soon as anything was wrong.

If Jesus is a gate like that, what does that tell us about him? Why might he have chosen this image to help people know about him?

Use white oven-bake modelling clay to make a flat model of a sheep. Once it's been baked and hardened, the children can use sticky tack to fix it beside their doorway. Each time they walk in or out, they can check in with their good shepherd, Jesus.

Jesus says
'I am the gate'

ROOM FOR ALL IN GOD'S KINGDOM

Readings

- Acts 7:55-60
- Psalm 31:1-5, 15-16
- 1 Peter 2:2-10
- John 14:1-14

Thoughts on the Readings

Jesus has given us the promise of a home in heaven with him. It is so lovely to think of Jesus' words, about his Father's house having many rooms – there is space for us all. And God's idea of who is included is always much broader than our own narrow view. It is interesting that Jesus says that we may believe in him because he tells us that he is one with the Father – or it may be because of the things that he does, things which will lead us to also act in a loving way, with God's priorities. Whichever way round this is described or understood, the creative loving God who formed the universe was also present on earth in Jesus, enabling him to heal the sick and come back from the dead. Because of this, we can do the same things as Jesus, bringing healing to others through our words and actions, and living confidently in the joyful knowledge that we will never be separated from God.

In the reading from Acts, we see how Stephen knew, even as he was put to death, that his relationship with and knowledge of a loving God would not end with death. Instead, he would have the chance to know Jesus even more closely as he entered into heaven. Following Jesus' example, he forgave those people who were killing him and asked God, in prayer, not to blame them for what they had done. It was only because Stephen knew God and was able to let himself be strengthened by him, that he was able to speak out these words of forgiveness and compassion, even while the sharp, heavy stones were being hurled at his body. This act of true bravery and strength is something that has inspired us in the Church as we remember Stephen and the other martyrs after him with respect and admiration.

As we are inspired by Stephen's faith, we too crave that closeness with God and the nourishment that comes from it. In the reading from 1 Peter, we are told to thirst after pure spiritual milk like newborn babies. For young babies, milk is the answer to all their needs, and they search for it determinedly, even wriggling their bodies along until they are close to their mother's breast. They open their mouth wide, turning their head from side to side until they are able to latch on and get a full mouthful of warm, sweet milk. Gratefully, they gulp it down, on a mission, concentrating hard. Nothing else matters. As they become full of milk, they visibly relax, starting to swallow less frequently, and their eyes close in bliss, until they release their mouth and rest, contented, in their mother's loving arms.

It is like this with us and God. It is good for us to seek and search for him, not giving up, because we know the joy that we will find when we are able to rest in his presence. Through choosing to pray with thankfulness, reading scripture, receiving communion and worshipping God with others, we draw near to God. We will find what we need, and what we didn't even know we needed. We will be filled with love and joy, so much that others will see it in us too. Heaven, and Jesus' presence, is nearby.

Discussion Starters

- **Stephen chose to speak with compassion about those who were throwing stones at him. What can help us to speak respectfully and with compassion about those who have hurt or offended us in some way?**

Intercessions

**As we come into your presence
feed us, Lord.**

Lord, we thank you
for the strength and joy that comes from you
when we are least expecting it.

We thank you for our church and its leaders,
and are grateful for those who came before us,
inspiring us and setting an example.
We think of the saints and martyrs
and those other, less famous people
who also led lives which showed
that they were close to you.
We thank you for their faith and courage,
their kindness and their holiness.
**As we come into your presence
feed us, Lord.**

We bring before you our world
with all its needs
and think of those places
where speaking out can result in punishment.
We also pray for anyone
who is discriminated against
because of their peacefully held beliefs.
We pray that you would bring
understanding, respect and peace
wherever fear and prejudice reign.
**As we come into your presence
feed us, Lord.**

Healing God,
we bring before you anyone
who feels worn down
by pain, tiredness or anxiety.
We pray that they would catch a glimpse
of your glory
and be encouraged by the knowledge of your love.
We pray for those known to us who have asked for our prayers, including . . .
As we come into your presence
feed us, Lord.

As we think of those
who are aware that they are near the end
of their life here on earth,
we pray that they would see
the glory of your heaven
and the welcome that awaits them.
We remember with love
those who have died, including . . .
As we come into your presence
feed us, Lord.

As we thirst for your Spirit
and search for you,
we pray that we would find all that we are looking for,
and more,
filling us, healing us and equipping us
to live for you.
Amen.

Children's Prayer

Jesus, to be close to you
is comforting and warm,
safe and calm.
When we are with you
we have all we need.
Amen.

Other Ideas!

Make a heart shape out of stones, to show how Stephen was able to know God's love even in the middle of violence and pain. You could also display the Bible reading about Stephen's martyrdom.

All-age Talk

Roll a sleeping mat and sleeping bag out on the floor. Pull up a chair. Blu Tack a poster of something you like on the wall or a pillar. Here's your room, made perfect just for you. Invite up someone else to join you. They want to put this pink blanket over the bed, and put a huge teddy on the chair. Invite someone else to join you both. They want to put up a different poster, and bring a pet (toy!) dog on a lead to live with them.

Imagine if we all had to share a room. Imagine if heaven was like one long room-share, with all of us from all of eternity squeezed into one space and bringing along everything that makes us the people we are. How would that ever work? We'd all end up with a cosmic headache!

Start taking everything out until your 'room' is empty. But Jesus doesn't want us to make our community of faith so bland that everybody fits. Our community of faith doesn't have to have magnolia walls that nobody really loves, and a plain duvet cover that doesn't excite anyone.

Jesus said, 'In my Father's house there are many rooms.' There is enough space for all of us, in all of our own ways, to be part of God's family home. The things that make us us can be celebrated, and we can enjoy the things that make other people themselves, too.

In my Father's house there are many rooms – and not only in heaven, in the eternity to come, but in the eternity we are already part of now. Our rooms can also be part of our Father's house. In my Father's house there are many rooms – and some of them are in Sheffield. And some of them are in Walthamstow. And some of them are in villages in Cornwall. As we offer all our rooms for God's use, what might we be making room for? Maybe to welcome others who need some space and company and share a pot of tea with them? Maybe to prepare resources for Sunday School? Maybe to host a refugee? God always uses what we offer in the way that fits us best.

Children's Corner

Have a collection of toy baby mammals and their mothers, so that the children can help the babies drink their milk. Maybe you can have some baby dolls too, so that the children can pretend to feed them as well. The children and their parents and carers can talk about how they drank milk when they were tiny (some of them may well still be nursing, too), about how babies need milk to grow and be happy and contented, and about how God fills us up with contentment like a baby at the breast.

The colouring sheet shows happy babies drinking their milk, with the verse from 1 Peter written to colour in.

Little Kids' Sunday School

Put picnic blankets on the floor with labels – bedroom, living room, kitchen, bathroom. As you call out an object or an activity (toothbrush! watching the telly! doing your homework! snoring!), the children go and sit in the right 'room'.

Houses come in all different shapes and sizes. Some have just a few rooms, some have lots of rooms. Each room is useful for a different thing, though. Jesus said to his friends, 'In my Father's house, there are many rooms.' There is space enough for all of us – for his friends so long ago, for all the Christians who have followed him through the years, for babies who aren't even born yet. All of us will fit in God's kingdom; nobody will be squeezed out.

The children can make a bug house to take home, full of lots of rooms! Give them each a paper cup, and provide them with paper straws, dry grass and leaves, and tiny sticks. They can cut and poke these into the cup to make a good home for tiny creatures, and hang it up somewhere outside ready for them to move in. If you have sticky labels, you can put a label on the cup that reads, 'In my Father's house, there are many rooms'.

Big Kids' Sunday School

Play a game of Sardines. Send one child off to hide, and after a minute or so, send the next child off to find them. Once they've found where they're hiding, they join the first child in their hiding place. Send the next child along, and the next, and so on, until everyone is squeezed into the hiding place the first child chose.

Just as well we all squeezed in, though it was touch and go at times. What about in the kingdom of heaven? Is there only room for some of us? Maybe Jesus only has space for the most special people?

Jesus said, 'In my Father's house, there are many rooms'. God's love is big enough to fit all of us in. Not just his disciples from long ago. Not just those of us who can fit inside our church. But there's space for everyone.

Look up the instructions for folding an origami house. On a square of paper, the children can write names or draw faces for lots of people they know, or have heard of, that they want to see enjoying being part of God's kingdom. Fold this paper up, following the origami instructions, into a house. They can write, 'In my Father's house, there are many rooms' on the front.

Like newborn infants, long for the pure, spiritual milk, so that by it you may grow into salvation

1 Peter 2:2

LOVE GOD AND EACH OTHER

Readings

- Acts 17:22-31
- Psalm 66:7-18
- 1 Peter 3:13-22
- John 14:15-21

Thoughts on the Readings

As Jesus promises the Holy Spirit to the disciples, Jesus describes all these blessings as coming from a position of love. If the disciples love him, then they will naturally do as he commanded – and we know what this is. Jesus' words are recorded for us, too. We are to love God, and love each other.

As our actions start to be in tune with God's priorities – listening, forgiving, caring, helping and loving – we are then in a position to be ready to receive the Holy Spirit. We will be ready to accept and receive the Holy Spirit as our helper, because we already love God.

This will give us the strength and tenacity to carry on caring for others and the world around us with joy, even when things are not easy.

Moving on to the reading from Acts, we hear Paul's speech to the people of Athens, talking about their altar to an Unknown God. Paul realised that these people already had knowledge of God, and wanted to worship, so he tells them more about God, how he created the earth and heaven, and how he wants us to be his children.

Sometimes people who do not go to church or would not consider themselves to have a faith can be aware of the presence of the Holy Spirit. They may recognise an atmosphere of peace within the church building, or the friendliness of an event they attend. If this happens, it is wonderful. It may be appropriate for us to tell them that Christians would describe this as the presence of the Holy Spirit, or it may not, depending on the person and their individual journey. We can pray for them, and continue to care for and welcome them. As we do this, obeying Jesus' command, the Holy Spirit will come and be present in that situation.

In Peter's letter today, we are told to keep on doing what is right and good, speaking respectfully to others and not worrying about what people might do if we speak out about our faith. It is better to get in trouble for doing the right thing than for doing the wrong thing! Hopefully we should not have to suffer for doing good to others, and speaking about our faith in a gentle and respectful way. But if we come across any opposition to this, then we know that God is with us, and we have made the right choice.

Discussion Starters

- **What can we do to create an environment where, together with those people who do not usually attend church, we can know God's love and the presence of the Holy Spirit?**

Intercessions

**Jesus, we love you,
send your Holy Spirit.**

Lord, as we come into your presence
and draw near to you,
we pray that we would know
the joy of being close to you.

We bring before you our church and its leaders
and ask that you would help us
to listen closely to you
and to act and speak at all times
with your love.
As we do this,
may you bless our worship
so that we can know your presence.
**Jesus, we love you,
send your Holy Spirit.**

Thank you for the acts of kindness
and selflessness
which we see in our world,
carried out by people of all faiths and none.
We pray that your empowering
and refreshing Spirit
would bless all those people whose actions show
that they care for others.
We pray too, that our churches would be known
as a place of peace and refuge,
healing and grace.
**Jesus, we love you,
send your Holy Spirit.**

We think of those people who are in need
of your healing, your love and your peace.
We bring them into your presence, and pray
that they would know the comfort
of your Holy Spirit
and that you would be with them
in whatever they face.
We particularly pray for . . .
**Jesus, we love you,
send your Holy Spirit.**

May the hope and joy of heaven
be close to those who are near the end of their lives
and may your comforting arms
surround those people

who have lost someone close to them.
We thank you for the people
who are now at rest in heaven,
close to you, and loved,
and remember today . . .
**Jesus, we love you,
send your Holy Spirit.**

As we go through this week, we pray
that you would be near us
in our thoughts, and words, and actions.
And as we do this, may we know again
your Holy Spirit.
Amen.

Children's Prayer

Jesus, we love you.
Make us wise and strong
as we choose kindness
in our lives every day.
Amen.

Other Ideas!

Cut out some small hearts from paper and card, and place these in a basket at the back of church. People can write their names on one of these hearts and then place them in the middle of a large heart (drawn onto a large piece of paper, or made out of a loopy length of rope). As they do this, they can think about how we are all within God's love, and that helps us to show love to others.

All-age Talk

Ask if there's anyone in the congregation who could come and help you out, as your best friend today.

Invite them up, and put some ears on their head (either stuck on an alice band, or on a strip of card that can go around their head) and give them a tail to wear (a leg of tights, tucked in their waistband will do).

Here's your best friend, your new dog Rover!

Rover doesn't know you that well yet. When you ask Rover to sit, he just sits and looks

quizzically at you. Give that a try. But he is your new pet dog, your new best friend, so you are going to spend some time playing with him and looking after him. Give Rover a nice bowl of dog biscuits and some water to drink. Find Rover a comfy dog bed. Take Rover for a walk around the church. Throw Rover a stick to catch.

After some time, you and Rover begin to understand each other, and begin to love each other. Rover is such good company, his fur is so soft, and he looks so funny when he runs around the garden. And Rover loves you too – you always give him just what he needs, food when he's hungry, a drink when he's thirsty, a scratch behind his ear in just the right itchy bit.

Because Rover loves you, he starts to do the things you want him to. When you go upstairs to brush your teeth, he stays at the bottom of the stairs, his tail wagging (Rover can wag his tail), because he knows you don't want dogs upstairs. When you ask him to sit, well, look what happens now! Try out a few simple dog commands, then maybe even some more complicated ones.

As we spend time in the company of our best friend, Jesus, we get to know him and love him more and more. Because we love him, we start to live in a different way, to live in God's way of love, caring for the world and for those around us. We don't do this because Jesus commands us, but we do it because we love him. The more time we spend in Jesus' company, the more we start to behave in a way that fits in with God's priorities, quite naturally.

Children's Corner

Cut up dishwasher sponges into the shape of hearts, and put out red and pink paint on saucers, and a large sheet of paper. The children can stamp hearts all over it, as they listen to Jesus in the Gospel speaking of love.

The colouring sheet shows children loving God, and loving each other. The words **'Love God, love each other'** are written across the top.

Little Kids' Sunday School

Play 'I Am the Wizard'. Sit or stand in a circle. One person holds a stick. This is their magic wand. They wave it and give everyone a command, which everyone then does (Stick out your tongue! Close your eyes! Touch your toes!) before passing on the magic wand to the next person. Make sure everyone gets at least one turn at being the wizard.

Some commands are easy and fun to follow. Nobody minds having to do something funny or silly. Some commands are more difficult. When mum asks you to help tidy the living room just as you're getting to the good bit in your game. When your little brother needs help to put on his shoes just as you're running into the garden to join in a game of football. Some commands are more difficult still – Jesus never said anything about recycling your newspapers, or not dropping litter, so how do we even begin to work out what command he's giving us here?

The secret is love. In our Gospel reading today, Jesus tells his friends, 'If you love me, keep my commands . . . Whoever has my commands and keeps them, is the one who loves me.'

If we love Jesus, if we spend time reading the Bible, praying and worshipping, watching what his other friends do, and spending time in Jesus' company ourselves, our love for him will grow, and we will know how Jesus would want us to behave in all manner of different situations. The better we know him, the easier we'll find it to follow him, and the more we'll want to.

The children can make a heart by threading beads onto a pipe cleaner and bending over the two ends at the top. Thread a ribbon through it, and the children can hang it up at home to remind themselves that they are loved by God, and this love helps them be loving in return.

Big Kids' Sunday School

Play a game of Twister, using the mat and spinner if you have one, or alternatively chalk-coloured blobs on the ground and call out 'left hand blue!' or 'right foot red!' etc. for the children to follow.

Some commands are very simple and clear to follow. When we are playing this game, the caller gives us commands and we do our best to follow them, although sometimes we do wobble a bit! Some commands are a bit more difficult. Can anyone think of a hard command they've had to follow? Maybe things to do with loading the dishwasher before they can go on their x-box, or doing half an hour's piano practice a day? Who are we happy to take commands from? Does it make a difference who tells us to do stuff?

Jesus says, 'If you love me, keep my commands . . . Whoever has my commands and keeps them, is the one who loves me.' Because we know and love Jesus, we are happy and eager to live in a way that matches up with his priorities, a way that fits in with his rule of love.

The children can make heart-shaped bath bombs to give out at church. In a mixing bowl, mix together 300g of bicarbonate of soda, and 100g of powdered citric acid. You can add a few drops of food colouring if you like. Spray on a little water, and start to mix it. Don't overdo the water – you need to stop just as it begins to be able to clump together in your hand. Squash the mixture into heart-shaped ice cube trays and leave for 20-30minutes to harden.

As people drop the hearts into their bath, they can think of how God's love washes around us, filling us with love ourselves and making us want to spread love to others, following Jesus' commands because we love him.

JESUS IS TAKEN UP TO HEAVEN

Readings

- Acts 1:1-11 or Daniel 7:9-14
- Psalm 47 or Psalm 93
- Ephesians 1:15-23 or Acts 1:1-11
- Luke 24:44-53

Thoughts on the Readings

As we think of Jesus ascending into heaven, our choice of psalms for today celebrates God ruling in heaven as King, and going up to his throne there. Jesus' disciples would have been familiar with these words, as they watched their friend and teacher, risen from the dead, be taken up to heaven in a cloud.

This glorious and wonderful event brought the disciples so much joy and confidence, that although they must have been sad to see Jesus leave them, this was overcome by happiness as they knew that his work on earth was done. Now Jesus would return to heaven, his eternal home, where they knew that they too would one day be able to join him again.

Jesus had told the disciples to wait in Jerusalem, because in just a few days they would receive the Holy Spirit. It is interesting that even after Jesus had entered Jerusalem on an ordinary donkey, been put to death on a cross, risen to life and appeared to the disciples and eaten with them, they still asked him whether he was going to give Israel its own king. Perhaps that idea of having a Messiah was so strongly linked to some sort of popular, powerful, earthly military ruler that it was hard to let go of this hope. Jesus again emphasises that he is not that sort of a king. He reassures the disciples that it is all in God's hands, and that they do not need to know the timing of when this might happen.

Sometimes we, too, have ideas of where God needs to move in power. We wonder why things have not happened yet. Surely God has promised us that things will change? Either we must have read Scripture wrong, or God has given up on us. But today our readings remind us that even if we don't see much change at the moment, things really are in God's hands. We don't need to worry about the how or the when. The best thing for us to do, like the disciples, is to spend time in prayer, listening and waiting. God will send his Holy Spirit to us and then we will have more than enough wisdom, strength and stamina to deal with anything that comes our way.

As the disciples stand, looking up into the empty patch of sky where Jesus had gone, two angels appear out of nowhere and speak to them. There is no point for the disciples to stand there looking at where Jesus had been a few minutes ago. There is more to look forward to. We can also be confident that our future and our church's future will be filled with the presence of Jesus, and blessed by the Holy Spirit.

Discussion Starters

- When is it helpful to look back to where God was at work in the past, and when can it stop us being open to God's new blessings, both now and in the future?

Intercessions

**King of heaven,
we look to you.**

King of heaven, we thank you
that you know us, and you love us
and you care about our lives and our world.
Thank you for the way
we can draw near to you as we pray.

We thank you for the opportunity we have
for our churches to show your glory,
both through being beautiful to look at
and peaceful to be within.
As we encourage each other
in our journey through life,
may we, too, show your glory
to the world around us.
**King of heaven,
we look to you.**

Thinking of our world,
we come before you,
bringing to mind those places
which have been waiting too long
for peace, justice and an end to conflict.
We pray that your Holy Spirit would come
and encourage those who long for change,
so that in the right time, and in the right way,
a new, peaceful future can be established.
**King of heaven,
we look to you.**

We pray for anyone who is in pain at the moment
or weary from dealing with the multiple challenges they face in life.
We ask that your gentle, holy and healing presence would be with them,

giving them the strength and the peace that they need.
Today we bring before you those people who have asked for our prayers, including . . .
King of heaven,
we look to you.

Jesus, as you reign as King in heaven,
we thank you that our home is with you, too.
We remember with love those who have gone before us,
who are in your presence in heaven.
We thank you for them, and name before you today . . .
King of heaven,
we look to you.

Lord, as we raise our faces
to see your glory,
may we know the joy
of your promises and your presence.
Amen.

Children's Prayer

Dear God,
as we look up and see
the clouds and the sky,
the stars, the moon
and the birds flying by,
it helps us imagine
heaven's glory
and we thank you that
    we can be
part of that story.
Amen.

Other Ideas!

Cut some cloud shapes out of white paper, and ask people to write on them something that describes heaven for them. These can be assembled together and stuck onto a larger piece of blue paper or card.

All-age Talk

We will be thinking today about how, although Jesus was taken up to heaven, hidden by clouds, and couldn't be seen any more, he is with us now. Heaven is not far away.

Make yourself a large cloud, perhaps from a piece of flipchart paper, a sheet or a big piece of card. Tell everyone that you need a bit

of help bringing this out to the front. You did try to make a floaty cloud but it didn't work very well, so we will have to make do with one made of card (or whatever yours is).

Gather a few churchy items together (the children can help bring them to you). These might include things like a hymnbook, a service book, a collection envelope, a biscuit, a cup, a candle and a teddy from the back of church. Let everyone have a good look at the items you have collected. Next, cover these up with your cloud. Ask people to see if they can name all the items that are now hidden.

Hopefully, with a bit of teamwork, people will be able to remember most of the things that are under the cloud. Lift it up and see if they were right. Although we were not able to see the things that were hidden, they were still there. They had not gone away or disappeared.

It is the same with heaven. When Jesus went up into heaven, taken up into the clouds, he could not be seen any more. But just because he could not be seen did not mean that he was not there any more.

Jesus promised that he would always be with us, and explained that once he had gone back to heaven he would send the Holy Spirit to help us. This is a promise not just for Jesus' friends who watched him go back up into heaven, but it is for us as well.

As we trust God, wait and pray, we will also be able to know the strength and joy which comes from the Holy Spirit.

Children's Corner

On a glass window or door if you have one, or a sheet of Perspex if you don't, spread a thin layer of petroleum jelly in the shape of a cloud, and allow the children to stick cotton wool balls onto it. As they build their cloud, they can think of how looking up into the sky sometimes makes us think of heaven, beyond our sight, and they can listen out for the cloud in the Bible reading today.

The colouring sheet shows Jesus, disappearing behind a cloud, as the disciples watch.

Little Kids' Sunday School

Lay some picnic blankets on the ground outside and encourage the children to lie down, looking up at the sky. What can they see up there? Trees waving in the breeze? Birds flying? Insects buzzing? Clouds floating past? What's the furthest they can see?

As you lie there, looking up, tell them the story of the Ascension, of how Jesus, after his resurrection, took his friends to the hills near Bethany. After telling them of the Holy Spirit he would send to them, it appeared to his friends that he was taken up into heaven and a cloud hid him from their eyes. Jesus couldn't be seen any more. His friends were left standing there, looking up into the sky.

The children can cover a paper cup with cotton wool balls to make a cloud. They can poke a hole through the base (now the top) and thread through a string. Tie a knot here so it doesn't fall straight through! Tape the other end to a small cardboard figure – this is Jesus. They can pull the string at the top, and the cardboard figure will disappear into the cloud. It doesn't mean that Jesus is no longer there, though, does it? Just that we can't see him right at the moment.

Big Kids' Sunday School

Give each child a glass and a small coin. Get them to put the coin underneath the glass. Can they still see it? Of course they can, it's still there, isn't it? Give them a jug of water, and have them pour the water into the glass. The water will refract the light, giving the illusion that the coin has disappeared. They can drink the water if they like, putting the glass back down on the coin. Ta da! The coin is back! And it never really went away.

Today is the day when we remember Jesus going back to heaven, the Ascension. Jesus was out on the hills near Bethany with his friends, after his resurrection. He'd been telling them about the Holy Spirit he was going to send them, when suddenly his disciples saw him go up to heaven. It was like a cloud was round him, and they lost sight of him. They were all standing around, staring up into the sky, when they were visited by angels who said, 'Why are you standing staring up into the sky? Jesus, who has gone away from you into heaven, will return the same way he has left.'

A bit like our coins, then. His friends couldn't see him any longer, but it didn't mean he wasn't there. And one day they would see him again.

The children can use white wool to make cloud pompoms, winding the wool round and round their hands, tying it round the middle, and snipping the ends. Once they have puffed their cloud out, they can tie on a piece of wool so they can hang their cloud from their ceiling, remembering the disciples seeing Jesus taken from them in a cloud, but like our coins, Jesus never really vanishing, and being with us all along, even when we can't see him.

GOD'S COMMUNITY OF FAITH

Readings

- Acts 1:6-14
- Psalm 68:1-10, 32-35
- 1 Peter 4:12-14; 5:6-11
- John 17:1-11

Thoughts on the Readings

Today Jesus reassures his followers, and us, that although things are changing, we are not to worry. He will be with them. And as we form a loving, supportive, heavenly community here on earth with each other, we will experience that same closeness as Jesus has with his Father in heaven. This will give us the strength, comfort and security that we need to deal with whatever life throws at us.

Although we are promised God's love, presence and protection, this does not mean that our external circumstances will be easy all the time, and we will never suffer. Quite the opposite, in fact. In the reading from 1 Peter we are told not to be surprised if our lives are made difficult because we choose to live God's loving way. This is just how it sometimes will be. But we do not have to worry about this – we can actually be happy, because if we are suffering for doing the right and kind thing, then this shows that God's Holy Spirit is with us.

As counter-intuitive as this may sound, we know that many, many people going through the most difficult times have found God's presence and strength with them in a remarkable way. All we need to do is to give our worries over to God, who cares for and loves us so much.

Somehow, in the context of heaven, our home, these earthly problems and difficulties do not seem nearly so impossible. We are able to see the bigger picture, and as we bring these things before God, we will know his amazing comfort, wisdom, peace and strength.

In today's reading from Acts, we again hear the passage about Jesus ascending into heaven in this remarkable way, taken up in a cloud. The extra portion of the reading, which we also have this week, tells us about what Jesus' followers did next. Jesus had told them that the Holy Spirit would come upon them, and that after this they would be able to tell all the rest of the world the good news of God's kingdom. While they were waiting, though, they met together, and they prayed. Then they met together and prayed some more. After this, they prayed and met together again.

The strength that comes from God is there for us in a special way when we pray together. We may not know what is happening next, we may not be sure of the way ahead, but the answer is always to pray. As we do this within a supportive and loving community, we will find that God's Holy Spirit is with us.

Discussion Starters

- **What opportunities do we have to meet together and pray? Are there any ways these could be more open and accessible to people who do not usually come to church?**

Intercessions

**God of hope,
be with us.**

As we come together to pray,
we thank you that we can bring our worries before you
because you love us, and care for us.

We bring before you our church
and thank you for the times
it has been a place of safety and love
to those who worship here.
As we pray together, may there be
a sense of peace and healing,
hope and welcome,
as we spend time in your presence as a community.
**God of hope,
be with us.**

As we think of our world,
we know that there are many areas
where the future is uncertain
and can seem frightening.
We pray that, as your people come into your presence in worship,
you would bring peace and wisdom,
strength and reassurance;
enough for their needs
and more.
**God of hope,
be with us.**

We bring into your loving care
anyone who is suffering at this time
and particularly those
who have had one thing to cope with
after another.

Help us to be a source
of support and strength
as we show your love
and speak your words of hope.
We particularly pray for . . .
**God of hope,
be with us.**

We think of those people who are nearing the end of life's journey
and pray that they would be aware of the loving welcome
that awaits them in heaven.
We also bring to mind our loved ones who have died,
now at rest with you.
We remember before you today . . .
**God of hope,
be with us.**

As we rest in your presence,
soak up your love
and gaze at your glory,
may we be filled with your Holy Spirit.
Amen.

Children's Prayer

All our worries
we bring to you,
knowing you love us
and care for us too.
Thanks that you always
want us to know
that we can talk to you
wherever we go.
Amen.

Other Ideas!

Have some stones for people to hold and place in a beautiful bowl or tray. As they do this, they can think of placing their worries in God's hands.

All-age talk

Bring along a bag of Lego or other bricks, as well as a large sheet. Spread the sheet out, and tip the Lego onto it, in the shape of a path. Challenge people to walk along the uncomfortable Lego path in their socks.

Explain how life is sometimes like this – and in the Bible it says that we shouldn't be surprised if sometimes it's like walking through fire (or along a lumpy Lego path). This is just the way it is sometimes, and it doesn't mean that God has left us, or that we have done something wrong. If we know that we have been doing our best to make the right, loving choices, we can be sure that God will always be with us.

Following Jesus does not mean that things will be easy, and we will never have any problems. It does not mean that we will become wealthy, have a guarantee of good health, or that everyone will like us all the time. Sometimes things will go smoothly, and sometimes they won't.

Ask three volunteers to try the Lego path again. The smallest person can stand in the middle, on the Lego, with their friends either side (shoes on, each side of the path). As the middle person makes their way along the Lego path, they can be helped and held up by the others who are accompanying them.

This is the way that it is for us, too. When things are not easy, God has given us a community to be part of so that we can support each other. As we meet and pray together, and help each other, we will find it easier to walk along the path that our life takes us. Supported by our friends in Christ, and helped by the Holy Spirit, we can journey through life with joy.

Children's Corner

The children can help the church teddies to do some difficult or uncomfortable things: build a tower with blocks, stand on one leg, abseil down a wool-rope from the dizzy heights of the table. The teddies couldn't do it alone, but with our help they could. Some things in life are difficult or uncomfortable, but Jesus says we don't have to do them alone. As we pray, his Holy Spirit will be with us, and our community of faith will support us.

The colouring sheet shows children and adults doing difficult things, and being helped by others. The writing says: **'Don't worry – you're not on your own' says Jesus**.

Little Kids' Sunday School

Take a bag full of dried butter beans (check the children know not to put them in their mouth, as dried beans are often toxic until soaked and cooked), and scatter them all around, either inside your meeting space, or even better, outside on some grass. Pick one child to pick them all up. Go! Gosh, it's slow, hard, work, isn't it? Does anyone have any suggestions how we could get those beans picked up faster? Yes! If everyone helps Casper to pick up the beans, it'll be much easier. Let the children scramble around to pick the beans up. You might find they love it so much that they demand to do it again and again.

After Jesus had gone back to heaven, his friends went back to Jerusalem to wait for the Holy Spirit that he had promised them. They knew there would be a big, hard job for them to do in the future. It was going to be difficult to follow Jesus if they couldn't actually see him any more. But they didn't try to do it by themselves. They met together to pray. And they met together and prayed some more. Just like you all helped Casper to pick up the beans, we can all help each other to live as Christians.

Give each of the children one of those tiny jam-jars, the size you get for breakfast in a hotel, if you can. They can draw faces on the beans using a permanent marker, and put the beans inside the jar. They can put a label on the jar to say, 'A community of human beans.' God calls us to live as a community so that we can support each other.

Big Kids' Sunday School

The children can practise carrying each other around, using their arms to make a seat. Two people stand opposite each other. One child grasps the other child's left wrist with their right hand, and their own right wrist with their left hand. The child opposite does the same. This makes a square shape that looks almost like a knot. If they lower this to the floor, another child can sit on it as a seat, and even if they're too heavy for one person to lift, both the children together will be able to manage it. Make sure the child being lifted holds on tight!

After Jesus had risen from the dead and gone back to heaven, his disciples knew it was going to be difficult in the future. They knew that Jesus was sending them his Holy Spirit, and that they'd have a big job on their hands to help God's kingdom come in the world. It was going to be hard to follow Jesus now that they couldn't actually see him any more, too. How would they know how to live? Once they went back to Jerusalem, they met together to pray, and they met again and prayed some more. Jesus had prayed, 'Let them be one, as we are one', and here they were doing just that, building a community. And we are part of that community of faith too, supporting each other to follow Jesus through bad times and the good times.

The children can be given two different-coloured lengths of paracord, and follow instructions online to tie a friendship knot. This is a knot used often by scouts and guides to tie their scarves, and looks very much like our hand-seat that we made earlier. It's a good symbol to use of how in the church we need to rely on each other, and how the community built of fellow followers of Christ should be a supportive and safe place for all of us. We all have our part to play in making that so.

THE GIFT OF GOD'S HOLY SPIRIT

Readings

- Acts 2:1-21 or Numbers 11:24-30
- Psalm 104:26-36, 37b
- 1 Corinthians 12:3b-13 or Acts 2:1-21
- John 20:19-23 or John 7:37-39

Thoughts on the Readings

The gift of God's Spirit is for everyone. We hear in the reading from Numbers, many years before the events of Pentecost, Moses recognised that gift of the Holy Spirit as some of the wise leaders he had appointed started to shout and call out like prophets in worship. At the time, we are told, this only happened once, but Moses spoke of the longing he had that one day all people would be able to worship God in this way.

The inclusiveness of Pentecost shows this being fulfilled. We are told that all the Lord's followers were in one place, and that would have included women, men and children – just as the prophet Joel had foretold. They had the confidence to speak out God's praises in all the languages which were spoken in that busy, multicultural city. We, too, can be enabled through God's Spirit to speak his good news of love, peace, hope and freedom to those around us, in whichever way makes sense to them. This might be through words or teaching, it might be through practical action, or perhaps through something creative or an offer of prayer. We may find that there are people within our congregation who do have the gift of speaking another language, and this could be used for God's glory too, perhaps through translating a poster for an event, or sharing a hymn or prayer.

Listening to the words of the reading from 1 Corinthians, we hear how the gifts that the Holy Spirit brings us are diverse too. We need everyone, together, as a community in order to have a complete set of all the wonderful things that God wants to give us. Both knowledge and wisdom come from the Spirit – two different, but very important gifts. Through talking and praying together we can learn from each other, and better understand each other as well as the world around us. It is the same with the other gifts which are described. As humans, it is our God-given diversity which is our strength.

Discussion Starters

- **What gifts do we have within our church community? Does anyone speak another language, or have practical or professional knowledge which could be useful to others? How could we allow these gifts to be used by God?**

Intercessions

**Holy Spirit,
we receive from you.**

Lord, as we come before you
in hope and expectation,
may we be ready to receive
your wonderful gifts.

We thank you for the way
that your Holy Spirit
has blessed and sustained your Church through the ages.
We thank you for those people
who have enriched our worship
and who have helped us to draw near to you in prayer.
Today, may we know your presence in this place
and receive your blessing once again.
**Holy Spirit,
we receive from you.**

We bring before you our world,
knowing that there are many places
where diversity of language and culture is not valued
and one group's wisdom is valued,
while another's is dismissed.
We pray that your Holy Spirit
would bring love and understanding,
so that everyone may know
that your gifts are given to the whole family of God
to share.
**Holy Spirit,
we receive from you.**

As we remember those people who are in need today,
we pray that your Holy Spirit would be with them,
bringing joy and peace,
whatever their circumstances.
We bring into your loving care . . .
**Holy Spirit,
we receive from you.**

With our mind set on the joy of heaven,
we remember with love
those who have gone before us
and pray for those who miss them.
As we worship, may we draw near to heaven
and know something of the love that you have

for all your children.
We name in your presence today . . .
**Holy Spirit,
we receive from you.**

Holy Spirit, we pray
that you would fill us again
and give us your good gifts,
so that we can help others.
Amen.

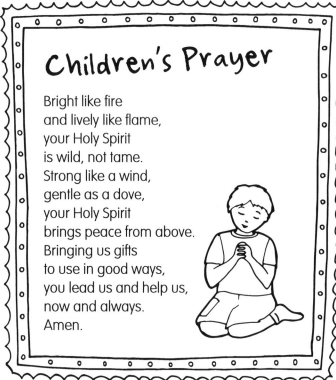

Children's Prayer

Bright like fire
and lively like flame,
your Holy Spirit
is wild, not tame.
Strong like a wind,
gentle as a dove,
your Holy Spirit
brings peace from above.
Bringing us gifts
to use in good ways,
you lead us and help us,
now and always.
Amen.

Other Ideas!

Make a flame collage with different
pieces of tissue paper, crepe paper,
cellophane (this could be from sweet
wrappers) etc.

All-age Talk

Roll up a large piece of paper or thin card to
make a trumpet shape, and ask some of the
children to come and help you fill it up with
paper 'flames'. These are best made out of
some sort of thin paper, such as tissue paper
or crepe paper, and it would be nice to have
different fiery colours too.

   The children can fold their piece of paper
a few times and cut out a simple flame shape
with round-ended scissors. You may need to draw the shape on for them quickly, or prepare
a template. When they have made some of these, they can pop them in your trumpet.

   Explain to everyone that we are making some flames to help us think about God's gift of
the Holy Spirit that came at Pentecost. God has given us all special gifts – sometimes we are

aware of them, and sometimes we don't realise that we have them. There are also new gifts and skills which God wants to give to us too. All of these can be used to help others, and to help the world, and this makes God happy.

As the children put the cut-out flames into the trumpet-shaped card, look at the flame and say what you think this gift might be. This might be something like speaking another language, having wisdom, knowing first aid, being good at looking after people, making a great cup of tea, being a fantastic listener, a good friend, patient, great at tidying up.

When you have had enough of pieces of paper being put in your trumpet, explain that we are going to stop for a minute and have a think about which gifts God has already given us that we know about, which gifts we have but are not so aware of, and which gifts we would like to receive.

Then, ask a volunteer to blow into the trumpet. As the flames blow out of the trumpet, the children can help to blow and flap them around the church. After this, ask the children to help catch them, and give one to everyone in the congregation.

As people receive this flame, they can also be open to receive that gift which they have asked for from God.

Children's Corner

Have some present boxes, filled with cut-out paper flames, wrapped up and tied with ribbon. The children can open these gifts, and play with the paper flames within, listening out for the gift God sent his friends in the reading from Acts.

The colouring sheet shows flames, and within each, a child using one of their God-given gifts.

Little Kids' Sunday School

Put on some music and turn on a bubble machine, so you can have a bubble-popping disco! Watch how the bubbles blow around in the invisible breeze.

After Jesus had returned to heaven, when the disciples were meeting in their room to pray together as usual, something rather strange happened. The people heard the sound of a rushing wind filling the room, a bit like our bubbles blowing all around. They saw what looked like flames on top of each other's heads. And they were suddenly filled with a feeling of courage, warmth, love and excitement. They were full to bursting with joy at the good news of Jesus' life and resurrection, and couldn't hold it in any more. They went rushing outside into the streets, to share this good news with everyone they could find. It didn't matter if they spoke the same language or not. Somehow God made sure everyone could understand what they were saying.

And this sharing of the good news didn't just stop then. The disciples kept on sharing it, with everyone they could, right through their life. The people they told got to know Jesus for themselves, and the joy from the Holy Spirit bubbling up in their lives meant that they went to share this good news too. And that carried on through the centuries right through to us!

The children can make bubble-print pictures to remind themselves of this story, of the breeze that blew their bubbles around, of the rushing wind filling the room at Pentecost. You can use flame-like colours, squeezing some liquid paint into a bowl, adding washing-up liquid and water, and letting the children blow air into the mixture through a paper straw. Make sure they blow, not suck! Once there's a big pile of bubbles on top of the bowl, they can press a piece of paper down on top.

Big Kids' Sunday School

Use Google translate to find out a variety of ways to say 'Jesus is alive!'. Write these on pieces of card, and write the names of the languages on other pieces of card. Scatter them around your meeting space, and the children can find them and match them up. Can they work out how to say any of these? Can any of your children share how to say 'Jesus is alive!' in their own home language?

Tell the children of how the disciples, praying together in a closed room, suddenly heard the sound of a rushing wind (get the children to make the sound of a wind blowing) and saw what looked like tongues of fire on each other's heads (light a candle). They were filled with love, courage and peace, and went rushing outside to tell everyone they could about their friend Jesus who had died and risen again. It didn't seem to matter who they were talking to, whether they spoke the same language or not. God made it so that everyone could understand in their own language.

And that good news spread right across the world, and right through the years to here, in this place, today. Can you imagine how many languages these words, 'Jesus is alive!' have been spoken in? Some of these languages aren't even spoken any more! The children can help to make some bunting to hang outside your church, so that anyone who walks past will read the good news in their own language. Even if you live in an area where there's very little linguistic diversity, you never know who'll be reading! Cut out triangles of fabric from an old sheet, and give the children permanent markers to copy out some of the phrases from the activity at the beginning. Staple these flags to a long strip of bunting tape. You can talk about who they know who speaks another language, and what different ways we might share the good news so that people can understand, even if they don't speak the same language as us.

FATHER, SON AND HOLY SPIRIT

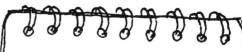

Readings
- Isaiah 40:12-17, 27-31
- Psalm 8
- 2 Corinthians 13:11-13
- Matthew 28:16-20

Thoughts on the Readings

In today's reading from Isaiah we hear a description of God which emphasises his enormity and his majesty as the creator of all that there is and all that there will ever be. We cannot even begin to understand how big God is. Compared to the creator of the universe who has been there since before the beginning of time, we are small and insignificant, and seeing God as creator alone, it would seem unlikely that he would have the time to be interested in us.

However, amazing and unlikely as it may seem, our God cares deeply for all of us, and is interested in the smallest details of our thoughts, our relationships and our lives. He understands us, he will strengthen us and encourage us, and his loving wisdom is more than enough for all of us. As we trust in God, we will find the strength, not just to keep going, but to do this with power and confidence. We know this power as the Holy Spirit, whom God has given to us to help us.

As Jesus sends out his disciples at the end of Matthew's Gospel, he tells them to baptise any new followers in the name of the Father, the Son and the Holy Spirit. We hear these words spoken so often that sometimes we can forget the real significance of them. As wonderful as it is to understand God as our creator, and the originator of all that exists, we also need to know God as Holy Spirit, that light and life within us which helps us to live in a kind and holy way as we travel through our lives. And of course, as Christians it is so important to us to be close to Jesus, our Saviour and friend. We know that he understands us because he has lived on earth as a human being like us, and through his earthly life he has inspired us.

Jesus tells us that through knowing him we will also know his Father in heaven, and he taught us to pray to our eternal creator as our Father too. As we do this, and draw near to God, we will experience his Holy Spirit in our lives as well.

Discussion Starters

- **What helps us personally to know more of God? Is it thinking of the beautiful and vast universe that he created, experiencing the encouragement and power of the Holy Spirit, or knowing that Jesus walked on earth as a human like us?**

Intercessions

Father, Son and Holy Spirit,
draw us closer to you.

As we come into your holy and loving presence,
we pray that we would know more of you,
as we gaze at your majesty,
hear about the life of Jesus
and know the strength and power of your Holy Spirit.

We thank you for our church
and for our neighbouring places of worship.
We are grateful for the way
that others have led us in worship
and brought us nearer to you.
We pray that together, we would come to know you more.
Father, Son and Holy Spirit,
draw us closer to you.

As we bring our world and its needs before you,
we thank you that you are always ready to listen
and that you care about everyone, and all your creation.
We pray that you would help us all
to find ways to treat the world we live in
with care and respect,
remembering that all things
were crafted by you.
Father, Son and Holy Spirit,
draw us closer to you.

We pray today for anyone who is feeling weary,
whether through long-term pain,
limited mobility,
anxiety or depression,
debt or addiction.
May your Holy Spirit renew, refresh and strengthen them,
bringing peace and a knowledge that you understand.
We particularly remember . . .
Father, Son and Holy Spirit,
draw us closer to you.

Give peace to those people who
are nearing the end of life's journey
and comfort those who love and care for them.
We remember with thankfulness
those who have gone before us,
and are now together with you in heaven.

We name before you today . . .
**Father, Son and Holy Spirit,
draw us closer to you.**

Holy and loving God,
you are wonderful,
and what we can see shows only a small part of
the size and beauty of your creation.
We are so grateful that you love us,
and that we can know you.
Amen.

Children's Prayer

God our Father,
Jesus our friend,
Holy Spirit who helps us,
your love will never end.
Amen.

Other Ideas!

Create a display using some plants and flowers which have leaves in three parts, a traditional representation of the Trinity.

All-age Talk

Bring along a telescope or binoculars of some description, some sandals or shoes, and a teddy.

Ask a volunteer to help you by coming up and having a look through the telescope/binoculars. How far away can they see? If we were to go outside on a nice clear night, with a really good telescope, we would be able to see some things that are very far away indeed. But no one's ever seen the edge of the universe (if it even has an edge!).

Even if we just think about the stars that we can see when we look up at the night sky, it is incredible to think that each of them is like our sun, and some of them have planets around them too.

How did all of this come into being? We believe all this beautiful creation was made by our loving God. But if the universe is so vast that we can't imagine it, how much bigger must God be?

What is so wonderful about our faith is that the same amazing, creative God who made the whole universe and all that there is, came to live on earth as a human being. He walked around on the same earth that we live on, and breathed the same air.

Ask a volunteer to try on the shoes or sandals and walk once around the church in them.

Jesus would have sometimes got sore feet, he sometimes would have felt tired, and sometimes would have been hungry. He understands what it is like for us humans too (ask the volunteer how they are feeling).

And when Jesus went back up to heaven, he promised that he would always be with us. We could always talk to him as we pray, whenever we wanted to, and he would send the Holy Spirit to be with us, to strengthen us, and to comfort us.

Ask for a volunteer to give the teddy a nice cuddle.

Explain that God wants to surround us with his love, just like our volunteer is cuddling the teddy. He cares about us, and he will never let us go. Even though he made the planets, the stars and everything that exists, he loves us and knows us each by name. What an amazing God!

Children's Corner

Have some old Ordnance Survey maps for the children to enjoy unfolding. They start off small, but the more you discover, the bigger they get. And the picture on them looks small but is actually a huge place, with each footstep across it being a day's walk. And they can fold up small enough to fit in your pocket (if you have a big pocket!). Our God is a bit like that. We know that he created the whole universe, and the more we look, the bigger we find it, and the more amazing we know him to be. And yet, he can also draw close to us, closer than inside our pocket, right inside our heart.

The colouring sheet shows a child looking in wonder at the universe in their hands. The writing reads, **'God, you are amazing and wonderful, yet we can know you and you fill us with your love'**.

Little Kids' Sunday School

Take the children outside and see if they can find a clover leaf hiding amongst the grass. It's a tiny little leaf, hard to see in all the green. It's small enough to pick and hide inside your fist. Although it's one leaf, it's made up of three leaves.

Tell the children that today is Trinity Sunday, when we think about our one God being Father, Son and Holy Spirit. Can any of the children guess why we went to look at clover leaves today?

Not only is it one-in-three like the Trinity but it's something that is hard to find. And it can be hard to get our heads around the idea of the Trinity. Some grown-ups, who've spent their whole lives thinking about it, still get their brain in knots! And it's also something that is small enough to hold in our hands. Because although God made our whole universe, he was also born as a human baby, just like us.

If you have a laminating machine, get the children to pick lots of clover leaves and scatter them inside a laminating pouch. You can feed it through the machine, and cut it up as bookmarks. Punch a hole and thread through some green ribbon at one end. The children can maybe give these out after church, so that as people read and learn and grow wiser and wiser, they'll remember that all this wisdom is held within the mystery of the Trinity. If you don't have a laminating machine, you can glue clover leaves on card and cover them with sticky-back plastic.

Big Kids' Sunday School

Give the children some ice to experiment with. Let them put it in a saucepan and heat it over a hob or a camping stove. Remind them to stay safe around the hot burner. What happens to the ice as it heats up? At what point does it stop being ice and turn into water? What happens to the water as it heats up? At what point does it stop being water and turn into steam? Could we turn it back again? Is it made out of different stuff?

Tell the children that this is Trinity Sunday, when we try to grapple with the idea of our one God being Father, Son and Holy Spirit. Can any of them think of why we experimented with ice today? How is it similar and how is it different from the Trinity?

Bring out a smoothie maker. Put some of your leftover ice inside, to symbolise God the Father, the creator of everything that is, standing solid through all of time, like this hard ice. Add some strawberries and raspberries. These are for Jesus, red for his blood, red for the love he showed us by being born as a human, living, dying and rising again. Add some orange juice. This is orange, like fire, for the Holy Spirit. Put the lid on tight and blitz it up. The children can share this, maybe with the rest of the congregation after church, and explain how it is made of three ingredients making one drink.

God, you are amazing & wonderful, yet we can know you & you fill us with your love

BUILDING OUR LIVES ON GOD

Readings

- Deuteronomy 11:18-21, 26-28
- Psalm 31:1-5, 19-24
- Romans 1:16-17; 3:22b-28 (29-31)
- Matthew 7:21-29

Thoughts on the Readings

The words from Matthew's Gospel at first seem quite harsh – that not everyone who calls Jesus 'Lord' will enter heaven. But doing religious activities is not the same as really following God's laws from the heart. The people Jesus describes were preaching and casting out demons, but unless this is done kindly, with love, humbly recognising the way that God tenderly cares for the poor and the oppressed, this is not in keeping with God's laws.

Our reading from Romans today seems to take a different angle on this issue – that it is through faith that we are saved, not by obeying some law. But this is when we are thinking of laws in terms of rules and regulations. As Paul explains, our faith actually makes the law more powerful. If, in our hearts, we hold and treasure God's law of love, this will inform and inspire all our actions.

We cannot possibly get it right all the time, and God understands this. A rule-based way of life is sure to fail us at some point, as so often one rule contradicts another. This is not how God wants us to live. As we spend time with God, and draw close to him, holding those difficult situations before him in prayer, we will come to be able to treat others with love and respect. Our words and actions will be inspired by God's wisdom and love.

Often there is not just one right or easy answer to the situations we have to deal with in our lives. Sometimes there seems to be no answer at all. But with love of God, and love of others at the centre of our actions, we can be reassured that we are on the right track. As Jesus explained, this is just like building a house on good foundations. Get this right, and everything else will fall into place.

Discussion Starters

- How can God's law of love be seen in our churches and our lives?

Intercessions

**As we build our lives on you,
thank you for your love.**

Thank you that we do not have to remember
complicated lists of rules
to follow you.
As we come before you,
may your good and kind law of love
stay close to us,
leading us and guiding us
through all that we do.

We pray that our churches
would be a place of acceptance and welcome,
where people can come to know your love
as part of a caring community.
Where our sense of worth
does not come from following rules correctly
or from being right all the time
but is simply a result of knowing
that we are loved by you
and we will treat others with care and respect
as part of your diverse family.
**As we build our lives on you,
thank you for your love.**

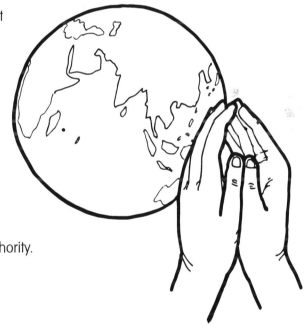

We bring before you our world
and think of those people
whose actions for justice and peace
have led them into conflict
with the laws of their own land.
We pray that your values
of love, respect and care
would be present in these situations
and in all the decisions made by those in authority.
**As we build our lives on you,
thank you for your love.**

We bring into your presence
anyone who is in need at this time,
or facing any troubles in their life.
We pray that you would be their strength,
their hope and their security,
whatever happens.
May your healing arms of love
surround those known to us
who are suffering at this time, including . . .
**As we build our lives on you,
thank you for your love.**

We remember today
all those who have gone before us
and have now been welcomed into heaven with you.
We pray for those who miss them at this time,
and ask that you would bring them your comfort,
healing and love.
We name before you today . . .
As we build our lives on you,
thank you for your love.

As we go out from this place,
we choose to build our lives on you,
knowing that this is the only way
to find true peace, purpose and freedom.
Amen.

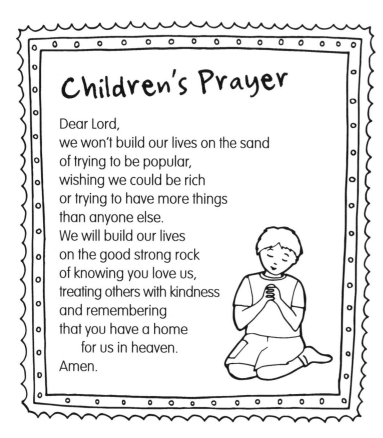

Children's Prayer

Dear Lord,
we won't build our lives on the sand
of trying to be popular,
wishing we could be rich
or trying to have more things
than anyone else.
We will build our lives
on the good strong rock
of knowing you love us,
treating others with kindness
and remembering
that you have a home
for us in heaven.
Amen.

Other Ideas!

Have a tray of sand and
some stones for people to
build with.

All-age Talk

Bring along some pieces of Lego, Duplo or
other bricks that fit together. Also bring along
a Lego or Duplo base plate that the bricks will
fix onto, and a tray of sand.

Explain that we are going to try out what
Jesus was talking about in the Gospel reading
today. Ask for a couple of volunteers. One
volunteer is to build a house with the bricks,

using the base plate as the foundation. Your other volunteer will also be building a house, but on the tray of sand instead.

Give your volunteers a time limit – maybe three minutes – to create something. They could each pick a helper if they wanted to.

As they start building, talk about how when Jesus spoke, he often used these practical examples and analogies to help us think about what he was saying, and remember his message. This was very different to the way that other people taught, and made Jesus' message accessible to everyone, from the youngest to the oldest.

Let's see how our builders are getting on.

Ask your helpers to tell you a bit about how they are finding the task. What's it like building a Lego house on sand instead of on a proper base plate? Perhaps it is difficult to get the pieces lined up, perhaps the sand gets in the way where the Lego is supposed to join together, so that it does not fit together properly. What about the house on the firm foundation? Is it fixed on? What if you turned the whole thing upside down? (We won't try this with the tray of sand!)

Jesus explained that if we build our lives on God's good law of love, everything else will fall into place. If we don't do this, and choose selfish priorities instead, we might be able to build a life that looks good on the outside, but when difficult times come, we will find it hard to cope.

The Lego house on the base plate could even be turned upside down and it would stay together. If we'd done that with the one on the sand, it would have been a messy disaster. God gives us his laws because they are good for us, and he loves us. He knows that if we remember to look to him and spend time in his company, and treat others and the world around us with respect, then we do not have to worry about anything else. That simple law covers it all.

Children's Corner

Use building blocks (natural wood slices of a fallen log are a more exciting challenge to build with) to build a house, either in a tray of sand or on a firm surface. You can provide a small jug or watering can so they can play the storms, too. Listen out for Jesus telling this story in the Gospel reading today.

The colouring sheet shows a house from Bible times, built firmly on stone foundations, as a house built on sand starts to slip in the storm. The Bible story reference is included so they can read this again at a later time.

Little Kids' Sunday School

Put the children in teams, or let them individually use building blocks or Duplo to build the tallest tower they can. You can either time them and see which tower is tallest when your buzzer goes, or count the blocks each time they build, so the tallest tower they manage overall is the winner.

When we build, it's hard to build up tall, isn't it? Very soon, the tower starts to wobble and then it all comes crashing down. The reason this doesn't happen with our houses and flats, and with this church, is that before the builders even start building, they dig into the ground to lay strong foundations to build on. Otherwise, every time it rained, the muddy ground would slip around, and every time we had a dry spell, the hard ground would crack, and our house would start to wobble and fall.

Jesus knew about builders. He'd seen people building houses, and probably enjoyed watching them when he was a little boy. Lots of little children love watching builders at work. He had been telling his friends how to get to heaven. It's not just about what you say, says Jesus, but about what you do, following God's rule of love, living as God wants you to live.

Jesus said, imagine your life is like a house. A wise builder decides to build his house on good foundations, on solid rock. When the stormy times come, the rain and wind blow all around the house, but it stands steady on the rock. A foolish builder decides to build his house on the sand. When the stormy times come, the rain and the wind flood the sand, which becomes wobbly and the house falls down.

Be like that wise builder, says Jesus. Build your life on the things Jesus says, not just saying them, but doing them too. Then even when bad things happen in your life, you will know you are safe and secure in God's love.

Give each child a jam-jar, and some grey modelling clay. They can use this to form a rock and stick it on the inside of the jam-jar lid. Use more modelling clay to make a house and stick that to the rock. Fill the jam-jar with water and eco glitter. Screw the lid back on, and they'll be able to see their house, standing firm on its strong foundations, even when the storm rages all around.

Big Kids' Sunday School

Collect as many large boxes as you can. Those shallow fruit boxes are good for this, that you find by the fruit and veg stall in the market. Give the children free rein to do some building. Can they make a house big enough for them to get inside?

Tell them the story of the wise and the foolish builders. Jesus had been talking with his friends about how they could get to heaven. It's not just what you say, said Jesus, but what you do. You need to do the will of my Father in heaven, to live in the way that God wants you to live, his way of love.

Imagine your life is like a house. The wise builder decides to start building on solid rock, so that his house has a good foundation. When the stormy weather comes, the rock stays solid and the house doesn't collapse. The foolish builder decides to build on the sand. But when the stormy weather comes, the sand shifts and the house wobbles and falls down. Be like the wise builder, says Jesus, building your life on the things that I say. Not just saying them, but doing them, living your life in the way I've shown you. Then when hard times come in your life, you'll know you are still safe and secure, held in my love.

Give the children jelly tot sweets and toothpicks so they can construct their own house, talking as you do so about how we build our lives, the choices we make, and what a life built on rock would look like.

MATTHEW 7:26

FAITH IN GOD'S PROMISES

Readings

- Hosea 5:15 – 6:6
- Psalm 33:1-12
- Romans 4:13-25
- Matthew 9:9-13, 18-26

Thoughts on the Readings

Reading the words in the passage from Hosea about God causing destruction can sound very challenging. Why would God want to hurt or harm anyone? What could this possibly mean to us today? Our psalm for today sheds some light on this. God destroys the plans of those in power who do not follow him. This is actually something that we hope and pray for as we think of difficult situations of violence, oppression, injustice and conflict. Any action which promotes these things is going against God's values of love, mercy and justice, and we can pray together and work together for things to change for the better.

In both our reading from Hosea, and in the passage from Matthew, we hear how God wants us to be faithful to him, rather than offering sacrifices or religious ritual. He is always faithful to us, and will keep his promise. Through this relationship of love, we can find that we are changed, transformed and equipped so that we can then act with kindness and mercy towards others. This is the way that our lives show that we are being faithful to God.

We also think today about what faith in God's promises means. We are reminded that Abraham had faith in God, and trusted him, even when becoming a father of many people seemed pretty much impossible. Yet because of his relationship with God, and the time he had spent close to God in prayer, Abraham was confident that God would do what he had said he would, one way or another. The woman in our Gospel story had this same faith. For 12 years she had been suffering from bleeding, and it must have seemed as if this would never end. Physically weak and emotionally weary, she did not give up, and was determined that if she just drew near enough to Jesus to touch his clothes, she would be healed. As she took this step, on her own, Jesus noticed and turned to her with love, already knowing what was on her mind. He reassured her that because of her faith, God had healed her.

We, too, may sometimes be in a place where we are not feeling particularly strong, successful or confident. The wonderful thing is that all God wants is for us to trust him, and draw near to him. He will cover us with his love, he will heal us, and he will protect us. He never wanted us to show off about how great we were anyway. When we come as we are, into God's presence, we are then in a position to receive his blessings and his promises.

Discussion Starters

- **What parts of our worship help us to come as we are before God?**

Intercessions

As we reach out in faith,
bless us and heal us.
Lord, we thank you
that we can come into your presence
just as we are,
trusting in your promises
and knowing that you love us.

We thank you for the way
that your church has been a place
of healing, community and belonging
through the years.
As we work with you
to bring about your kingdom,
we pray that we would know your love
and share it with those around us.
As we reach out in faith,
bless us and heal us.

We pray for our world
and all those places and situations
where violence and injustice
seem to have the upper hand.
We pray that your love would triumph over fear
and that those with the power to change things
would have the confidence and strength
to take action for peace.
As we reach out in faith,
bless us and heal us.

We bring before you those people
in need of healing –
those who have been suffering for many years,
those who feel ashamed, embarrassed or isolated
because of their condition
and those who have been told
that there is no effective treatment or cure.
We pray that your healing love,
your peace and your presence
would surround them as we pray.
We name before you . . .
As we reach out in faith,
bless us and heal us.

We pray for those people
who are on the last part of their earthly journey.

May your promise of heaven comfort them
and give them peace at this time.
We also remember those who have recently died
and those who are missed at this time of year, including . . .
As we reach out in faith,
bless us and heal us.

As we travel through this week, we pray
that you would fill us with your love
as we come before you,
just as we are.
Amen.

Children's Prayer

Dear Jesus, we're so grateful
that all we have to do
is to reach out and touch the
edge of your clothes
and we'll be healed by you.
Amen.

Other Ideas!

Have a picture of Jesus – perhaps
of one of the times he healed
someone, if possible. Provide a
pack of post-it notes and a pen,
so that people can write the
names of those they know who
need healing, and place
the names before Jesus.

All-age Talk

Ask a volunteer to dress up in some sort
of cloak – this could be a small cassock,
if you have one, or an old curtain or towel
draped around their shoulders. Not sure how
authentic the costume is for our Gospel story,
but it will do! Ask some of the other children
to come and be the 'crowd' around Jesus,
and tell them you are going to secretly tap
one of them on the shoulder. This is going
to be the person who touches the edge of
Jesus' clothes.

When you have done this, the children can all crowd around Jesus, while the person you
have chosen tries to touch the edge of the cloak. When they have done this, they can let you
know and everyone can sit down.

So, did the person with the cloak on feel that someone had touched it? Could they make a guess as to who it was?

In our Gospel reading today, we hear how Jesus knew just who it was when a woman who had been ill for years and years touched the edge of his cloak. He knew why she had done it, and he knew she wanted healing. He loved her, and cared for her, even though there were lots of other people around as well.

The woman hadn't thought she was good enough to ask to speak to Jesus, or to ask him to pray for her, but she had faith that just by getting close to him, she would be healed.

We, too, can sometimes feel that our worries and problems are not big enough to worry God with. Or we might feel that he is too busy to listen to us. Jesus shows us that this is just not true. God has got time for us, he loves us, and wants the best for us. He cares about everything that is going on in our lives, and wants us to talk with him about it all. We don't need to pretend that we already know it all, or are doing everything right – if we just creep up close to Jesus, and reach out to touch him, we will find that we can know his peace, love and healing too.

Children's Corner

The children can take it in turns with their parents and carers to dress up in a cloak, and to have someone touch their cloak, and listen out for Jesus healing the woman who touched his cloak, in the Gospel reading.

The colouring sheet shows Jesus in a crowd, with the woman creeping up to touch his cloak.

Little Kids' Sunday School

Dress up one of the children in a cloak. If you don't have a cloak, a sheet or blanket tied around their neck or tucked in their collar will do. They stand in the middle of a circle of children and close their eyes. You point to one of the children who has to creep to the centre of the circle and touch their cloak before creeping back. Once they're seated again, the cloaked child can guess who it was that touched their cloak. They'll have to listen really hard for the direction of the footsteps.

Jesus was very popular. Everywhere he went, he was surrounded by huge crowds of people, all eager to hear what he had to say. He told funny stories, but stories that challenged people and made them believe that a better world was possible. He made them feel loved and accepted just as they were. Sometimes he would do amazing things, and they'd see someone who was sick get healed.

This day there was a woman who had been sick for 12 long years. She'd tried everything but hadn't got better. She was sick and tired of being sick and tired. She decided that if she could just touch the edge of Jesus' cloak, she would be healed, and so she made her way through the crowd. She crept through quietly, not wanting to make a show, not wanting to get Jesus' attention, and touched his robes. But Jesus turned and saw her! 'Take heart, woman,' he said, 'your faith has healed you.' And she suddenly felt in her body that she was better!

And this is true for us, too. We only need to creep towards Jesus, to reach out and touch him, to know his healing and his peace.

217

Cut the letters 'FAITH' out of sandpaper, for the children to stick on a piece of card. They can reach out and feel them, like the woman reached out to feel Jesus' cloak, and as they do so they will be reminded that it was her faith that healed her.

Big Kids' Sunday School

Tuck a hanky or scarf in the waistband at the back of one of the children. Tell them you'll be choosing a child to take it out, but they won't know who it is. Gather the other children and whisper to them either 'it's not you', or 'it's you!'. The child with the scarf has to walk from one end of the room to the other, surrounded by all the other children. The child you picked has to try to take the scarf and keep it hidden. At the other end of the room, can the child who had the scarf guess who took it?

Jesus was often surrounded by crowds, drawn to him because he told such brilliant stories, because he challenged them, because he made them believe in a better world, because they felt loved and accepted. People brought their children so he could bless them, and people who were sick came in the hope that he would heal them.

Today was no exception. Jesus was walking in the middle of a crowd, when a woman who had been sick for 12 years managed to make her way to him. She didn't want to be noticed, she didn't grab his attention, but simply reached out to touch his cloak. Despite the crowd all around, Jesus noticed her. He looked at her with love and said, 'Take heart, woman, your faith has healed you.' And she realised that she was actually better!

Provide the children with letter beads for 'FAITH' and other coloured beads, and get them to thread them to make a bracelet. As they wear this bracelet, it will remind them to reach out to Jesus with faith, like the woman in our Gospel story today.

JESUS SENDS OUT HIS DISCIPLES

Readings

- Exodus 19:2-8a
- Psalm 100
- Romans 5:1-8
- Matthew 9:35 – 10:8 (9-23)

Thoughts on the Readings

When Jesus sends out his disciples, he equips them with all the gifts they need, but he also warns them that it is not going to be easy. Sometimes people will reject them and will not listen to their message. If this is the case, they are not to stay there, trying to convince or persuade them. They are to move on to the next town. Perhaps those people would later hear from their neighbouring town about God's good news, and would be ready to accept and understand it then.

We, too, sometimes need to make sure that we respect people's right to make their own choices about their faith, beliefs and practices. We don't know what is going on between them and God, and it can be counterproductive for us to try to persuade, cajole or pressure them to either believe things in a certain way, as we do, or to attend church events that we would like them to come to. If they come, they come. If they don't, they don't. We don't want people to feel that they are expected to take on board a certain set of beliefs before they are ready, but that they are welcomed just as they are.

In the reading from Paul's letter to the Romans, we are told that it is 'by faith' we have been made acceptable to God. It is because of his love that we are part of his family. What does this faith mean? It is knowing God, trusting him, drawing near to him, turning our lives towards him and being ready to be open to his love. It is not because of our own knowledge, or because we have said the right words or performed the right actions. When thinking about helping others in their journey of faith, this reminds us of the sort of attitude we should have. We can show others love through our words and actions, and we can also openly, honestly and gently share our own experience of the relationship we have with our loving God.

Today's psalm reminds us that God's love is for the whole world – everyone on earth can shout praises to God together. And he loves us all, and cares for us, like we are his sheep. As we look at those around us, we can remember that we are all part of that same flock, loved by God, who wants us to know him.

Discussion Starters

- **How easy is it to 'brush the dust off our feet' when people reject church or the message of the gospel?**

Intercessions

Lord, our God,
we belong to you.

We thank you, Lord,
that you love us and care for us
like the sheep of your pasture.
May we learn to rest in your love
and receive your blessings.

We pray that our church
would be a place of love and welcome,
reaching out to those in the community around us.
As we remember
that we are all the sheep of your pasture,
may we come together in love
to seek you and to serve you
in everything we do.
Lord, our God,
we belong to you.

We bring before you our world,
knowing that you have given all people
the ability to choose to live with love
or to live with fear.
We pray for those places where
fear has given rise to hatred and discrimination
and we pray that through your love
people would find the confidence and courage
for kinder thoughts, words and actions.
Lord, our God,
we belong to you.

Surround with your healing love
all those who are facing difficult times in their lives,
whether through poor health or difficult personal circumstances.
We pray that you would give them strength and hope
and an awareness of your presence at this time.
We name before you today . . .
Lord, our God,
we belong to you.

As we remember with love
those who have died
and now rest in your presence,
we thank you for your love and faithfulness
through every circumstance we face in our lives,

and the promise of a home in heaven with you.
Today, we particularly remember . . .
**Lord, our God,
we belong to you.**

Lord, we thank you and we praise you,
together with all your people around the world.
We give thanks that you are always with us
on our journey through life.
Amen.

Children's Prayer

Lord, we want to help
to build your kingdom,
bringing love, peace
and hope
to everyone on earth.
Amen.

Other Ideas!

Have a picture up of a field of
wheat ready to be harvested,
with the words from Matthew
9:38 (about asking God to send
workers to bring in the harvest).

All-age Talk

Cut out some heart shapes from card, and
prepare some envelopes with the words
'Peace be on this house' written on them.

Ask some children to come up to help you
with some letters. They can enjoy putting the
card hearts in the envelopes, and sticking the
envelopes shut.

Explain that Jesus sent out his disciples to
help tell all the people the good news that God
loves them, he cares for them, and he wants
them to be his friend. Jesus knew that although God loves everyone, not all the people would be
ready to welcome the disciples and listen to them. Their job, though, was to offer this message
of love and peace to everyone. If people were ready to listen to them, the disciples would be
able to use the power given to them by Jesus to heal all kinds of illnesses and diseases.

Once the children have finished sorting out the envelopes, they can deliver them to the
people in the congregation. Explain that everyone has a choice whether to open their envelope,
just like people have the choice whether to come close to God and enjoy being part of his
family. He does not force anyone to love him.

What we can do is to show other people God's love, through caring for them, listening to them and making our church into a place where they are welcomed into a community. We can offer to pray for them, and talk about times our prayers have been answered.

As we work together, we can help God's kingdom to come.

Children's Corner

Provide a box of raisins or tiny breadsticks or similar, and the children's job is to make sure that each of the church teddies is offered one. They can see if the teddies are hungry and want to eat them, and help them eat them up. Some teddies might not feel hungry today. That doesn't matter. Our job was to make sure that all the teddies were offered this good thing; it's up to them to choose to eat it. Listen out for Jesus telling his disciples to offer a good thing – God's peace – to the people they visit, regardless of whether that peace is gratefully received or not.

The colouring sheet has the words **'Peace Be on This House'** and patterns to colour, so they can stick it up as a blessing in their own home.

Little Kids' Sunday School

Sit the children in a circle, to play 'Knock, Knock, Can I Come In?' One child walks around the outside of the circle. They choose a child and 'knock' (gently!) on their head, saying, 'Knock, knock, can I come in?' If the child says no, they move on to another child. When a child says yes, they swap places and the new child begins to start moving around the circle, knocking on the doors.

Jesus knew that there were lots of people living nearby who needed to hear about God's peace. So he gathered together his disciples and told them they had a job to do. They were to travel around the whole area, to give God's peace to people. Jesus told them to ask when they arrived somewhere new, for someone to let them stay in their house. As they arrived, they would share God's peace with the house. The people in the house might listen and accept it. Or they might not be interested, and not want anything to do with them. Don't worry, said Jesus. That bit's not your job. Your job is simply to share God's peace with them. They can choose whether to accept it or not.

Let the children roll out some clay, and press the word 'PEACE' into it, using wooden letters or fridge magnets. When it dries, they can display it at home, as a reminder that God's peace is offered in their home, and they simply need to accept it.

Big Kids' Sunday School

Give each child a bowl full of a different type of snack (popcorn, crisps, chunks of cheese, crackers, slices of apple, for example). They can take it in turns to walk around the group, and offer their snacks to the children. Some children may not want some of the snacks, and that's fine. They can just say, 'No, thank you', and the offering child can move on.

If we offer someone something, there's no compulsion there, is there? Alastair didn't want the popcorn, and that was fine. Lois didn't want the cheese, and that was fine too. And the children offering the snacks very sensibly just moved on to the next person. Nobody tried to pin Alastair down on the floor and make him eat a piece of popcorn, wrestling the popcorn into his mouth! That wouldn't have been very kind at all! And it would have meant he hadn't been offered the popcorn at all, just that you'd made him have it. Who knows if the other popcorn eaters really wanted the popcorn, in that scenario?

Jesus gathered his friends together in order to send them out, to bring a message of God's peace to the people in the surrounding area. Jesus told them that when they entered a new place, they were to find somewhere and ask if they could stay. They would give a message of God's peace, and if the people opened up their house to them, they would stay. If the people didn't welcome them, and didn't want to listen, they were to shake the dust off their feet and simply leave.

Accepting God's gifts can't be forced. For a gift to be a gift, it has to be freely received. A bit like with our snacks earlier.

Have ready-cut a pile of bendy branches and greenery, and some florist's wire. The children can bend it round into a wreath to go on their door – not a Christmas wreath, but a wreath of peace. A laurel wreath has traditionally meant peace as well as victory. They might like to include some symbols of peace as they weave. You could have cut-out pictures of doves, or peace flags. They can hang their wreath on their door, as a sign of God's peace in their house.

224

GOD KNOWS AND LOVES US

Readings

- Jeremiah 20:7-13
- Psalm 69:8-11 (12-17) 18-20
- Romans 6:1b-11
- Matthew 10:24-39

Thoughts on the Readings

We have some challenging words today from Jesus, in our reading from Matthew's Gospel. Jesus tells us that he has come to bring trouble, not peace, and to turn family members against each other. This doesn't sound right – surely Jesus has come to bring peace to the world, love, joy, hope and all the wonderful things that we hear about usually in church?

Thinking about this in the context of the reading from Jeremiah, and the psalm for today, where the writers are going through really tough times, this can make more sense. Sometimes, through standing up for what is right, we can make enemies. And sometimes, these are people who are quite close to us.

It is not always the right time to say these things, but we will know in our hearts when we need to trust in God, draw on his strength, and use our voice to speak out for love, understanding and justice. If we keep quiet, it is likely that those people who need to hear God's message of love for others, justice for the poor and oppressed, and freedom from the love of money and things will assume that we agree and support their own view.

As we are reminded in the reading from Romans, we have left our old selves behind on the cross. As we are now living in God's light, with his strength, we really have no choice to stay silent over injustice, discrimination, unkind treatment of other people, or the destruction of the beautiful world God has given us.

It won't always be easy, people won't always like it and we may lose friends. Sometimes a situation may be quite complex, and sometimes those in authority may seem reluctant to listen. We may sometimes, like the writer of today's psalm, feel like we are sinking in the mud. But God will be with us. He will help us know what to say and what action to take, and he will support us. Together, as the family of God, we are stronger than we think.

Discussion Starters

- **What, if any, campaigns are we involved with as a church? Are there any issues which we need to speak out on?**

Intercessions

**As we walk through life,
you are with us, Lord.**

Father, we thank you
that we are part of your family,
loved and guided by you.
We pray that we would always listen
and be ready to speak out for others
and show your love.

We bring before you our church
and thank you for the opportunity we have
to speak out and change things
for the better,
in our community and in our world.
We pray that you would help us to work together with others
To bring in your kingdom.
**As we walk through life,
you are with us, Lord.**

As we think of our world,
in great need of your justice and peace,
we particularly pray for those places
where the comfort and relative calm
of the current situation
needs to be disrupted
before a good, right and true solution
can be found.
Help us to speak out, and take action
in your strength.
**As we walk through life,
you are with us, Lord.**

We bring into your loving care
any situation where family relationships
are difficult, and where communication causes pain.
We pray that your healing and love
would bring understanding and peace.
We also pray for anyone who is in any kind of pain,
particularly those whose condition is little understood.
We bring before you those known to us who have asked for prayer, including . . .
**As we walk through life,
you are with us, Lord.**

We remember with love
those who are now in heaven with you.

227

We thank you for that promise we also have
of an eternal home, where we can rest in your love.
We name before today . . .
**As we walk through life,
you are with us, Lord.**

Thank you, Lord, for your saving love.
May we always remember
to come to you and trust in you,
whatever life may bring.
Amen.

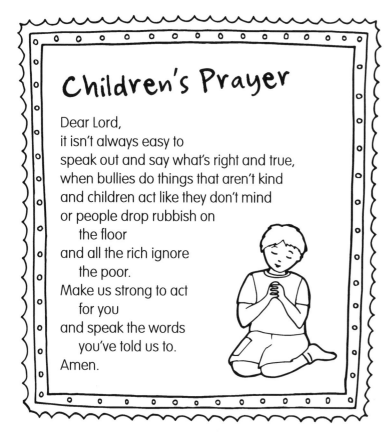

Children's Prayer

Dear Lord,
it isn't always easy to
speak out and say what's right and true,
when bullies do things that aren't kind
and children act like they don't mind
or people drop rubbish on
    the floor
and all the rich ignore
    the poor.
Make us strong to act
    for you
and speak the words
    you've told us to.
Amen.

Other Ideas!

Give people the opportunity to
fill in a charity campaign card,
or provide the online link for
this. Put up a display about
the issue or situation, so that
people can find out a bit more
about it.

All-age Talk

Bring along a bag or pillowcase with some
toy animals in it – these could include plastic
insects, fluffy toy birds, cuddly giraffes and
the like.

   Ask a volunteer or two to come up and
help you find out what is in the bag. They can
take out an animal, one at a time. We'll have
a think about all the lovely animals that God
has made.

Hold up the first animal. A centipede (or whatever has come out of your bag). Does God care for the centipedes? Yes, he does! He knows exactly how many legs they have (no, it's not 100) and cares if they hurt one of them.

What's next? A giraffe! Does God care for the giraffes? Yes, of course he does! He made their beautiful long necks and is interested in the way that they stretch their tongues out to gather the leaves that he has provided for them.

Continue this with the other animals, thinking together about how God knows about them and cares about all the things they do.

Now, ask for another volunteer. Here is our last creature! What does this creature like to eat? (Ask them!). Does God care for this lovely human person? Yes of course he does, and he cares for each and every one of us. He knows all the things that we do, he even knows how many hairs are on our heads. He is interested in what we like to eat for breakfast, and in what we like to do for fun. He knows how hard we try to do what's right, and it makes him so happy when we care for others and look after our world.

Living God's way is not always easy, but he cares for us so much. He loves us, and he will look after us, whatever happens in our life.

Children's Corner

Fill a tub with some gloopy mud and provide some small world characters to try to walk over it. When they begin to sink, the children can rescue them and pull them out of the mud. They can listen out for this in the psalm for today, and whisper about how God rescues us when we feel we are sinking.

The colouring sheet shows a parent holding a child's hand as they squelch through mud. The muddy-looking writing has words from the psalm.

Little Kids' Sunday School

Bring along some small containers that have little holes in. The kind of plastic tubs children play with in the bath, maybe. Stick some googly eyes on them, if you like, and let the children squash playdough inside so it squeezes through the holes as their hair.

Who can count how many playdough 'hairs' their person has? You have to know them pretty well, and get up close for that, don't you? In the Bible reading today, Jesus says that God can number every hair on our heads! Can you count your own hairs? Have a little try. For God to even know how many hairs we've got, he must really know us very well. He must be close to us, and love us a lot! So, no matter how scary things get in the world, we don't need to fear. The God who is in charge of the whole universe knows us and loves us, even to the hairs on our heads.

Make a hairy person by cutting up wool and sticking it on a paper plate. You can cut long bits and tie them in plaits, or short bits to stick all over the top. Draw on a face, and on the back, write, 'Matthew 10:30'.

Big Kids' Sunday School

Have a 'Hair Race'. Hole punch all around the top of a few paper plates, enough for one for each child. Put a basket of cut-up wool (around 10-15cm lengths) at one end of the room and tape the plates, sticking up, to the edge of a table, so the holes are free. The kids can draw a face on the plate, and then run backwards and forwards to the wool, carrying only one piece at a time. They thread it through and tie it, then run back for another bit. When all the wool has gone, count up who has made the Hairiest Plate Person.

Sometimes when things are scary or difficult, we can feel insignificant, as if we don't matter, as if nobody knows us or what we are going through. But in our Gospel reading today, Jesus tells us that God even numbers the hairs on our heads. You have to be close to count hairs, we've already found that out this morning. You have to spend time, and be in intimate contact, to count hairs. What a picture of our God, cherishing us so much.

The children can make grass head people to take home, to remind them that God knows them well enough to even number the hairs on their heads. You'll need some tights, some grass seed, some sawdust, and maybe some googly eyes. Sprinkle some grass seed into the toe of the sock, and fill it with sawdust until it's the size of a tennis ball. Tie it off, cut below the knot, and stick on the googly eyes. When they get home, they can balance it so that the bottom bit of the tights dangles in some water in a cup. They may need to spray it too, to keep the grass seed moist so it can grow into green hair.

WITH YOUR FAITHFUL HELP
RESCUE ME FROM SINKING
IN THE MUDDY PIT

SHOWING GOD'S LOVE TO OTHERS

Readings

- Jeremiah 28:5-9
- Psalm 89:1-4, 15-18
- Romans 6:12-23
- Matthew 10:40-42

Thoughts on the Readings

Our Gospel reading for today is short but to the point. We are to welcome, help and offer hospitality to others, and this is where we will find our reward. We may think of this in terms of a heavenly reward, but Jesus may not have only meant this. Many people recognise that certain jobs and activities can be 'rewarding', including people who would not describe themselves as having a faith. However, this is still all part of what Jesus is talking about.

But how can we welcome prophets now? And who would we identify as prophets? Looking back to the reading from Jeremiah, we can see that a genuine prophet is one who speaks out the truth, even when it is difficult and people do not want to hear it. This often makes them very unpopular, particularly when there are other people claiming to speak out a much easier and reassuring truth, which does not require any sacrificial changes. Thinking about the prophets in our lives and in our communities, these may be the people who speak out a message of peace and justice in difficult circumstances, and who may ask us to step outside our comfort zone and take action for the environment, on homelessness, on equal rights or on another issue. As a church, welcoming and supporting these prophets can make us unpopular too. We may be accused of meddling, of being too political, or of having selfish motives. This could be why Jesus tells us that those who welcome prophets are also given the same reward as a prophet.

Jesus then goes on to tell us that if we welcome a good person, we will be given the same reward as a good person. We often come across people outside the church who are wise, kind, generous and are taking action to make the world a better place. God loves and welcomes these people, as they are also working towards his kingdom, although they may use different words to describe this. We can welcome the God-given wisdom from those who would not identify themselves as Christians, and value what we can learn from them.

Lastly, Jesus tells us that we will be rewarded for giving to and helping those who are not considered big or important, even if this is just a cup of cool water on a hot day. Who are these people Jesus is talking about? Perhaps they might be the people in the church who seem the most ordinary, who are sometimes forgotten. Perhaps they might be the toddler with the runny nose, playing with a rather loud and beepy toy in the church aisle. Perhaps they are those people with dementia, or a learning disability, who have a beautiful faith but are unable to express this in words. Or maybe they are the homeless person who prays as they settle down in their sleeping bag for the night. We know that throughout scripture God speaks out as a voice for the poor, the marginalised, and those who have been forgotten or ignored, and as we also make this our priority, valuing those who God values, we will find our work and worship more meaningful and rewarding too.

Discussion Starters

- How can we make our church more accessible and welcoming to all of Jesus' followers, from the youngest to the oldest?

Intercessions

**God of love,
may we love like you.**

Lord, you have called us
to love, welcome and help
all those who are working for your kingdom.
As we do this,
may we be ready
to learn and receive from them, too.

We pray for our church
and we thank you
for the prophetic and wise leaders
who have helped us in our journey with you.
We pray that we would be ready
to recognise these gifts in others
and to welcome them.
**God of love,
may we love like you.**

We thank you for our world
and all those who work together to make it a better place.
We particularly pray for those
who take a risk to speak out
for what is right,
even if this is not a popular message.
We bring before you those
whose lives have been made difficult
because they have stood up for truth.
**God of love,
may we love like you.**

As we think of those known to us
who are suffering in any way.
We particularly pray for those
who feel forgotten, and whose voices are not heard.

We pray for those who feel weary
from coping with a disability or long-term illness
and those who feel misunderstood.
We name before you today . . .
God of love,
may we love like you.

We bring into your loving presence
all those who are nearing the end of their journey through life.
We pray that those who love them
would be comforted and supported by your care at this time.
We also remember with love
those who have made that journey before us,
and name before you today . . .
God of love,
may we love like you.

Lord, we thank you that you
welcome us into your presence
and surround us with your love.
We pray that you would help us
love and welcome those we meet this week.
Amen.

Children's Prayer

As you welcome us, Jesus,
we will welcome others.
As you love us, Jesus,
we will love others.
As you help us, Jesus,
we will help others.
Amen.

Other Ideas!

Display a pottery jug full of water, and some cups or glasses, with the words from Matthew 10:42: 'And whoever gives even a cup of cold water to one of these little ones in the name of a disciple – truly I tell you, none of these will lose their reward.' People can pour water into the cups and offer it to others after the service.

All-age Talk

Prophets aren't real prophets if they only tell us what we want to hear.

Bring along two large cardboard boxes or shoeboxes. Fold a large, shiny piece of paper in half and cut out the shapes of a heart, a dove and a cross. Place a set of shapes in each of the boxes. Wrap both the boxes up in nice bright paper, and tie ribbons around them.

Ask two volunteers to come up and help you. Tell them that they are going to open these lovely presents for the congregation, that there is something wonderful inside, but not to show anyone what it is until you say so.

Before they start opening the boxes, explain that one of the volunteers is going to tell the truth about what is in their box, and the other is going to tell people what they want to hear is in the box! It might be best to choose your older volunteer for this second job. Quietly whisper to each of the volunteers which their job is.

Now they can start opening these wonderful presents! Let's guess what's inside! Is it magical ice-cream that can make you fly? Is it an expanding racing car? Is it a folding climbing frame that can go at the back of church? Or perhaps it is a lifetime's supply of chocolate!

As your volunteers to describe the contents of the presents (one real, one pretend), ask the rest of the congregation which present they would like best, and who they think is telling the truth.

Thank your volunteers and ask them to show everyone what really was inside their boxes. Sometimes people try to tell us what they think we want to hear, and lots of people listen to them. These are like the pretend prophet in our reading today. But other people tell us the truth of God's love, how we can follow Jesus, and how the Holy Spirit can help us. It is not always easy to do the right thing and live in a loving way all the time, but God will help us, and this is really the best present of all because it will last forever. These people are like the true prophets, and Jesus says that he wants us to welcome them and listen to them. We can learn from them, and their wise words will help us all through our lives.

Children's Corner

Provide a toy tea set, and a big jug to fill the little teapot with water. Maybe lay it out on a towel in case of spills. The children can enjoy pouring out cups of water to share with their adults, each other, and the church teddies, and can listen out for Jesus telling us to do this in the Gospel reading.

The colouring sheet shows an empty jug and empty glasses, with some thirsty-looking children. They can colour water in the jug and colour water in the glasses, so that everyone in the picture has something cool to drink.

Little Kids' Sunday School

The children can run a relay race, pouring water into a cup, and carrying it to the end, before tipping it into a container. See who can fill the container first.

It's lovely when someone pours you a glass of water when you're thirsty. In our Gospel reading today, we hear Jesus telling us to pour a glass of water for the people who are seen as little and unimportant. Sometimes they get a bit lost in all the busyness around. Jesus reminds us to offer a welcome to everyone.

Create some posters with 'WELCOME' written on them in various community languages. If you live in a linguistically non-diverse area, choose some other languages that visitors might know or have a connection to. The children can decorate these with pens, stamps, and stickers, and practise saying the words. Stick them up in your church building, to show that you are a place of welcome to all.

Big Kids' Sunday School

Play a game of 'You Are Welcome Here'. Send a child to go and sit on a picnic blanket or mat. They have to decide on an attribute, such as people with long hair, people wearing blue, people wearing sandals, but they don't tell the group. One by one, the children go and ask, 'Am I welcome?'. The child replies either, 'Yes, you're welcome here' at which they join them on the mat, or 'No, you are not welcome', at which point they go away. When all the children have asked the question, they can try to guess which attribute it was that the child on the mat chose. You can play this until everyone's had a turn on the mat doing the welcoming.

It's a nice feeling when you're welcomed, but not so nice when you're turned away. In our Gospel reading for today, Jesus speaks to us of welcome. He talks of us welcoming prophets, those difficult, sometimes irritating people who speak the truth when we don't always want to hear it. He talks of us welcoming the righteous people, people who live good lives, not necessarily people who are part of our community of faith. And he talks of us giving a glass of water to 'these little ones', those who aren't seen as important. Our welcome should be expansive, and reach out to everyone.

The children can use long strips of old plastic bags, or long strips of old fabric, to weave a welcome mat to put by their door, reminding them to offer God's welcome to anyone who comes. You can wind round and round the width of a table to create the warp, and weave in and out of that. Once it's done, cut it off the table, and trim any longer bits, tying the ends of the warp together to stop it unravelling.

RECEIVING GOD'S REST

Readings

- Zechariah 9:9-12
- Psalm 145:8-15
- Romans 7:15-25a
- Matthew 11:16-19, 25-30

Thoughts on the Readings

God will bring peace, he is faithful, and he will help those who stumble or fall. He is the one who will bring peace, and take away weapons meant for war. He is a gentle and kind King, and we hear in the reading from Zechariah how he is humble and rides on a donkey – something which came to be fulfilled as Jesus rode into Jerusalem.

Jesus knew that many people would be familiar with this prophecy, and chose to show in a very visual and remarkable way that he was that kind and gentle King. There would be no doubt about it. He was not there to be a military leader, or to gain power through force. Even those weapons, kept as security just in case, are described as being broken, decommissioned, and taken away.

In our reading from the book of Romans we are reminded how hard it is for us as humans to get it right all the time. We cannot do it on our own, and just through trying hard. The good news is that we don't have to worry. Jesus will rescue us, and he will help us to live that life of peace, forgiveness, compassion and love that God wants for us.

Then, as we read the passage from Matthew's Gospel, we again hear that contrast between the way we are as humans, often finding it a struggle to do the right thing, and the hope that we have in Jesus. It does not need to be difficult or complicated. As we lay down our burdens before Jesus – whether these are things to do with our relationships with others, our work, our worries about our own or our family's health, our sense of responsibility towards our community and our world, or anything else – we can know his love, and find a place in his company where we can rest.

After this, Jesus says, we can take up his yoke. As we do this, in obedience and out of the desire to follow, learn and grow closer to our Lord, we will find that it is not exhausting and difficult any more. With Jesus, we will no longer feel that we are weighed down with worry, pressure and others' expectations. He will look after us, he will care for us, and in him we will find all that we need.

Discussion Starters

- **In what areas of our life do we need to swap our own burdens for Jesus' yoke?**

Intercessions

**Jesus, we lay our burdens down
and come to you for rest.**

Lord, as we come before you,
we bring those things
which weigh us down
and give them to you.

We bring before you in prayer, our church,
and thank you for the way that it has been a place
of rest and refuge to those who need peace.
We pray that through the worship that takes place here,
we can place before you those things we can no longer carry
by ourselves
and find your love and strength.
**Jesus, we lay our burdens down
and come to you for rest.**

As we think of our world,
we pray for those nations, groups and individuals
who are holding on to weapons
out of fear for their own security.
We pray that through your love,
trust and respect would increase,
so that tension and the threat of violence
become a thing of the past.
**Jesus, we lay our burdens down
and come to you for rest.**

We bring into your loving care
all those who feel weighed down
by illness, injury, mobility issues,
financial worries or their employment situation.
We pray that you would help them to find a place
of rest, peace and healing.
We particularly pray for . . .
**Jesus, we lay our burdens down
and come to you for rest.**

Remembering those who have gone before us
and now are at peace in heaven with you,
we thank you for your promise
that you will always be with us
and that you will never leave us.
May your love and peace be known
by those who have lost someone close to them,

and by anyone who is nearing the end of their life at this time.
We remember those who have died, including . . .
**Jesus, we lay our burdens down
and come to you for rest.**

May we receive from you today
all that you have for us
and leave with you, in your care,
those things which worry us.
Amen.

Children's Prayer

Jesus, we will come to you
if we are tired and stressed.
We know that you will care for us
and you will give us rest.
We'll tell you all our worries
and we'll leave them safe
with you.
Your strength will help
us carry on,
we know that this is true.
Amen.

Other Ideas!

Cut out some suitcase shapes from card or paper, and give them to people as they come in to church. Suggest that people either think about or write down something that is a heavy burden to them, and place the suitcase in front of a cross or picture of Jesus. As they do this, they can release the burden to God.

All-age Talk

Bring along a couple of large supermarket bags, preferably the big heavy-duty ones, filled with some large and heavy items. These could be things like hymn books, tins, bottles of water or lemonade etc. Also have a stand-alone cross nearby.

Leave the bags at the back of church and ask a couple of small volunteers to help you bring your bags up to the front. As they do this, thank them and tell them how strong they are – those bags are such a struggle to carry!

Sometimes we feel like this in our own lives. The things we have to do, the things we are worried about and the things that we want to fix but we can't, feel like big heavy bags that we have to carry around with us.

We can't just leave them behind as there are people who rely on us, and sometimes we don't feel we have anyone to help us carry the bags either.

Thankfully, Jesus has told us that we do not have to do this all on our own. He says that we can bring our burdens to him, and we don't have to carry them around by ourselves any more.

Bring out the cross, and ask your volunteers to unpack the bags, laying the heavy items in front of the cross.

Explain that all these things are like our worries. Jesus wants us to bring them to him. He actually has told us to unpack our bags of worries, and he will give us rest (your volunteers can have a nice sit down once they have done this!).

How do the bags feel now? Much lighter? Jesus said that we can take up his yoke instead – this is much easier than our own heavy old bags (the volunteers can now carry the empty bags back to where they started). With Jesus, we don't need to struggle on our own. He is always with us, he loves us, and he wants to help us.

Children's Corner

Give the children bags to pack with 'shopping' – tins of beans are nice and heavy and non-breakable. They can enjoy packing them, trying to pick them up, and unpacking them. They can listen to Jesus in the Gospel today, telling us that he will give us rest.

The colouring sheet shows someone walking on a path with heavy bags, and sitting in the shade of a tree, not carrying their bags any more. The writing reads, **'Come to me, all you who are heavy-laden and I will give you rest'**.

Little Kids' Sunday School

Play 'Port/Starboard'. Name one side of the room Port and the other Starboard. Call out instructions for the children to follow: port, starboard (run to the right sides), captain's coming (salute), scrub the decks (hands and knees scrubbing the floor), climb the rigging (stand up and pretend to climb), hoist the mainsail (pull an invisible rope).

Are they puffed out now? Sometimes we can get exhausted and overwhelmed, trying to do lots of things at once, to please different people, to fit everything in. Jesus said, 'Come to me, all you who are heavy-laden, and I will give you rest.' We can be heavily laden with things to do, as well as stuff to carry. We can be heavily laden with guilt, or sadness, too. Jesus promises us all rest if we come to him.

Give the children deco pens suitable for drawing on wood so they can decorate a wood-mounted coat hook. They can screw this onto their wall, and every time they hang up their coat and bag, they can remember that God has promised to give the heavily laden rest, and give to God some of the other things that they are carrying at that time.

Big Kids' Sunday School

Put numbers 1-6 beside lots of different heavy objects: tins of beans, pairs of wellies, saucepans, etc. Each child has a backpack or bag, and you pass dice around the group. Whatever they roll, they have to pick up and put in their bag, until all the objects are gone. Then they can put their backpacks on, or pick up their bag, and see who can get to the other side of the room first.

It's hard, moving when you're so heavily laden. All those heavy things in your backpack or bag meant that your body really noticed every step! You must have been relieved to sit back down and put your bag on the floor.

In the Bible reading today, Jesus says, 'Come to me, all you who are heavy-laden, and I will give you rest.' Although rest is lovely when you are heavily laden with a big bag, what other kinds of things make us heavily laden? What other things do we carry around in our lives and in our minds and hearts?

Give the children fabric pens to decorate a plain cloth bag with the words, 'Come to me, all you who are heavy-laden, and I will give you rest.' Every time they pick it up and carry it, they'll be reminded of this promise of Jesus, and can pass over to him some of the other things that are weighing them down.

Come to me,
all you who
are heavy-laden
and I will
give you rest

THE STORY OF THE SOWER

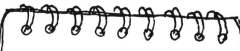

Readings

- Isaiah 55:10-13
- Psalm 65:(1-7) 8-13
- Romans 8:1-11
- Matthew 13:1-9, 18-23

Thoughts on the Readings

The reading from Isaiah likens God's words to the water cycle – the snow and rain waters the earth, and as it does so, it helps the crops to grow, fills the rivers and provides thirst-quenching drinks to people and animals. Having done all these wonderful and fruitful things, the water then evaporates, ready to fall again on the earth.

God's love and blessings are just the same. They do not run out. They are not lost over time. Again, and again, and again we can experience God's blessings just as fresh as when they first fell from heaven. His blessings are for the past, the present, and the future. We don't have to pine after days gone by, or wish the time away for a future revival. If we just reach our hands out to God, we will receive those refreshing raindrops and gentle snowflakes of God's words of love, peace, belonging, healing and freedom.

In the reading from Romans we hear how we just need to let God's Holy Spirit live in us, and that will be the way for us to find life and peace. Contrary to the ideas often around us in the world that we need to 'do more of what makes us happy', or 'follow our dreams', if we put aside that desire to make our own lives nicer, and just tune into God, we can find true happiness and fulfilment.

Then, as we hear Jesus' parable about the farmer sowing seed, this highlights for us how important it is to make sure that we are in a place in our lives where we can receive that watering and nourishment from heaven. We must not waste our time or energy trying to get rich or creating a pleasant life for ourselves. Like those seeds, we need to put down good roots and patiently wait and listen for God's words and blessings. We don't need to wander around looking for these, checking to see if anyone else has got more than we have. As we faithfully wait and rest in God's loving presence, we will find his strength and love right where we are.

Discussion Starters

- **In a society with much talk of 'measuring' happiness and people trying to 'find happiness', how can our churches communicate a message of God's true joy and peace?**

Intercessions

**As your rain falls from heaven,
bless us, Lord.**

Lord, as we come before you,
we pray that you would help us find that place
where we can rest in you
and receive your nourishment, blessing and love

We thank you for our church
and pray that you would bless us
and any other worshipping communities
who are our neighbours.
As we gather together
to come to know you more,
we pray that we would hear your words
and be refreshed and strengthened by your love
and your wonderful presence.
**As your rain falls from heaven,
bless us, Lord.**

We pray for our world
and bring before you those situations
where wealth has led to misery
instead of happiness
and where inequality
has brought uncertainty,
unrest and division.
We pray for a shift of priorities
to focus on your love, and your kingdom.
**As your rain falls from heaven,
bless us, Lord.**

We bring into your loving care
anyone feeling weary from life's demands
and those who are finding it hard to cope.
We pray that they would discover
the refreshing and strengthening love
of your Holy Spirit
and the peace that comes
from being rooted in you.
We name before you those who are ill or in need, including . . .
**As your rain falls from heaven,
bless us, Lord.**

As we think of your heavenly kingdom,
we pray for anyone close to death,

that they may know your welcoming
and loving arms around them at this time.
We also remember in your presence
those who are now in heaven with you, including . . .
**As your rain falls from heaven,
bless us, Lord.**

As we spend time with you,
resting in your presence,
may we experience your Holy Spirit,
strengthening and refreshing us
in our lives.
Amen.

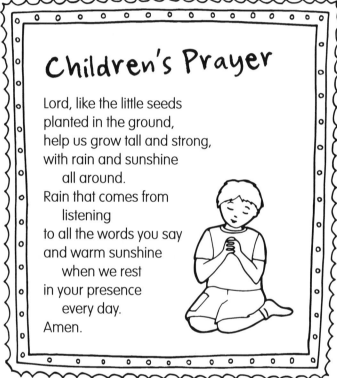

Children's Prayer

Lord, like the little seeds
planted in the ground,
help us grow tall and strong,
with rain and sunshine
    all around.
Rain that comes from
    listening
to all the words you say
and warm sunshine
    when we rest
in your presence
    every day.
Amen.

Other Ideas!

Bring some wildflower seeds
and put these in a bowl. Cut out
some small squares of paper.
People can take a pinch of the
seeds, and wrap them up in the
paper square. When they take
them home, they can scatter
them around somewhere they
can grow.

All-age Talk

Bring along a flowerpot, some compost,
some seeds and a watering can with a bit
of water in. You'll need a tray, too.

Explain that today you have brought
along some seeds to plant. Let's look at the
packet – what's inside? They are going to be
lovely sunflowers / tomatoes / leeks / rocket
(or whatever you have brought with you).

You're sure that it's very easy to plant
seeds, so you won't need to look at the instructions, so let's get started. As convincingly as you
can, go to shake the whole packet of seeds straight into the empty flowerpot.

Hopefully someone will try to stop you! What's the matter with this? Aren't you supposed to put the seeds in the flowerpot? Ah! We need some compost?

Bring out the bag of compost. Is this better? Let's scoop some into the flowerpot (ask a volunteer to help with this). That seed needs some good compost to give it food, and to hold water around it so that it does not dry out. Ask another volunteer to plant your seeds into the compost.

Put your flowerpot on the tray, and bring out the watering can. Ask if anyone would like to help give the little seeds a nice drink. If you only put a small quantity of water into the watering can, then your pot will not be deluged, even if your helper is very enthusiastic.

Now, what would be the best place for our seeds to grow? Let's find a nice sunny window or a patch outside. Those seeds won't like it if they are stuck in a dark cupboard.

Explain that this is like Jesus' story in the Gospel reading that we heard today. Those seeds with only a thin bit of soil to grow in, or the ones on the rocky ground, didn't have all the food they needed to grow. Just like seeds need water, soil or compost, and sunshine, we need to be fed too. But our food is God's wisdom, love and kindness.

As we spend time with God in prayer, and as we listen to the special words from the Bible or in our favourite hymns, we can receive that watering and nourishment from him. This is what will give us the strength to keep going, to grow and to thrive, sharing God's love with others around us, all through our lives.

Children's Corner

Give the children a bowl of water and some white sponges. They can use the sponges to soak up the water, then squeeze the sponges so the water trickles back into the basin. As they listen to the reading from Isaiah, they can show how the water can be sucked up into the clouds, and rain again, without ever running out, just like God's blessings.

The colouring sheet shows a raincloud over the hills, raindrops dropping to the ground, a stream carrying them past crops, trees, and flowers, and back into the sea. The writing is taken from the Isaiah reading.

Little Kids' Sunday School

Choose one child to be the 'farmer', carrying a basket of ball pit balls. These are the seeds. The other children are hungry birds. The farmer walks around, scattering the seeds, and the birds fly down to eat them. When the farmer has run out of seed, see which bird has eaten the most, then give another child a turn to be the farmer.

Jesus told a story about scattering seed. He must have seen farmers busy sowing their crops, and the people he was telling the story to would have known all about this too. As you tell the story, you can walk around your room, scattering some seed on the 'path', where the birds can come and peck it up, and scattering some seed on 'rocky places', where it grows quickly but hasn't got enough soil, so when the sun comes up it scorches and dies. Scatter more seed amongst 'thorns' so it grows but then gets choked. And scatter more seed on good soil, where it grows well and produces a good crop.

This is like people, says Jesus. Some people listen and don't understand the good news. Some hear the good news with joy but because they don't have a root, when things get difficult, they stop believing. The seed among the thorns is like people whose faith gets choked by the things of this world. And the seed that falls on good soil is like those people who hear the good news, and let it change their life.

Help the children to shake out the seeds from poppy seed heads, or whatever other plant you have that has started to produce seeds already. Poppies are fun though, as they're like little shakers. They can pour some of the seeds into those brown paper money envelopes, and label them up. As they scatter them in their gardens or a local green space, they can remember the parable of the sower.

Big Kids' Sunday School

Put the children in a circle, and go round naming them, Sea, Cloud, Rain, River. When you say one of their names, they have to race around the circle back to their place. When you say Water Cycle, they all have to race around the circle and back to their place.

In the Bible reading from Isaiah, we hear of how God sends the rain, and how it doesn't return again until it's watered the ground, bringing forth crops. God says that's like his word, that leaves his mouth and doesn't come back until it's succeeded in its purpose.

Give the children a clear glass or a jar each, and three-quarters fill it with water. Fill some small cups with food colouring and water, and put a pipette in each. Spray some shaving foam on the top of the water in the jar – this is the cloud. The children can drip some coloured water onto the top of the cloud, and watch it 'raining' from the bottom of the cloud. What is it that God sends us? How does it change us? How does it change the world?

THE WEEDS AND THE WHEAT

Readings

- Wisdom of Solomon 12:13, 16-19 or Isaiah 44:6-8
- Psalm 86:11-17
- Romans 8:12-25
- Matthew 13:24-30, 36-43

Thoughts on the Readings

The theme of our readings today is that of present suffering yet hope for the future, as we trust in God's promises. As we picture those prickly, tangled weeds growing alongside the good, straight, golden wheat we can see how these things cannot be separated from each other without causing damage to the crop. In the same way, our lives sometimes seem tangled together with prickly and difficult situations, and sometimes we live through challenging circumstances where there seems to be no easy answer.

We may at first think that it would be wonderful if these difficult things were taken away, but as we bring the situation before God it becomes clear that there are many different things and people that are connected in relation to this. Jesus' message is that we do not have to worry if life feels like we are growing in a field full of weeds. We are not doing anything wrong, and it is not a sign that we have misread God's will. This is just how life as a human being sometimes is.

All that we need to do is to trust in God, and come to him for strength. Then those things around us will no longer be overwhelming, frightening or impossible to face. With Jesus, we have a promise that all this will be taken away at the end of time, as there is no place for this trouble and pain in heaven.

In the reading from Romans, we hear creation described as being in pain like a woman in labour. Strong, powerful pain, that can't be ignored. But this is also positive and creative pain, bringing new life. Our suffering on earth can be seen in this same way, as we go through difficult times. The pain will not last for ever, it is natural pain, and through drawing near to God in the middle of all of this, experiencing his presence and Holy Spirit, we will find peace, strength and healing.

Discussion Starters

- **How can we, as a church, be a place of blessing for people living through difficult times, those who are carers, and people with disabilities? And how can we find that balance between praying for God's healing, and drawing alongside others who are suffering, accepting that this may be how things are going to be in this life?**

Intercessions

**Lord, as we grow in you,
may your kingdom come.**

Lord, we come before you
with all those things
that worry or concern us today.
We pray that you would give us wisdom,
strength and patience
for every situation.

We thank you for our church
and pray that we would be a place
of strength, support and community
for those who feel like their lives
are tangled with problems
and choked with challenges.
We pray that your Holy Spirit
would bring comfort, peace and wisdom
as we worship together.
**Lord, as we grow in you,
may your kingdom come.**

We pray for our world, with all its needs
and think of those places
where a complex and long history
of fear and misunderstanding
has led to violence and conflict.
We pray that there would be a realisation
that for lasting peace,
all people need to live respectfully alongside
those who had been seen as different,
or as the enemy.
**Lord, as we grow in you,
may your kingdom come.**

We bring into your loving care
all those who are living with
a long-term physical or mental health condition,
particularly those for whom
there is no effective treatment or cure.
We pray that your peace and promises
would surround and strengthen them.
We name before you those who have asked for our prayers, including . . .
**Lord, as we grow in you,
may your kingdom come.**

As we think of the home in heaven
that you have promised to those who love you,
we respectfully remember
those who have died
and who are missed at this time,
and give thanks for their lives.
We name before you today . . .
**Lord, as we grow in you,
may your kingdom come.**

As we go out from this place of worship,
we pray, Lord, that your Holy Spirit would be with us,
inspiring us, and giving us wisdom each day.
Amen.

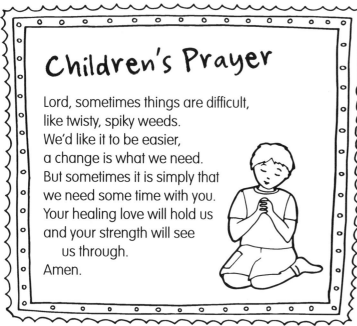

Children's Prayer

Lord, sometimes things are difficult,
like twisty, spiky weeds.
We'd like it to be easier,
a change is what we need.
But sometimes it is simply that
we need some time with you.
Your healing love will hold us
and your strength will see
  us through.
Amen.

Other Ideas!

Collect a few flowering weeds
and put them in some water
in a jam-jar. The challenges in
our lives can also sometimes
be a blessing when we look at
them in a different way.

All-age Talk

Bring along some lentils or dried peas, some
flour, a sieve, a bowl, a spoon and a tray.

Ask a volunteer to mix together the
lentils and the flour in the bowl. No, we're
not making a cake to have with coffee after
church, you'll be glad to know!

Would anyone like to try to pick those
lentils out now? You may have a keen helper,
but it is much too big a job to find all those
little lentils and separate them from the flour.

This is like Jesus' story of the wheat field, with weeds growing in it. It would have been much
too difficult to separate all those weeds, and by doing so the wheat might have been pulled up
and damaged, too.

Jesus explained that this is like our lives. Sometimes there are difficult and horrible things in our lives. Where we can, we try to make things better, for ourselves and for others. Sometimes there is a solution, and that is great. Sometimes there is a medicine that can help us get better, or perhaps our friend doesn't move away after all. But other times, there is not an easy answer. We can't always get rid of the things that are difficult in our lives.

Jesus tells us that we don't have to worry about this. It does not mean that we have made a mistake, or that we have got muddled about what God's will is for us in our lives. Our life on earth, though wonderful in many ways, is not always easy.

The good news is that even through the most difficult times, God will be with us. He loves us, he cares for us, and he won't ever leave us. He has promised that his Holy Spirit will stay with us and help us. And as we go through our sometimes confusing, messy and complicated lives, we will know God's joy and peace in the most surprising of circumstances.

And at the end of our lives, when we come to live with God in heaven, those sad and painful things will be all left behind, as we know God's glory and peace.

Now we need the sieve. Ask your helper to tip the flour and lentil mixture into the sieve, making sure that it is positioned over the tray! They can give it a stir, as the flour sprinkles through the holes in the sieve, leaving the lentils behind, just as God has promised to separate out the things that have caused pain and sadness, as we enter into our eternal and heavenly home with him.

Children's Corner

Fill a large tray with sticky weed/cleavers and a bag of salad. Mix it around, and see if the children can untangle the salad from the sticky weed and put it in a bowl. Tricky, isn't it? (It doesn't matter if they accidentally eat some sticky weed instead of salad, as it is edible!) Listen to Jesus talking about untangling the good crops from the weeds in the Gospel reading.

The colouring sheet shows a field of wheat, growing amongst weeds, with the Gospel reading reference so they can look it up later.

Little Kids' Sunday School

Pick a big bunch of sticky weed/cleavers (you can find it growing in most scruffy patches of green space) and have a sticky weed fight! Because it has little hooks, when you throw it, it catches on your clothes and sticks there. It doesn't hurt, though.

Jesus told a story about wheat growing in a field full of weeds like this. They were growing all around the wheat, and tangling around it. The farmer had a good look to work out what to do. He didn't want to cut it all down, as that would have got rid of the good wheat as well as the weeds. He didn't want to start chopping into it, in case he damaged the good wheat as well as the weeds. So, he decided to leave it, growing together, knowing that when it was harvest time and the wheat had been cut, it would be an easy job to separate the wheat from the weeds. That's a bit like our lives, isn't it? Sometimes, our lives feel a bit like a tangled mess. But Jesus promises that when we go to heaven, only the good parts of our lives will be there in heaven. All the tangly mess will be left behind.

Give the children a piece of thick card covered in double-sided carpet tape. Peel the paper covering off the tape, and they can stick down a tangle of string, winding it all around and making a muddle. They can use this to print, dipping it in a tray of paint, then pressing it onto paper. The prints can act as a reminder for them of this story Jesus told, of the mess and the muddle of our lives, and of how Jesus promises that in heaven all the tangling weeds will be gone.

Big Kids' Sunday School

Bring along a bag of tangled wool, and tip it out so you can all work at untangling it.

It's a really difficult job, isn't it? But some of this wool can be really useful. It's just what we need. So, although it was tempting to throw the whole lot in the bin, we didn't want to get rid of the good stuff alongside. And although it was tempting to cut or rip out the wool, we didn't want to damage the good stuff. So, it was worth taking our time, easing it gently.

Jesus told a story about some wheat growing in a field. The field also had a lot of spiky weeds, and some of us who have gardens might know all about that. The wheat was growing nicely, but as it grew, so did the weeds. They grew high, and they grew all around the wheat. The farmer could have been tempted to chop it all down and throw it all on the fire, but he didn't want to lose his good crop. He might have been tempted to have a bit of a chop at the weeds, but didn't want to risk damaging the good wheat. So, he let it grow, knowing that when it was harvest time, it would be easy to separate the ears of corn from the weeds.

Our life might feel like it's full of weeds, squeezing into the good bits of our life. But we don't need to worry, Jesus says. At the right moment, and not before, all the bad things will be separated off from the good things. We don't need to worry that when bad things happen to us, we're somehow doing something wrong. It's just that life can be difficult sometimes; and the promise is that in heaven it'll only be the good that remains.

The children can choose their favourite colours of wool to twist into a braid and tie round their wrist. They might like to have a go at Nordic Slinging Braids. There are several videos available on the internet for you to watch and work out what to do! When they wear their braids, it will remind them of the tangled mess the wool used to be in, and what beautiful order they created out of that mess, and that this is the promise God makes about our lives.

MATT 13:24-30, 36-43

SEEKING GOD'S KINGDOM

Readings

- 1 Kings 3:5-12
- Psalm 119:129-136
- Romans 8:26-39
- Matthew 13:31-33, 44-52

Thoughts on the Readings

As Solomon asks humbly for wisdom from God, that wise choice in itself helps him to be able to receive even more than he has asked for. Because if we really, truly seek wisdom, everything else will fall into place.

Wisdom is not the same as knowing lots of things, it is not the same as being able to influence people, and neither is it the same as being able to analyse situations. The wisdom that comes from God is deeper than this. Intuitive, based on love, with a desire to really understand others, this is the sort of wisdom that can bring resolution to the most difficult of conflicts and the most complex of situations.

The psalm for today, too, emphasises that desire for understanding God and knowing him more. Rather than asking God to do this or that, the Psalmist, like Solomon, only wants to tune in to what is on God's heart.

As we think about the words in the reading from Romans, we hear how the Holy Spirit can help us when we don't know what to pray. Sometimes when we are faced with a difficult situation, we don't need to ask God for one particular outcome or another. All we need to do is to bring these things before him, in the gentle and loving presence of the Holy Spirit. God knows what we need. He knows the whole situation, even the really tricky and hidden parts of it. He knows what is in each person's mind. This is how we can pray with wisdom. By realising that we don't have all the answers, and trusting in our kind and loving God to resolve things in the best way for everyone. He has an eternal perspective, which is so different to our small and local view. What we know for certain is that his love and heavenly kingdom last for ever, and he loves us and cares for us so much. The wonderful words at the end of this reading remind us that God will never leave us, and nothing in the universe can separate us from his love.

Just as Solomon longed for God's wisdom above everything else, Jesus' parables in the Gospel reading illustrate how those who long and search for the kingdom of God are rightly treasuring and valuing something which is more precious than any other gift. And while Jesus' harsh sounding words about the separation of the good from the evil people at the end of time may be challenging to our ears, perhaps the point of Jesus emphasising this is that we are not to waste our worry and energy on trying to judge and punish people in this life. We just need to leave these things to God. As we trust in him and draw nearer each day to his kingdom, we will find that real treasure of closeness with the one who created us and loves us so much.

Discussion Starters

- **Solomon asked God for wisdom, and he was given it. He was also given other blessings which he had not asked for. If you could ask God for two things, wisdom might be one of them, but what would the other be?**

Intercessions

**Lord, as we seek your kingdom,
may we know your ways.**

As we bring our concerns before you, Lord,
we pray that your Holy Spirit
would lead us, and help us to pray.

We thank you for our Church,
both here and around the world
and pray that all those who lead us
would be inspired by your wisdom
and strengthened by your presence and love.
We pray for any situations
where differences of opinion
have led to division
and we pray that you would bring
understanding, respect and peace.
**Lord, as we seek your kingdom,
may we know your ways.**

Lord, we think of our world
and pray for those in authority,
that their decisions may be made
with wisdom and love.
We pray that where there is conflict,
you would give light
to understand the way ahead
for the common good.
**Lord, as we seek your kingdom,
may we know your ways.**

May your loving and healing care
surround anyone who is struggling
with pain, anxiety, addiction
or any other challenges in their life.

Be with them as we bring them before you
and may your Holy Spirit surround them
and enable them to draw near to your holy presence.
We name before you today . . .
Lord, as we seek your kingdom,
may we know your ways.

We remember with love and respect
those who have gone before us
and have been welcomed into your heavenly kingdom.
We think of them giving worship to you
and dwelling in your holy presence.
We remember those known to us
who are missed at this time of year, including . . .
Lord, as we seek your kingdom,
may we know your ways.

As we go out into our lives this week,
may we go equipped with your wisdom,
filled with your love
and inspired by your Holy Spirit.
Amen.

Children's Prayer

Dear Lord,
all we want is to know you more,
to be wise and prepared for
    all that's in store.
As we reach out towards
    you, give us what
    we need
to make the world better
    and plant love like
    a seed.
Amen.

Other Ideas!

Fill a box with 'treasure' of
sparkly and shiny things,
and display the words from
Matthew 13:44.

All-age Talk

Find a cardboard box, and put these things inside: the word 'wisdom' written on some bright
and sparkly card, some shiny necklaces or bracelets, a line of paper dolls holding hands, and
a crown.

Hold up the box, and explain that in today's reading, God asked Solomon what he would like as a gift. Now ask a helper to unwrap the box for you. What did Solomon ask for? Read out the word on the card inside.

Yes, Solomon asked God for wisdom. He was already wise enough to know that if he was able to understand God's ways and his priorities, everything else would fall into place. Solomon knew that on his own he would not be able to do all the things that God had asked him to do. He was aware that he was quite young, and that he did not know everything. By being honest with himself, Solomon was able to come to God in humility and ask for the one thing that would really make a difference. He did not ask for a long life, lots of money or fame. He wanted to serve God, and to try to do a good job at leading the people in his care, and this was more important than anything else.

God then told Solomon that because he had asked for such a good gift of wisdom, he would give him those other things as well. He would make him rich (bring out the shiny necklaces), he would give him friends who liked and respected him (show the line of paper dolls), and he would also be a strong and good king (hold up the crown). You could ask some helpers to hold these up.

Jesus also told stories about seeking God's kingdom, an understanding of his ways and his wisdom, as the most precious treasure of all. This is worth more than all the other riches put together.

And as we, too, choose to ask for that wisdom from God, we will find that the other things in life come together too. If we find it difficult to understand someone else, and we end up having arguments – the answer is God's wisdom. If we are worried about money – the answer is God's wisdom. If we are struggling and going through difficult times – the answer is God's wisdom. And if, like Solomon, we have a difficult or challenging task ahead of us, we need that wisdom and strength that comes from God, more than anything else in all the world.

The good news is that God is delighted to give us his wisdom. As we spend time in prayer with him, and look at the situations around us, we will receive that understanding and peace that can only come from our heavenly Father. And, like Solomon, we may be surprised at what other gifts we are given by God too.

Children's Corner

Provide a treasure box full of shiny precious things to look through and enjoy, buried inside a large tub, under soil, shredded paper, or leaves. The children can dig out the treasure box, and see what's inside, as they listen to the words of Jesus in the Gospel, talking about treasure. They can whisper about what treasure it is that we find, and the treasure of wisdom that was given to Solomon.

The colouring sheet shows King Solomon, standing in prayer, and the words to colour read, **'Lord, give me your wisdom'**.

Little Kids' Sunday School

Get the children to help you mix together some simple bread dough. Mix 500g of strong white flour with a sachet of yeast and 2 teaspoons of salt. As you tip in the yeast, show the children what it looks like and explain that yeast is a type of fungus and as the yeast grows, it eats up carbohydrates and gives off carbon dioxide. Yeast grows fast, and the gas it gives off in the bread dough makes little bubbles that make the bread rise. Mix in 3 tablespoons of olive oil and 300ml of water, and knead well. Children are often quite good kneaders, so make sure they've washed their hands and let them loose to bash away!

As you knead, you can talk about how in the Gospel reading today, Jesus is explaining the kingdom of God. One of the pictures he uses to help us understand what the kingdom of God is like, is yeast. He says it is like the yeast a woman gets and mixes into her dough until it's worked all the way through.

How might the kingdom of God be like yeast? What is our yeast in our dough going to do? How is the kingdom of God like that?

The children can shape handfuls of the dough into something that makes them think of the kingdom of God – a crown, maybe, or a heart or a cross. Then once the dough has risen, you can bake it in a hot oven for 20 minutes.

Big Kids' Sunday School

Play a game of 'Mustard Roulette'. Make a plate of tiny butter sandwiches, just the size of a mouthful, but add a thin layer of mustard to the inside of a few of them. If they're brave enough, the children can take a sandwich in turn, and see who gets the mustard one! Any children with a mustard allergy can be Official Supervisors, on hand with a glass of water for emergencies.

It doesn't take much mustard for us to really notice it, does it! It packs a punch much bigger than its size. Jesus used mustard to tell us about the kingdom of heaven. Look at this tiny seed, he said, probably holding out one just like this (you can sprinkle some mustard seeds onto your hand). It is so tiny that you can hardly see it. And yet, if you plant it, it grows into a shrub big enough for birds to nest in. Jesus didn't mention, although he must have known, that the mustard seed would grow into a plant making more mustard seeds, and imagine how much food could be made spicy with all of them!

As you grow mustard seed egg-head people (boiled egg shells, with faces drawn on them, full of cotton wool, with mustard seeds sprinkled on the top) you can talk about what Jesus might have meant by this. How is the kingdom of God like a mustard seed? In what ways is it small? In what ways does it grow big? In what ways does a little of it go a long way?

JESUS FEEDS 5000+

Readings

- Isaiah 55:1-5
- Psalm 145:8-9, 15-22
- Romans 9:1-5
- Matthew 14:13-21

Thoughts on the Readings

The disciples must have been surprised when Jesus asked them to give the people something to eat. Surely he must have seen that they were not lugging great bags and baskets of food with them to cater for everyone? And this was not usually the deal, that people coming to hear Jesus would also get a free lunch!

But the disciples did what Jesus said, and brought the five small loaves of bread and two fish to him. Sometimes we may feel that we are being asked by God to do something that we do not in any way have the resources to do. We may see the great need around us, in our community and in the world, and think that the little that we have is not enough to make any difference. Today's Gospel reading reminds us that being able to bring God's blessing to others is not about already having a wealthy, extensive resource base. We just need to offer what we do have – even if it is something quite small. God can do the rest. Perhaps we also need to overcome the feeling that what we have to offer is not good enough – whether this is a skill, some knowledge, an item or an amount of money. What we have may be just what is needed to catalyse actions from others and create a bigger change.

The reading from Isaiah also echoes that abundance of God's blessings – likening them to the best food and drink in plenty, without having to pay, while today's psalm tells of God's care for his creation, and the way that he provides food and help when the time is right. As part of God's family ourselves, and wanting more of his kingdom, we can offer what we have to help others.

It can be a privilege and joy to be part of God's purpose to feed and provide for those who are in need. There are opportunities all around us to take action and to help to share what we have with others. Perhaps this is by sponsoring a child through a charity, buying 'alternative gifts' of food parcels for refugee families and tools or seeds for farmers. Or maybe there are opportunities closer to home, to donate to a foodbank when at the supermarket, give to a homeless shelter, or open the church for free tea and toast. This week let's open our eyes to see where God is giving us the opportunity to share our own loaves and fishes.

Discussion Starters

- **What might be one thing that we can offer to God from our resources to address a need? Are there ways we can work together with others to multiply this blessing?**

Intercessions

**Lord, we offer what we have,
use it for your glory.**

Lord, we come before you in prayer,
seeing the need in the world around us.
We offer ourselves
to work with you,
helping to provide for those in need.

As we bring our church before you,
we thank you for the way that you have blessed us
and provided for us.
May we always be ready
to value what others in our church family
have to offer,
from the youngest to the oldest.
And as we bring these things before you,
may you use them to bless the world around us.
**Lord, we offer what we have,
use it for your glory.**

We pray for our world
and see the need around us:
people without enough to eat
and those who cannot afford nutritious food.
We know that the miracle we need
is that of a change of attitude,
so that those who have more
will choose to live more simply,
and share what they have with others.
**Lord, we offer what we have,
use it for your glory.**

We pray that your nourishing care
would bring healing to those
who are hungry for affirmation,
that they may know how much you love them
and that they are a part of your family.
We also pray for anyone for whom
food causes anxiety, worry or guilt
and ask that they would find
reassurance, freedom and hope with you.
We now bring into your presence those known to us
who are unwell or in need at this time, and name before you . . .
**Lord, we offer what we have,
use it for your glory.**

We remember before you
those who are now at rest,
having come to the end of their life here on earth.
We thank you for your promise
of an eternal home with you.
We name before you today . . .
**Lord, we offer what we have,
use it for your glory.**

Lord, whatever we have to offer
we bring to you to use:
our skills, the things we own
and our knowledge.
We pray that together
these gifts you have given us
would make the world a better place.
Amen.

Children's Prayer

Dear God,
we know that you love the world
and we know that you love us too.
Thank you for the gifts you have given us
of food, clothes, and the
         things we are good at.
As we offer these to you,
    we pray
that you would show us
how we can use them
to help others
and help our world.
Amen.

Other Ideas!

Have a basket displayed with
some items around it which
could represent the things that
we can offer for God to use.
These could include things like
a book, a phone, a toy dog,
knitting needles and wool, a
wallet, car keys or a toy car,
a packet of biscuits, tea bags etc.
People can prayerfully choose
one of these items and place it in
the basket as they offer that thing
to God for him to use.

All-age Talk

Beforehand, fold some blue or grey tissue paper over as many times as you can, so that you
have multiple thicknesses. Cut out a fish shape, twice. Keep the layers of paper together and
secure them with a small piece of tape on each side, so that it looks like you just have two fish.
Do the same with some brown paper, and cut out five circles to be the little loaves in today's
Gospel story. Place your five loaves and two fish in a lunchbox or tin.

At the beginning of your talk, give the lunchbox to a small child who doesn't mind helping. Ask them to keep it closed until you tell them to open it.

Explain to the congregation that today you had planned to treat them all to a gourmet lunch. You were going to book the caterers, and there would be plenty of delicious food for everyone. Cakes, crisps, posh sandwiches, little jellies and everything! Are they feeling a bit hungry? Unfortunately, the caterers were on holiday, and also your budget didn't quite run to that.

Ask your helper to come up. This lunchbox looks like there might be some food inside. Would they be ok to share it? Yes? Oh, that's wonderful, there's enough for everyone in here!

Open the box up, and show the five loaves and two fish. I wonder how we can share these among everyone? There are only going to be a few crumbs each if we break them into pieces.

Tear off the pieces of tape as you do this. The separate tissue paper shapes will then be released and you can give the tin a shake to separate them some more. Show everyone the lunchbox now – there is plenty for everyone!

Ask your helper (and some friends) to take the lunchbox around the church so that everyone can have something from it.

Just like Jesus showed when he fed the five thousand people, with God there is more than enough for everyone! His love goes on and on, and he cares for and blesses people all through history and all around the world.

All he needs us to do is to offer what we have for him to use. We might have some food that we can share with others, or we might have some toys we can share to make others happy. Perhaps we can play a musical instrument and we could share that skill, or maybe we are good at giving people lifts in the car. On their own, each of these things can seem quite small, but together, when we offer them to God, he can do more than we could ever imagine!

Children's Corner

Have a lunchbox containing some bread rolls and fish-shaped snacks (fish-shaped sweets or crackers). The children can open up the lunchbox, and share out the snacks inside as they listen to the Gospel story about the young boy sharing his lunch with thousands of people.

The colouring sheet shows Jesus and the young boy sharing his lunch with the thousands of people sitting down to eat on the hillside.

Little Kids' Sunday School

Bring along a lunchbox with some small treats inside. Play 'Pass the Lunchbox': when the music stops, whoever is holding the lunchbox can open it to eat a treat.

Tell the children the story of the little boy with a lunchbox. How he had gone to listen to Jesus, maybe with his family. They were out on the hillside, thousands of them, all listening to

Jesus telling stories. Jesus was good at telling stories; they made you laugh but they made you think, too. But it was well past lunchtime, and everyone was getting hungry. It was too far to pop back for lunch, but nobody really wanted to leave; they didn't want to miss anything Jesus said. The little boy looked at his lunchbox. He had five little rolls of bread and two small fishes. He suddenly saw it as something quite different from just a lunch for himself, and imagined what it would be like to share it, so that other hungry people could be fed too. He decided to take it to Jesus, who rather than making him feel stupid for thinking his little lunch could be of any use at all, took it and blessed it, and his friends started to hand it out. Suddenly there was enough lunch for everyone!

The children can make loaves and fishes edible necklaces, by threading five pieces of hooped cereal on a thread, and using a needle, two fish-shaped sweets. As they wear these, they can remember the story, and when they get hungry enough to eat them, they can share with those around them. What else do they have that they can share?

Big Kids' Sunday School

Play 'This Is Not a Bread Roll'. Pass a bread roll around the group. They each take it and say, 'This is not a bread roll, it's a . . .' Their ideas can be anything they like. That bread roll could be anything from a juggling ball to a trampoline for a mouse.

In our Bible story today we hear of a boy who was able to see his lunch, his bread rolls and little fishes, as something else. Thousands of people had come to listen to Jesus, to hear his stories, to catch his vision of a better world, and a better them. They'd all left their towns and villages and were sitting on the hillside, starting to get hungry! The boy looked at his lunch and was able to see it not as something to eat himself, but as a way of feeding other people. He went and offered what he had to Jesus, not worrying that maybe he was making a fool of himself, or that what he had wouldn't be enough. And Jesus, taking the bread and fish and blessing them, made sure his vision of everyone being fed became reality.

Give the children squares of origami paper, and follow some instructions online to make an origami box. If you make two, you can slot one over the other as a lid. On tiny bits of paper, they can write what it is that they have that they can offer to Jesus to use, then pop these in their origami 'lunchbox'. What else might their talent on the piano, their ability to make a cup of tea, their capacity for coming up with great playtime games, turn into once Jesus has blessed them?

STEPPING OUT IN FAITH

Readings
- 1 Kings 19:9-18
- Psalm 85:8-13
- Romans 10:5-15
- Matthew 14:22-33

Thoughts on the Readings

Faith is something special, in our hearts, which enables us to make the choice to become vulnerable like Peter and step out into the unknown and trust in God. Peter already had that trusting relationship with Jesus. He knew Jesus well and understood that he would not want him to come to any harm. But to walk out onto the water was something that required a lot of courage. For us, too, it is our relationship with God, cultivated day by day as we spend time in his company, which helps us to have the courage we need to step out in faith too.

Elijah, too, had that faith. He could have become impatient, waiting for God to speak, and perhaps given up when God's voice was not heard in the earthquake, fire or wind. Or he might have been tempted to make up something and convince himself that this was what God wanted to say. However, because he had such a close and trusting relationship with God, he was able to recognise God's gentle voice when the time was right.

Our reading from Romans describes this same faith. Those people who have faith – that trusting, close, loving relationship with God – don't need to be convinced by argument about the existence or the nature of God. Their own experience is more than a theoretical discussion. This is the good news that we can share with others. Sensitively and respectfully talking with other people about our experience of and relationship with God is a very different thing from trying to persuade people to think or believe the same things that we do. Faith is not forcing yourself to believe something which cannot be either proved or disproved in a scientific way, and as Christians we need to make this clear. We are not into some sort of brainwashing and we certainly don't want people to feel that they have to pretend to themselves or others in order to belong to the church 'club'. Faith is instead the real and genuine encounter with God, leading us to put our trust in him because we love him and we know he loves us too.

So how can we share this with others? First of all, we need to make sure that we are making the space in our own lives for God. Are we in the habit of giving thanks to him when we see a beautiful sunset or a bright butterfly? Do we chat to him about our day, the things we are worried about, the things we are grateful for, and are we honest with him about the mistakes we have made and the attitudes we have held which were less than loving? If we do these things, when we speak to others it will be natural to explain our faith in terms of relationship and experience, giving them the opportunity to know Jesus too.

Discussion Starters

In what ways have other people led us closer to God and into a deeper faith? What can we learn from this?

Intercessions

**As we walk in faith,
we put our trust in you.**

Lord, we want to grow closer to you
day by day,
so that we can know you more
and share your love with others.

We bring our church before you,
the community with whom we worship
week by week.
We thank you for those people
who have led us closer to you
and who have inspired us in our faith.
We pray that you would help us to be a place
where your loving welcome is shown to all those around us.
**As we walk in faith,
we put our trust in you.**

As we think of the world around us,
we thank you for those innovative groups
who are helping communities adapt to climate change,
making possible what had seemed impossible.
We pray that you would show us
where our small actions, taken with an attitude of faith, generosity and love
can make a real difference to others
and to our world.
**As we walk in faith,
we put our trust in you.**

We pray that your gentle voice of love
and your caring presence
would surround and encourage all those
who are in need or pain.
We pray for anyone struggling with past trauma

and for those who long for closeness with you.
We also bring before you anyone known to us
in need of prayer, including . . .
As we walk in faith,
we put our trust in you.

We remember before you
those who have made the journey
from this world to the next
and give thanks that they can now worship you
surrounded by your loving presence
for all eternity.
We particularly remember today . . .
As we walk in faith,
we put our trust in you.

Lord, thank you that we can know you as a friend.
Thank you that you are always with us through our lives
and in every circumstance.
Amen.

Children's Prayer

Jesus, we love you,
Jesus, we trust you,
Jesus, we know
that you will always
   be with us.
Amen.

Other Ideas!

Have some very small post-it notes
and some different coloured pencils
or gel pens for people to write out
and keep a Bible verse to encourage
them. This can remind them that like
Elijah found, God can speak in a small,
gentle and quiet voice. Have some
Bibles open at the readings for today,
so that people can choose a verse or
two that means something to them.

All-age Talk

Cut some long strips of blue and green crepe paper, and write the words 'debt', 'fear', 'loneliness', 'illness', 'bereavement', 'stress' and 'tiredness' on them. Ask a couple of helpers to lay these down on the floor to be the lake in today's story, but don't read the words out at the moment. Position your helpers at either end so that they can help wave and wiggle the paper strips to be the stormy waves.

We're lucky enough that there is a nice strong floor underneath the waves. They're not that wet either! But when the disciples saw someone walking on the water, it's no surprise that they were more than a little bit scared.

Once Peter realised that it was Jesus, though, he trusted in him completely. He stepped out of the boat and placed his feet on the surface of the water (ask a volunteer to stand in the middle of your wiggly waves). Looking at Jesus, he walked towards him.

But then the waves became bigger and stronger (ask your helpers to wave them more fiercely). Peter was scared. He started to sink! The cold water splashed his face and soaked his clothes. It wouldn't be very nice to swim in this rough water. Peter knew just what to do. He reached out with his hand and straight away, his friend Jesus took it and helped him up, out of the water (act this out).

Jesus and Peter both walked back to the boat together, and the waves calmed down (your helpers can now lay the strips of paper down on the floor).

Sometimes we, too, feel like we are sinking. Not necessarily in a deep cold lake, but sometimes things are just too much for us to cope with by ourselves. Now ask someone to read out the words on the strips of paper. Whatever the reason, we know that we can reach out to Jesus, and he will take our hand. He will rescue us, and we won't be on our own.

As a church, we can be there for each other too, supporting each other and helping each other up when we feel like we are sinking. We can show God's love to each other like this, as we look to him for strength.

Children's Corner

Provide a container of water (on top of a towel in case of spillages) and a variety of objects for the children to experiment with, to see if they sink or if they float. They can listen to the story of Peter walking on the water, and then sinking beneath the waves, before Jesus comes to reach out and hold him safe.

The colouring sheet shows Peter sinking in the water, and Jesus reaching his hands out to rescue him.

Little Kids' Sunday School

Put a big container of water in the middle of your group, and a pile of objects next to it. You can go around the circle as the children choose an object, say if they think it will float or sink, and then try it out to see if they were correct.

Jesus' friends were out in the boat one day, floating on the sea. You can put one of your floating objects back in the water as you speak. They had been out fishing all night, as the wind was too high to go back to shore. Now it was dawn, and they suddenly spotted something that gave them a fright. They saw a figure walking out to them, over the water! You can put another floating object back in the water. They were terrified, but suddenly heard the voice of their friend Jesus, speaking to them. 'Don't be afraid,' he said, 'it's only me.' Peter called out to him. 'If it is you, call for me to come to you over the water.' Jesus called back, 'Come!' So Peter climbed right out of the boat, and started walking over the water to Jesus. Put another floating object back in the water. But suddenly Peter remembered the wind and the waves, and the watery depths beneath him. He began to be afraid, and started to sink. Put one of the sinking objects in the water. But just as he started to sink, Jesus reached out to him and rescued him, and together they walked back to the boat. What kinds of things make us feel like we are sinking?

Give the children a lump of plasticine each to mould into a boat and see if they can create a boat that floats. Allow them to try placing pennies inside. How much can their boat hold before it starts to sink? They can take their boats home to play with in the bath, remembering that when we feel like we are sinking, Jesus reaches out to us and pulls us to safety.

Big Kids' Sunday School

Do some apple bobbing, with apples floating around in a bowl of water, that the children have to pick up using just their mouth.

The apples float on top of the water, don't they, until they get pushed down by our hungry faces. In our Bible story today, we hear of Peter and the disciples out in their boat. It was a windy day, and the sea was quite rough. Suddenly they saw a figure walking out to them, over the water. They thought it was a ghost – what person can walk on top of the water? But then they heard Jesus' voice calling out, 'Don't be afraid, it's me.' He called Peter to come and join him, and Peter climbed out of the boat and began to walk to him over the water. But Peter heard the wind and began to be afraid. He started to sink. Immediately, Jesus reached out his hand and caught him, and they went back to the boat.

Can you imagine being one of the disciples on the boat? How would you feel? What would you see? Or can you imagine being Peter?

Make a submersible out of an old plastic bottle and a pen lid. Weight the bottom of the pen lid with a small lump of sticky tack. You may need to play around with this to get the weighting right. Fill the bottle right up to the top, drop the pen lid in, open end first, and screw the cap on tightly. You want your pen-lid submersible to float just below the surface of the water. If it is right on the top or drops right to the bottom, take it back out and change the amount of sticky tack. Gently squeeze the full bottle. As you squeeze, the submersible will drop. As you let go, the submersible will rise to the surface again.

As we are squeezed by the pressures and fears of life, we can become like Peter, sinking in the water. We need to trust that Jesus will reach out to us and pull us back up, like the submersible in our bottle.

GOD'S BLESSINGS ARE FOR ALL

Readings

- Isaiah 56:1, 6-8
- Psalm 67
- Romans 11:1-2a, 29-32
- Matthew 15:(10-20) 21-28

Thoughts on the Readings

God's blessing is available to everyone. But we need to turn towards him with a right attitude to receive what he has for us.

In the Gospel reading, Jesus talks about those things which really make it difficult for us to worship God. Jesus' disciples worried that he had offended the Pharisees by saying that eating the right sort of food was not what made people clean. This was something that was very important to them as a religious law, and many of those food and hygiene laws originally had sensible practical purposes. But what the Pharisees had lost sight of was that the rules were given by God to make life better, easier and healthier for them – not as a way of excluding or judging others.

Jesus then goes on to explain that it is unkind, selfish and hurtful words and actions which put us in a place where we are not able to worship God. We need to leave these behind. The cultural practices which may have gone along with religious tradition for many years are not the same thing. Behaviours, such as eating certain foods, which do not cause hurt or harm to others or the world do not matter in terms of our worship of God. Jesus warns us to guard against a judgmental attitude which excludes others.

As we continue with our Gospel reading, we hear how Jesus healed the daughter of a Canaanite woman. She had followed behind Jesus, asking him for help, and although the disciples wanted Jesus to send her away, he did not do so. Perhaps the gentle tone of Jesus' words has been sometimes forgotten when he talked about not taking the children's food away to feed it to the dogs. It seems unlikely, knowing what we do of Jesus, that he would have said anything to make this woman feel unloved and unimportant. Instead, we can imagine Jesus saying these words with a knowing smile as a tongue-in-cheek 'quote' from those traditional religious groups who would not have wanted anything to do with this woman. As he said it, she would have known it was not something that he held as his own personal opinion, which then gave her the space and confidence to reply with faith and humour, that even the dogs eat those crumbs from under the table! There may have been some dogs wandering around doing that very thing, tidying up some scraps from the floor, as Jesus and the Canaanite woman spoke together.

Our reading from Isaiah also speaks about how God's promise is for all people, no matter which country or cultural background they are from. In Psalm 67, all the nations worship God together. Perhaps we can think about what this means for us today, with technology giving us a window into the world, at the same time as living in communities with people from many different countries, speaking different languages. Our cultural practices won't all be the same – we may eat different foods, or dress in different ways. But if our hearts are ready to worship God, this does not matter. As we seek him and try to live his way, with love, kindness and respect, we will draw near to our Creator in worship, and find peace within ourselves, and with others.

Discussion Starters

- Are there any cultural practices which the church has required people to conform to, in order to participate in worship? These may be current examples or those from years gone by.

Intercessions

**Lord, we worship you
with our whole hearts.**

Lord, we come before you,
leaving behind any unkind thoughts,
so that we can draw near to your love
and worship you.

We think of our Church,
both here and around the world,
and give thanks for
its rich diversity of worship.
We pray that we would learn from each other
and share together in friendship and respect
as we come into your presence.
**Lord, we worship you
with our whole hearts.**

We bring before you our world
and all its needs.
We particularly pray for any groups
who are excluded or marginalised
because of their different traditions,
ways of dress, or cultural practices.
We pray that you would give us understanding and insight
as we look to you to guide us
in ways of love, welcome and inclusivity.
**Lord, we worship you
with our whole hearts.**

We bring into your loving care
anyone who is in need of your healing.
We particularly pray for those
who are living with a little-understood health condition
and for anyone who is waiting for a diagnosis.

We also bring before you
those who care for them.
We name before you today those known to us who have asked for our prayers, including . . .
Lord, we worship you
with our whole hearts.

As we remember those who have died,
we thank you that you welcome
everyone who comes to worship you
and we thank you that these people
who have gone before us
are now able to praise and worship you in heaven.
We remember today in your loving presence
those who are missed at this time, including . . .
Lord, we worship you
with our whole hearts.

Lord, we pray that you would help us
to remember and prioritise
those things which help us to worship you,
to love others and to treat them with kindness and respect
and to speak with your words of love.
Amen.

Children's Prayer

Whatever language we speak,
we love to praise you, Jesus.
Whatever food we like to eat,
we love to praise you, Jesus.
Whatever clothes we like to wear,
we love to praise you, Jesus.
If we've got long, short or
    curly hair,
we love to praise you, Jesus.
With all of God's family from
    all round the world,
we'll praise and
    worship you, Jesus!
Amen.

Other Ideas!

Display a globe with the words
from Psalm 67.

All-age Talk

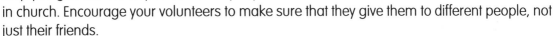

Jesus shows that people from another culture and religion are included in God's family and blessing.

Prepare some envelopes with a piece of shiny card inside, looking like a special invitation. On the card, write the words 'God's blessing is for you!' If possible, make enough for everyone in the congregation.

Ask a couple of volunteers to come and help you give the envelopes out to the people in church. Encourage your volunteers to make sure that they give them to different people, not just their friends.

As the people open the envelopes, ask them to read out what is on their card. God's blessing is for them! How wonderful!

You might not have had enough shiny card to make one of these for everyone, but don't worry! God's shiny and golden wonderful blessings are for the rest of you as well!

But what we heard in our Gospel reading today was that God's blessings are not just for one group of people, or even one country, or for people who worship God in one particular way. They are for everyone, all around the world! This is good news. As we hold our golden card in our hand, let's think about someone else we know from a different background to ourselves, and thank God for them. Let's bring them before God and pray that he will bless them with his love, hope and healing.

And as we think about those people, loved by God, let's resolve to be a welcoming community, ready to listen and ready to learn from others.

Children's Corner

Allow the children to play with and explore a large world map, preferably a laminated one or one that's made of fabric or is a floor mat. Give them some packs of smiley face stickers, and they can put these anywhere they like on the whole world. As it says in Psalm 67, 'May all the peoples praise you.' So wherever they put a smiley face sticker, there'll be someone there, praising God.

The colouring sheet shows a world map, with pictures of people wearing traditional dress, praising God in different ways in different places. The writing reads, **'May the peoples praise you, God, may all the peoples praise you!'**

Little Kids' Sunday School

Play 'Party Time!' under a parachute, or failing that, a very large sheet. Hold the edges of the sheet and when you say a category e.g. brown eyes, curly hair, had cornflakes for breakfast, those people can run under your puffed-up sheet (hold the edges and waft it into the air) and have a mini party! Think in terms of a three-second disco without the music.

As humans, we often put people into categories. People like this. People like that. These are the ones we like. Those are the ones we don't. But God shows us a different way. In his kingdom there is no 'them and us', but only 'us'. His blessings are for everyone. What's important isn't the cultural rules we follow, but how we live God's love in the world. You can puff up the sheet and let everyone go underneath for a three-second disco!

Give each child a blob of clay, and shiny things to stick all over it. This is their disco glitter ball. They can use it as a paperweight and as it reflects light all over the place in all different directions, it will remind them that God's blessings scatter over everyone.

Big Kids' Sunday School

Play a game of 'Giants, Dwarves and Wizards'. It's a bit like rock, paper, scissors, but played as a team game. Each team chooses which they're going to be: Giants stand up tall, Dwarves crouch down low, Wizards cast a spell. On the count of three, they step forward and do their stuff. Everyone in the team is the same character. Giants beat Dwarves because they can stamp on them. Dwarves beat Wizards because they can poke them with their swords. Wizards beat Giants because they can cast a spell on them. If both teams present the same character, they start again. The winning team chases the losing team back to their base/wall, and anyone captured becomes part of the winning team.

As humans we are very tempted to divide people into them and us. Just like in our game, when we're thinking about 'our' team and wanting to beat 'their' team. The Bible readings today show us a different way of living. Jesus tells the disciples that it's not following this or that particular cultural rule that really matters. And straight on the heels of that, we hear how a Canaanite woman – a woman from outside the Jewish community – followed him, asking for healing for her daughter. 'Even the dogs get to eat up the crumbs from under the table', she says. If even dogs can eat the bits of good food, then what about God's blessings? They are for everyone.

The children can make a sign to show this. Write a letter 'M' on a circle of card and attach it with a split pin on a bigger piece of card. Write a letter 'E' next to it. They can show how it is tempting to think that God's blessings are for me, and people like me. But God turns this upside down. You can spin the 'M' and turn it into a 'W', reading 'we'. With God, them and us ideas cease to make sense. God's blessings are for all of us.

ONE BODY IN CHRIST

Readings

- Isaiah 51:1-6
- Psalm 138
- Romans 12:1-8
- Matthew 16:13-20

Thoughts on the Readings

Our gifts, skills and qualities are given to us by God. Our faith also comes from God, and is expressed and understood in different ways. Some people might be drawn more to prayer, and others to action. Both these things are needed, and we should not worry about whether others' experience of faith is the same as ours. This is between them and God. As humans our diversity is our strength, and this includes our spirituality as well as our gifts and personalities. We may also come across people in whom we see God at work, who encourage us with their wisdom and help us in practical and compassionate ways, but who would not choose to use religious language to describe their beliefs. It is good, if we can, to talk together and share our own experience of faith, while also genuinely listening to others.

In the Gospel reading we hear how God gave Peter the understanding that Jesus was the Messiah. This was not just something that he had worked out on his own, but from wisdom and insight that came from God. In the same way, the reading from Romans describes how we are not to feel that we are more important than others because of the particular gifts that we have. They all come from God, and they are all important for us to work together.

Isaiah, too, tells us how we are chipped from the same rock as Abraham. We are part of that same good blessing, given to Abraham by God all those years ago. However, we need to recognise that this is the source of our strength and the thing that enables us to choose to live in a kind and godly way. Today's psalm is full of praise for God's rescuing and help. It is he who brings courage and protection. Through recognising this, and coming before God in honesty and humility, we are able to receive the gifts and blessings that he has for us.

Discussion Starters

- **What gifts in others have helped us in our lives and in our journey of faith?**

Intercessions

**Lord, with the gifts we have,
we will serve you.**

As we come before you in prayer,
we ask you to help us understand
how we can use the gifts you have given us
to help others.
We thank you for the church
and for all the members of the body of Christ
who offer their lives to serve others.
Please bless us all in our calling,
whatever that may be
and help us to recognise the value
of others' gifts too.
**Lord, with the gifts we have,
we will serve you.**

We pray for our world
and think of those groups
whose voices have not been heard
and whose skills have not been appreciated.
We pray that you would help us to value
the wisdom and gifts of those around us,
being ready to listen and to learn.
**Lord, with the gifts we have,
we will serve you.**

We bring into your loving presence
anyone feeling that they are not useful
or that they are unable to make a contribution.
We pray for your healing and love
to bring wholeness, and an understanding
of how precious they are.
We also pray for those
who are suffering with an illness, disability,
injury or pain
and pray that you would bring your peace and healing.
We name before you today . . .
**Lord, with the gifts we have,
we will serve you.**

As we think of those people
who have now completed life's journey
and are able to worship you in heaven,
we pray for those who miss them
and ask that you would surround them
with your comfort and love.

We particularly remember today . . .
**Lord, with the gifts we have,
we will serve you.**

As we rest in your presence,
we receive the gifts you have given us.
May we use them wisely, sensitively
and confidently
for your kingdom.
Amen.

Children's Prayer

Lord God, you have given us
so many good things.
A clever brain,
kind hands
and a caring heart.
May we always use them
to help others
and to show your love.
Amen.

Other Ideas!

Have some gold 'coins' cut out
of card, with a treasure box or
basket for people to place them
in. As they do this, people can
think of a gift or skill that they
have, and offer it to God.

All-age Talk

Cut up some mirror card (this can be bought
from a craft shop or on the internet) into
squares, big enough for people to see their
reflection in. Put these into a bag or pillowcase.

Explain to everyone that today you have
brought along a special lucky dip bag with a
present for everyone inside! All the presents
are different, and they all show something that
is very important for helping to bring about
God's kingdom of kindness, goodness and love.

As you pass round the bag, and everyone takes a piece of mirror card, explain that in
today's reading we heard how God gives us all different gifts to help other people, and to help
the world. In this bag there are pictures of people who are good at helping in practical ways
– tidying up, changing the lightbulbs, climbing up ladders to fix the guttering. There are also
pictures of people who are good at encouraging others – who will notice things that people
have done, and tell them 'well done!' These people also notice when others are feeling a bit
sad or low, and always have some kind words for them.

There are some other pictures in the bag too. Some people are really good at organising things, and making sure that they happen. They can see the bigger picture and can draw others around them to help them, too. Then there are also pictures of people who can explain about the Bible to us, and can help us in our prayer and worship. These are the people we know we can ask to pray for us if things are tough.

Let's have a look at these pictures, and think about the person you can see in there. What gifts do you have? Whatever it is, God can use us. He wants us to work together and to care for each other. None of us can do everything – we need each other. And when we do this, amazing things can happen!

Children's Corner

Find or make some jigsaw puzzles about the human body, so the children can practise putting a body together out of all its parts.

The colouring sheet shows a body, drawn like a jigsaw puzzle so that all the parts fit together to form the whole. The writing reads, **'In Christ, we, though many, form one body'**.

Little Kids' Sunday School

Sing 'Head, shoulders, knees and toes', missing out a word each time until you're doing it in silence. Then sing it through again, loudly and lustily!

Our bodies are so useful! They're made up of lots of bits, and we need all of them. Our head does a different job from our feet, and our hands do a different job from our tummy, but all of them are important. In the Bible reading today, we hear how the church is a bit like a body. How might that be?

The children can make paper plate people. They need four long strips of paper, which they will fold in a zigzag. These need to be glued on to be the arms and the legs. The paper plate is the body. Cut out a smaller circle and stick it to the top to be the head. They can take this home to remind them of how, just like our body is made up of lots of parts, so is the church, and all of us are important, needed, and wanted.

Big Kids' Sunday School

Play that game where you roll the dice and if you get a six you get to come into the middle to use a knife and fork to eat a piece of chocolate. The catch today is that when you throw a six you go into the middle to wait for someone else. The first child to throw a six puts their arms behind their back, and the next child puts their arms through the holes to be their new arms, cuts up some chocolate and feeds it to child number one. Then the second child can wait by the chocolate for someone else to throw a six and come and be their arms.

In today's Bible reading from the letter to the Romans, we hear that just like the human body is made up of lots of parts, all doing their own job, so too is the church. And just like in our game, when we couldn't feed ourselves the chocolate, we all need each other. Because each of us has our own things to contribute.

Cut some lengths of elder wood, about a couple of centimetres long each, and help the children poke out the inside with a tent peg. Starting at the 'head' they can thread a folded-over length of string down through the 'head' bead, bundling some wool at the top to be the hair and stop it coming through. Split the doubled-over string so that one half threads through a couple of beads, through a short bead at the end, then back through those 'arm' beads again. Do the same for the other side. Thread both lengths of string through one bead to be the body, and do the same for the legs as you did for the arms. Their little wooden bead people can remind them of this reading from Romans, and as you work with the wood and the string, you can talk about what each other's special skills are, and how everyone is needed.

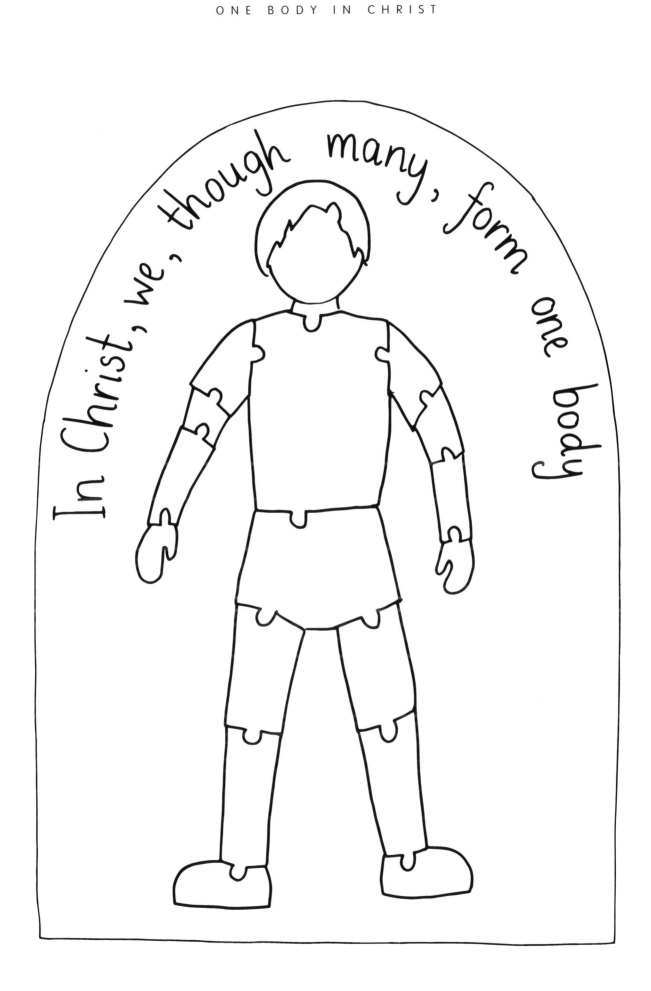

In Christ, we, though many, form one body

TAKING UP OUR CROSS

Readings

- Jeremiah 15:15-21
- Psalm 26:1-8
- Romans 12:9-21
- Matthew 16:21-28

Thoughts on the Readings

When Jesus' disciples tried to reassure him that God would not allow him to suffer or be killed, Jesus brushed this aside. So many people seem to think in this way, but life does not work like this. Sometimes difficult and challenging things do happen in our lives, and sometimes we wonder why things are not working out the way that we hoped.

Jesus explains that to follow him, we need to take up our cross too. If things are sometimes painful or hard, we are not to worry that we have done something wrong, that God has forgotten us, or that he has wilfully 'allowed' us to go through tough times. The disciples were right that God would not purposefully make bad things happen to us, but what they did not understand was that the most important thing of all is for us to seek a close relationship with God, to know his love through the most difficult of times, and to share this with others.

The reading from Romans explains in practical terms what this would look like. We are to help those in need and welcome strangers into our home, and make friends with people, not looking for fame or status. If our enemy is hungry and thirsty, our job as Christians is to act with compassion and give them something to eat and drink. These are challenging words. We are to be patient when difficult times come, and when people treat us badly, we should not look for revenge. There is certainly no implication that our life will be easy or trouble-free.

This can sometimes be a challenge to us when those outside the church ask why God can allow suffering. Perhaps it may help for us to explain that our understanding of God comes from a different perspective. Our relationship with God, knowing that he loves us, understands us and cares for us, is the thing which can help us keep going when things are tough. Being part of a supportive community of faith is wonderful too, as we can all help each other, both in practical ways and with emotional support.

Sometimes other Christians, like Jesus' disciples, may suggest that if we pray hard enough, or with enough faith, God will take away all our problems and bless us in material ways. However well-intentioned, this attitude can cause pain to those who have lost a loved one, are living with a long-term physical or mental health condition, or who are struggling with money issues. As a caring and supportive church community, we can provide a safe place where people don't have to feel that their lives need to be perfect and problem-free to be accepted. Together, we can give an opportunity for friendship, healing and hope.

Discussion Starters

- Do we prefer to pray for specific outcomes, or for comfort, strength and wisdom? How do we find the right balance?

Intercessions

Lord, in our journey through life,
we choose to follow you.

As we come before you, Lord, in prayer,
we acknowledge those things in our lives
which are not easy
and we thank you
that you are always ready
to love us and to help us.

We bring before you our church,
giving thanks for those who lead us in worship,
who listen, care and pray.
We ask that you would help us
to be a supportive community of faith,
so that we can be a place of safety, hope and healing
and show your love.
Lord, in our journey through life,
we choose to follow you.

We pray for our world,
remembering anyone without a safe home,
those who are separated from loved ones
and anyone living in areas of conflict.
We pray that you would help those in power
to work together for a solution
and give strength to those going through difficult times.
Lord, in our journey through life,
we choose to follow you.

We bring before you
anyone living with a long-term
physical or mental health condition
and those who cope day to day
with disability or pain.

We pray for sick and premature babies
and their families,
asking that you would surround them all
with your healing and love.
We bring before you in prayer today . . .
**Lord, in our journey through life,
we choose to follow you.**

As we remember those family members and friends
who have now died and are at peace with you for eternity,
we pray that you would comfort those who miss them.
We name before you today . . .
**Lord, in our journey through life,
we choose to follow you.**

Lord, as we choose to follow you,
we receive your love, peace and strength.
We pray that we would grow closer to you
day by day.
Amen.

Children's Prayer

When things are hard,
dear Jesus,
give us your love, we pray.
We want to walk with you
and know
your strength in us
each day.
Amen.

Other Ideas!

Give out wooden holding crosses or hearts, to help with prayer and to show God's love. People can either keep these for themselves as an encouragement and a way of feeling that God is close when things are tough, or they may have someone in mind who they would like to give it to as a gift.

All-age Talk

Bring along a selection of characters e.g. a toy pirate, a toy dragon, a superhero, a teddy, a monster, a doll, and perhaps some Lego or Playmobil characters of various descriptions.

Also bring along a toy tea set, or some plastic cups and plates (one for each of the toys), and a packet of biscuits.

Ask a small volunteer or two to come and help you to set up a tea party for all the toys, and to give them a biscuit each. As they do this, give a running commentary. ('Oh, I see Superman has a cup of tea – he'll like that! I'm sure the dragon will love crunching his biscuit with his big, strong teeth!' etc.)

Explain how the children have actually been teaching us something this morning. This is what God wants us to do. Some of those characters are 'baddies' in the story that they come from, and some of them are 'goodies' (the children can help you identify which is which). But our lovely helpers have generously given them all drinks and biscuits.

In our reading today we heard that if our enemy is hungry, we should give them something to eat. And if they are thirsty, we should give them something to drink. This isn't always easy to hear, or easy to do, but with God's help we can be welcoming and generous to those who are different from us, and even those who in the past have made our lives difficult or caused us pain. This goes along with Jesus' message of loving our enemies and forgiving others. Not only does it show God's love, but it brings peace and freedom to us as well.

Now your helpers and some other volunteers can help to eat up the biscuits for the toys!

Children's Corner

Give a collection of lots of different crosses for the children to pick up and feel. They can listen out for Jesus in the Gospel reading, telling us to take up our cross and follow him.

The colouring page shows someone carrying a cross along a road, and the writing reads, **'Take up your cross and follow Jesus'**.

Little Kids' Sunday School

Play 'Follow My Leader'. The children can take it in turns to be the leader, taking you on a trip around your meeting area, moving in different ways as you copy them.

When we are following our leader, we have to copy them, to move the way they move, to do the things they do. Jesus said, 'Take up your cross and follow me.' When we follow Jesus, we know that we will be following him, not just past the lilies of the field and the birds of the air, but also through his cross and suffering. What might our cross be? What does a cross look like in our lives?

The children can make a cross to take home by choosing two sticks and wrapping them together with a pipe cleaner. As they choose their sticks, either from a pile you've collected or from somewhere outside your building, you can talk about the times when it feels hard to follow Jesus, and the times when it feels easy.

Big Kids' Sunday School

Tie a long rope into a loop. The children hold it all around the edge. Get them to form it into a square. Now get them to form it into a triangle, but this time without talking. Now get them to form it into a cross, maybe even with their eyes shut.

How did we know how to move? We had to listen to each other, and follow each other's lead. Leadership isn't always about one person at the front beckoning us onwards. In the Gospel reading today, Jesus tells us to 'take up your cross and follow me'. As we follow Jesus, watching for what he does and trying to do the same, we will naturally find ourselves in some similar situations. We may not end up carrying a cross to our crucifixion, but we will probably find ourselves in some uncomfortable places, on the receiving end of some unkindness or negativity, because of the way we are following him. That doesn't mean we're following him wrongly. Sometimes we get the impression that the Christian life is all about joy and gladness. And in a way, that's not wrong. But the joy and gladness sometimes come despite the situations around us rather than because of them.

The children can make a cross to take home. Give each of them a rectangular piece of wood and help them bang eight nails in, two at each end of the cross. They can wrap embroidery thread around them to show the shape of the cross.

Take up your cross

and follow Jesus

LISTENING AND SPEAKING OUT

Readings

- Ezekiel 33:7-11
- Psalm 119:33-40
- Romans 13:8-14
- Matthew 18:15-20

Thoughts on the Readings

Ezekiel was told by God to tell the people to turn back to God's ways. They may not listen, but he was to give this message anyway, whether it was well-received or not. However, what God really wants is for the people he has made to turn back to him, to choose to live in a loving, kind and godly way, rather than in a way which leads to selfishness, isolation and unhappiness.

In today's Gospel reading, Jesus explains how best to address a situation when one person has done wrong to another. He says that first of all, we should talk to that person in private. This may be all that is needed. It doesn't have to result in an argument or conflict, because if we listen to God, he will help us to bring the subject up in a respectful and sensitive way. However, if that person does not listen then we can bring one or two other people along and talk together. After this, the issue should be brought to the church, and only if that solution does not work, then Jesus said that the person should be treated as a Gentile and a tax collector (and when we think how Jesus treated these people, it was to help them realise their worth in God and turn their lives to receive his love).

The reading from Romans describes how all God's rules are summed up by realising that we should love our neighbour as ourselves. Everything else can be seen in this light. Are we acting in a loving way towards others? Are we passing judgement because we think a rule has been broken, when actually this most important law of all is still intact? Or perhaps it is the other way around – we need to be careful that things we accept and do not challenge, and perhaps consider normal, are not actually breaking God's law of love. This can sometimes be the case when we are not aware of how our own language and actions come across to others, perhaps causing people to feel judged and excluded by the church. Another example might be where we have overlooked opportunities to make our buildings and services more accessible to others, particularly people with disabilities, limited mobility and those on a low income. If we really are loving others as we love ourselves, we would make sure that they were able, as much as possible, to join in with all the things that we enjoy too.

Discussion Starters

- How can we understand and take on board God's law of love in our church and in our lives? Are there any practical steps that we can take – perhaps buying a ramp for the step, stocking Fairtrade tea and coffee, twinning our church toilets, attending training so that we can make our church more dementia or autism friendly, or something else?

Intercessions

**Lord, your laws are built on love,
may we show this love to others.**
As we come into your presence,
we thank you for the love and sense of belonging
that we find in you.

We thank you for our church,
for those who provide care and love,
those who lead us in worship
and help us understand what you have to say to us.
We pray that you would fill us with love for our neighbours:
those who live, work or worship near our church,
so that we can be a place of blessing
in our community.
**Lord, your laws are built on love,
may we show this love to others.**

We think of our world
and all those places
where love, understanding and respect
are precious gems
in situations of conflict, violence and injustice.
We pray that the decision makers who hold power
would bear in mind your law of love.
**Lord, your laws are built on love,
may we show this love to others.**

We bring before you
all those who are in need,
particularly anyone who has experienced being excluded,
misunderstood, or discriminated against for any reason.

May we have humility
to be ready to listen and learn,
so that we are ready to hear the voices
of those who have sometimes been ignored.
We also pray for anyone who is in any kind of pain at this time, including . . .
Lord, your laws are built on love,
may we show this love to others.

We remember in our hearts
those who have now died
and are at rest in heaven with you.
We pray that you would surround their family and friends
with your love, healing and care.
Today we particularly think of . . .
Lord, your laws are built on love,
may we show this love to others.

May we go from here
ready to learn from others,
ready to listen
and with our hearts full of your love.
Amen.

Children's Prayer

Thank you that you love us,
may we love others too.
Thank you that you hear us
when we call out to you.
Thank you that you
    always care
and always understand.
We're so glad for the
    way you hold us
gently in your hand.
Amen.

Other Ideas!

Cut a big heart out of a large sheet of paper or card (or a few pieces taped together). Write the words 'We bring to God's love . . .' in the middle. Provide some coloured pens and pencils for people to draw or write their prayers on the heart, to be surrounded by God's love.

All-age Talk

Today we are thinking about speaking out for what is right, and being ready to listen to the wisdom of others.

Bring along a couple of yoghurt pots or syrup tins, with small holes made in the base. Bring in, too, a long piece of string without any knots or breaks in it.

Ask a couple of children to come and help you make a yoghurt pot telephone. It would be interesting to see whether they have made one of these before or not. It might be a good chance to ask older members of the congregation whether they remember playing with these. They're great phones – a bit basic on extra features though.

Push one end of the string through each of the yoghurt pot holes, from the outside to the inside (taping round the end of the string can make this easier), and tie a good-sized knot to keep it in place.

Now, a church is a good place to try out our telephone, as it is nice and long. Ask one child to carry their end of the telephone to the back of the church, and the other child to stay with you. Then they can pull the string so it is nice and tight, but not so tight that the string comes out!

We heard in our readings today how sometimes God speaks to us, through others, and we hear his message of love. Sometimes we need to speak to others about things that are not right, and this is not always easy. God will help us to speak to others with love and respect, even when we feel tempted to argue with them or say something unkind.

Let the children try out the telephone now. Remind them that they don't need to talk in a loud voice, and they need to have the yoghurt pot to either their mouth or their ear – not both at the same time!

How was that? Could they hear what was being said?

By listening closely, we can also hear what God is saying to us. If we tune in to his law – to love our neighbour as we love ourselves – all the other rules will be put into perspective. And if we do need to speak to others about something that is not right, we can do it in a gentle way, like speaking on that telephone, and we can also make sure that we take it in turns to speak and to listen, as the children are showing us today.

Children's Corner

Let the children play with either old or toy telephones. They can practise speaking into them, and listening to them, as they play at having conversations. And they can whisper about how sometimes we need to be listening to God, and sometimes we need to be speaking his message to others.

The sheet shows lots of different types of phones to colour in, with interesting dials and buttons. The writing reads, **'We listen to God and we pass on his message'**.

Little Kids' Sunday School

Stand in a line and pass a message along to a person at the other end, telling them to open the packet (of crackers/hoop cereal/raisins), then telling them to put some in the bowl, then telling them to come up the line and offer everyone a snack!

It was important we did really good listening in this game, wasn't it, so we could all end up with a snack to eat. We talk a lot about good listening. Our parents want us to listen, our teachers want us to listen, at church we talk about listening to God. But that wasn't the only important thing we had to do. We had to pass on a message too. And being brave enough to speak out is also important.

Jesus tells us in the Bible reading today, that if someone is doing something wrong, we need to go and tell them. That can feel quite scary! None of us like being told off, and we don't want to make someone angry. But unless we are brave enough to take that first step, the person may not realise what they're doing. It's up to us to pass on that message.

Help the children to make paper cup telephones with cups and string, so they can practise both listening and speaking.

Big Kids' Sunday School

Play 'Air Mail'. This is as simple as it sounds. Form pairs, and each child sits on opposite sides of the room. They fold a paper plane, and write something on it. They throw it to their friend, who reads the message and replies.

We talk a lot about the importance of listening. We are told at home and at school how important it is to listen to our parents and our teachers. We hear at church about how we should listen to God. But we don't always hear about how important it is to speak up. When we were having our plane conversations, it would have been very boring if only one of us was 'talking'. In the Gospel reading today, Jesus tells us how if someone is doing something wrong, we need to go and speak with them about it. That's quite scary to do. We worry about how someone will react. But if they aren't told, they aren't given the chance to fix things. So, it's worth doing. We need to pass along that message of how to live in a loving way, in God's way.

Make a large speech bubble on paper or card. Give the children post-it notes so they can fill them with things they feel they want to say. If they have something that is just between them and God right now, they can draw a small symbol, like a cross or a heart on the post-it note, and they don't need to share it right now. You might like to play some reflective music as they do this to create a calm and thoughtful atmosphere.

We listen to God and we pass on his message

FORGIVENESS

Readings

- Genesis 50:15-21
- Psalm 103:(1-7) 8-13
- Romans 14:1-12
- Matthew 18:21-35

Thoughts on the Readings

That first slave in Jesus' story owed a really eye-watering amount of money – although it's hard to calculate exactly how much ten thousand talents would be, it's likely that today's equivalent would be millions of pounds. Something which would be virtually impossible ever to pay back. Jesus chose this example to illustrate how much God has given to us by forgiving us all our sins. We may not realise the extent of this, as we excuse ourselves for our unkind or judgmental words or thoughts, our wasteful and greedy use of the world's resources, and the times we are too wrapped up in ourselves to see our neighbour's need. However, as we acknowledge these things and bring them before God, he gladly and generously forgives us and helps us to have a new start.

Jesus continues his cautionary tale as the first slave then refuses to forgive the debt of someone else who owed a small amount of money to him. Things don't end well. That first slave had not realised or acknowledged the extent of the king's generosity. Perhaps he had convinced himself that he deserved that good treatment, and others did not. In the same way, we must not be tempted to take God's grace and forgiveness for granted.

Why should we forgive? Is it because it is good for the other person – who might not even notice or care? No, it is because God knows that it is the only way that we can find freedom and release from the things that have caused us pain in the past. We can still acknowledge that these things were wrong and bad, and there can still be consequences for the people who have done these harmful things, but the chains of resentment that stop us finding peace will be broken through forgiveness.

If we humbly acknowledge God's gift of forgiveness, we are then in a position where it will be only natural to forgive others. Sometimes it will be harder to do this, and sometimes it will be easier. But if we make that choice to forgive, instead of being knotted up in anger, we will receive freedom, peace and joy.

This is why Jesus answers Peter's question about how often we should forgive others with a bigger number than Peter expects. Jesus understood that sometimes we have to keep on forgiving that person, every time we see them, acknowledging and releasing those feelings of pain and hurt in the presence of our loving God. And as we do this, we will gradually find peace.

The reading from Romans also reminds us that we are not to pass judgement on others who have different religious practices to our own. It is what comes from the heart which is important, and when people's actions are for the purposes of worshipping God, this is what matters. We can be sensitive to others by observing the same practices they do when we are together, out of respect, even if we do not do this the rest of the time. This is wise advice for us, who like Paul, also live in a society with a wide variety of cultures and beliefs. It is good for us, as Christians, to visit other places of worship to learn and make links, and to welcome others to visit our churches too.

Discussion Starters

- Why does Jesus say that forgiving others is so important?

Intercessions

**For your mercy and kindness,
we thank you, Lord.**

As we come into your loving presence,
we thank you
for all you have done for us.

We thank you, Lord, for the church where we worship
and for our Christian sisters and brothers around the world
with different traditions and customs.
We pray that you would help us
to share and learn together
as we worship you.
**For your mercy and kindness,
we thank you, Lord.**

We pray for our world,
for a greater understanding
between people of different beliefs,
backgrounds, languages and cultures,
so that prejudices are broken down
and hatred melts away
as people encounter each other
as fellow humans living together on earth,
part of your family.
**For your mercy and kindness,
we thank you, Lord.**

Healing God, we bring into your loving presence
anyone crippled with the pain of past trauma
and those who have known little care or love
in their lives.
We pray that through your faithful, kind and gentle presence
they would know a sense of worth in you
and find a release from those things which cause pain.

We also bring into your presence
anyone who is unwell or in need at this time, particularly . . .
**For your mercy and kindness,
we thank you, Lord.**

We pray for those who are on the last stage
of life's journey, and those who love them.
And we also bring to mind those people
who have left this life on earth behind
and now dwell in eternity with you,
at peace.
We remember in your presence today . . .
**For your mercy and kindness,
we thank you, Lord.**

As we receive your blessings in this place,
give us the strength and courage
to make peace with others
and to choose to forgive.
Amen.

Children's Prayer

Dear God,
forgiveness isn't easy
but it's what we'll
choose to do,
knowing that you
love us
and that we're
forgiven, too.
Amen.

Other Ideas!

Make a collage or a slideshow
of pictures of people around the
world worshipping God in different
ways (a charity website may be
helpful with this), with the words
from Romans 14:11.

All-age Talk

Bring along some strips of paper and a few
glue sticks. Ask some of the children to come
up to the front and help you make some
chains. Ours are just paper but we will be using
them in a minute to help us think about the
story Jesus told which we heard today.

While the children are busy, talk about how in our reading, we heard how the first man owed a huge amount of money to the king. He asked and pleaded to be let off the debt, and the king very kindly agreed. However, someone else owed the man a small amount of money and he refused to pass on the kindness and let him off! The king was very cross and sent him off to be tortured.

Pretty tough, isn't it? But really, when we choose not to forgive others the wrong they have done us, whether this is something big or something small, whether it was on purpose or by mistake, we can end up torturing ourselves over the whole thing, waking up feeling resentful and upset again and again, and being overwhelmed with anger and a desire to get our own back if we have to see the person. We may find ourselves wishing that bad things would happen to that person, and that they would get a taste of their own medicine.

How's that paperchain getting on? Ask for a volunteer who does not mind being wrapped up in the chain, and wind it around them.

This is not the way that God wants us to live. He loves us, and wants us to live a life of joy and peace, so that the gifts he has given us can grow and blossom, and be a blessing to others. To be able to do this, we can tell God about all these things that have hurt and upset us in the past. Forgiveness does not mean pretending that these things have not happened. But once we have done this, we can start making the choice to forgive, and this will bring us freedom.

Now ask your helper who is wrapped up in the paperchain to burst out of it, so that they are free! How does this feel? When we forgive others, it may or may not make a difference to them. But we can be sure that it will make a difference to us, and it will be a good one.

Children's Corner

Collect some blackboards and chalk, and maybe whiteboards and whiteboard pens too, if parents and carers can be trusted to supervise their children closely! The children can see how they can make marks on the board, and then wipe it clean, and whisper about how when we do things that are wrong, Jesus forgives us, and when others do things that are wrong, we should forgive them.

The colouring sheet shows people worshipping in a variety of different ways – churches from different traditions, worshipping in different cultures round the world. The words at the bottom of the sheet read, **'However we worship, we all worship the Lord'**.

Little Kids' Sunday School

Draw with big chalks over the space outside your meeting place, or on the walls. Then give the children buckets and brushes to scrub it all clean again.

In the Gospel story today, Jesus is asked about forgiveness. How many times should I forgive my brother or my sister who sins against me? And he answers with a story, of a servant who owes lots of money. Write a very large amount of money on a blackboard. The servant is summoned to the master, who threatens to sell him and his family as slaves to pay their debt. The servant begs for mercy and the master is merciful. Wipe

the large amount of money off the board. The servant goes outside and finds a man who owes him money. A much smaller amount of money. Write this on the blackboard. He starts to threaten this man, who can't pay either, but this time there isn't any mercy shown, and the man is thrown into prison. When the master hears of this, he is angry. 'You have had mercy shown to you', he thunders, 'so you should show mercy to others!'

We have all had mercy shown to us. God forgives us, every day. So we should forgive other people too. Wipe the blackboard clean again. Once we've been forgiven it's like a fresh start. Once we've done forgiving, it's like a fresh start too.

Make little blackboards out of slices sawn from a branch – wood cookies – and paint them with blackboard paint. The children can take them home with a chalk so they can practise drawing and rubbing out again, and remember that as they have been forgiven, so they should forgive.

Big Kids' Sunday School

Give each child a heart cut out of J cloth. They can scribble on it with washable markers. That's a bit like our heart, when we mess ourselves up through sin. When we are unloving and unkind, when we are selfish and self-centred, it's like this scribbled-on heart. But when we ask for God's forgiveness, it's like it's washed clean again (wash your hearts in some soapy water).

Peter came to Jesus and asked, 'How many times should we forgive our brother or sister who has sinned against us? Up to seven times?' Jesus replied, 'Not up to seven times, but seventy-seven!' And then Jesus went on to tell this story.

Choose a child to be the first servant, and pass them a letter reading 'You owe me £££££££.' There was a servant who owed his master lots of money. He was summoned to the master, who threatened to sell him and all his family as slaves. (Send the first servant to another child who can look threateningly at him and point to the debt letter.) The servant fell to his knees (they can do this) and begged for mercy. And the master was merciful (he can rip up the letter and throw it away). As the servant came out of the master's house, he met with another servant who owed him money. (Give another child a letter saying, 'You owe me £.') The first servant grabs the second servant and demands his money back. The second servant begs for mercy, but the first servant throws him into prison. (Your prison can be under a table or behind some chairs.) The master gets to hear of this and is angry. 'You were shown mercy, and yet you did not show mercy!' he thunders. And the first servant is thrown into prison after all.

When we are forgiven, it's like we are washed clean. But we need to have the courage to forgive other people, too. Because holding on to our anger, our resentment, is like a prison for us. Being brave enough to forgive, gives us our freedom.

The children can use old soap scraps to make new soap. Grate them, mix them with a little water, and melt them, either in the microwave or over a basin of hot water. Once they are softened, squash them into rubber or silicon cupcake moulds or ice cube moulds. After a while, they'll have hardened enough to be gently tipped out into paper bags. The children should leave them a few days before using them. When they wash their hands, they can think of God's forgiveness making them clean, and remember to ask his help so they can forgive others.

HOWEVER WE WORSHIP, WE ALL WORSHIP THE LORD

GOD'S GENEROSITY TO US

Readings
- Jonah 3:10 – 4:11
- Psalm 145:1-8
- Philippians 1:21-30
- Matthew 20:1-16

Thoughts on the Readings

Today's psalm tells how God is 'slow to anger and abounding in steadfast love'. And in the reading from Jonah, God did not carry out the destruction he had threatened in Nineveh, because the people had turned from their evil ways. Jonah was jealous, and not best pleased about this – it did not seem fair that after all Jonah had gone through to bring this message to the people, they escaped any consequences through a last-minute change of heart. But God explains that he loves and cares for those people so much, and what he wanted was for them to change – not for them to be punished.

In the parable Jesus tells in the Gospel reading, those labourers who had worked hard all day long felt a real sense of injustice and disappointment. Those people who had come to work just for the last hour or so of the day were being paid exactly the same wage as they were, and it was not right. They felt that they should have been paid more than the daily wage for which they had agreed to work. However, the landowner in the story defends his decision. It was his choice to be generous, and those who had worked all day have not been underpaid. Basically, the message to them is to stop being jealous, and be grateful for what they have.

This radical method of apportioning pay for workers is an interesting point of discussion for us now, as it would have been then. The money was given because of the generosity of the landowner, the willingness of the workers to take that opportunity, and would have been the usual basic daily wage which would really have been needed to buy the basics on which to survive. This leads us to think about concepts such as a universal basic income as well as welfare payments which are based on need rather than whether the person has earned it in any way. At the time when Jesus was speaking, there would have been nothing like this, and this attitude of the generous employer would have led people to think about money completely differently.

Of course, the point that Jesus was making with this parable was that God's love and the promise of a home in heaven with him is something that is open to everyone. We don't earn a VIP place in heaven because we have happened to become a Christian at an earlier stage in our lives. We are not better or more deserving because of this. The workers who were standing around in the market place waiting for employment were wanting to work just as much as the people who were there at the beginning. People are often seeking spiritual meaning and fulfilment in their lives for some time, but at a later stage of life may discover that wonderful relationship with God which brings them peace and wholeness.

Discussion Starters

- Where do we see similar attitudes to the labourers who had worked all day, and how can we show these people that they are valued, while still supporting those who are in material need?

Intercessions

Generous God,
you give us all we need.

Lord, we come before you
knowing that we have not earned
your blessings and love.
We are so grateful
for all that you give us.

May our church embody
your generous welcome
and open-hearted love,
so that those around us
in our community
may be drawn towards you
and come to know all that you have to give to them.
Generous God,
you give us all we need.

We pray for the world we share
and think of those people
who are not paid enough to live on,
as well as those people
who, in spite of high income levels,
feel unhappy and unfulfilled.
We pray that your generous love
would help us to create
a generous and sharing world.
Generous God,
you give us all we need.

We bring into your healing presence
anyone feeling weighed down with problems,

anyone weary with pain
and anyone who feels that they are not valued
or listened to.
We also pray for those known to us
who are in any kind of need, including . . .
Generous God,
you give us all we need.

Remembering those who are now at rest
in heaven with you
and thinking of those
who love and miss them,
we name before you . . .
Generous God,
you give us all we need.

We thank you for the gracious way
you forgive us, bless us
and choose us to show your love.
Amen.

Children's Prayer

Lord, you are so generous,
Lord, you are so kind,
help us to share all that
    you give us.
Amen.

Other Ideas!

Cut out some gold coins from
card for everyone, with a heart
drawn on the back. Display
them in a basket with a sign
saying, 'God's love is enough'.

All-age Talk

Bring along three pretend cheques (make
these out of A4 paper cut into thirds) and a
thick pen which will show up. The cheques
don't need to be that accurate or detailed
– just with somewhere to write a name, the
amount and some sort of signature. Staple
the cheques together so that they look like
a chequebook. Also bring along a duster, a
dustpan and brush, and a broom.

Let's see if we have some willing workers here in church. There's a £100 pretend cheque for everyone who works today!

Hopefully you will have a helper or two. Give them the broom and set them to work.

Praise them for their hard work, and have a look at your watch/clock/phone. You still need some more work done, so let's see if anyone else is willing to do some work. Oh yes – great – they can have the dustpan and brush.

Run your finger over one of the surfaces and hold up the duster. Is there one more person who could do some work? Hand them the duster, and set them to work. But almost as soon as they have started, look at your watch/clock/phone and announce that it is the end of the day and everyone can finish working and come to you to get their pay.

Write them each out a cheque for £100, with a flourish, thanking your helpers for all their work.

Your helpers may not have made a fuss, as unfortunately these are just pretend cheques, but in Jesus' story the workers who had been slaving away were really jealous of those who only worked for a little while, but still got the same pay.

Jesus explained that God is generous like this. We don't get extra points or a special chair in heaven because we have been his friend for longer than other people. It is a wonderful prize already to know God and be able to talk to him in prayer, surrounded by his love. God loves everyone, and wants us all to be part of his kingdom.

Children's Corner

Build large building blocks or Duplo into a winner's podium, with different heights for first, second and third place. Have some teddies who can argue about who gets to be the best and most important. How can the children rebuild this podium to make things fair? Listen out for Jesus' story about being fair in the Gospel reading.

The colouring sheet shows a variety of people praying and worshipping: from a little toddler waving a shaker and a tambourine, to an organist, a guitarist, and an old person on their knees. The writing reads, **'God's love for us is the same size, no matter who we are'**.

Little Kids' Sunday School

Have some bananas and a blunt knife. You want to give everyone a snack. How can you do it fairly? Get the children's ideas. Count the number of people in the group, and work with them until you've shared the bananas fairly.

We like things to be fair, and we've made sure we've all had the same amount of banana. Jesus told a story about how things are fair in the kingdom of heaven, and it's not in the way we might think. Hold up a clock with movable hands, reading 6am. Make the sound of a cock crowing. It was very early in the morning, but the marketplace was already full of people hoping and hoping to be picked to get some work today. If they didn't get picked, they wouldn't get paid, and would have to go home to their families without any money. It was harvest time in the vineyard. The owner of the vineyard went down to the marketplace to hire some people to work in his vineyard, cutting grapes. Some of the children can get up and follow the owner, and start work, cutting grapes. But there were lots of grapes! So at 9am (move the clock hands), he went back down to the marketplace, and found more people to hire. Choose some more children to go and cut grapes. He went again at about noon (move the clock hands) and at about 3pm in the afternoon (move the clock hands). Each time there were still people looking for work, and they came with him to cut the grapes. Around 5pm, he went back to the marketplace for a final time. He asked the people there, 'Why have you been standing here all day doing nothing?' They replied, 'Because nobody has hired us.' So they followed him up to the vineyard, and cut grapes until the sun went down.

At the end of the day, it was time for all the workers to get paid. The workers hired last were called up first, and paid a denarius, a whole day's wage. They were happy! They would have worked all day if they could, and had been worrying all day about how they wouldn't have enough money to take home to look after their family. The workers coming after saw how much they'd been paid and got excited, thinking they'd be paid even more. But each of the groups of workers were paid the same, one denarius. They started to feel resentful. Hadn't they worked harder than the others?

What do the children think? Was the vineyard owner fair? What would have happened if he had paid them more money the longer they'd worked? Was it the 5pm workers' fault they hadn't got picked earlier? Did their families not still need money to buy food?

The children can make a clock out of a paper plate with two clock hands held on with a split pin so they can move. They can write 'God is generous all the time.'

Big Kids' Sunday School

Have a 'standing on one leg' competition. The longer you can stand on one leg, the more chocolate buttons you win.

Who got the most? Who got the least? Did the person who lost try as hard as the person who won? Did the person who lost want the chocolate buttons as much as the person who won? Was it fair? Can anyone think of a different way to share out the chocolate buttons?

Jesus told a story about a vineyard at harvest time. Early in the morning, the vineyard owner came down to the marketplace where all the workers were waiting, hoping to get picked for work that day. He chose some of them, and took them back to the vineyard to pick grapes. There were still more grapes, so he came back down to the marketplace to choose some more workers. And then again. And then again. It was now getting late, and there were still grapes needing to be picked. He went down to the marketplace one more time. There were still some people waiting there. He asked the people there, 'Why have you been standing here all day doing nothing?' They replied, 'Because nobody has hired us.' So they followed him up to the vineyard, and cut grapes until the sun went down.

When it was time for everyone to finish work for the day, they were called up to receive their pay. Those hired last were paid first, and were given a whole denarius, the equivalent to a whole day's pay. They were delighted! They'd been worrying all day about going home without enough money for their family, and now they'd have enough to buy food for everyone. Those waiting behind them got excited. If those guys, working for so little time, were getting paid so much, then how much more would they get paid? But as each worker was called up, each worker was given one denarius. They started to mutter that it was unfair. They had worked much longer in the hot sun. Why should they get paid the same amount as those who had only worked a little time? The owner of the vineyard replied, 'I have paid you a day's wage. Don't be angry just because I choose to be generous.'

How is this story similar to the competition we had at the beginning of our session? Are being fair and being generous different things? Why do you think Jesus told this story? What did he mean? What does it mean for us?

The children can make their own denarius to take home, by moulding clay or modelling clay into a flat coin shape, and covering it in silver foil. Let them see a picture of a real denarius, and they can use a pencil to engrave the foil so it looks the same. They can take their denarius home as a reminder of the vineyard owner's generosity, and God's generosity to us.

CHOOSING TO DO GOD'S WILL

Readings

- Ezekiel 18:1-4, 25-32
- Psalm 25:1-8
- Philippians 2:1-13
- Matthew 21:23-32

Thoughts on the Readings

God judges fairly – everyone is responsible for their own actions. We do have choices that we can make, whatever our circumstances or background, and God in his love and compassion knows exactly where we are. He is merciful and will forgive us if we turn to him. Our psalm reminds us that we need to realise our own need of God, that we have not always done everything right, and that we need him to lead us.

Through consciously putting others' needs first, listening to others, really trying to empathise and understand, taking practical action to make the lives of others better, even if this is people we have never met or are likely to meet, if we make this our habit, then we will be well on our way to living a holy life, as God wants us to. The reading from Philippians tells us that in humility, we should think of others as better than ourselves.

This is not about regarding ourselves as unimportant or no good. In fact, the opposite. We can know that we are loved and valued for who we are in God's sight, and through this can then have the confidence to appreciate others for who they are, too. We can become more aware of the skills and gifts that others have, and enjoy them without being jealous. And we can also put ourselves in others' shoes, shaking off the temptation to see inequality as part of the normal order of things.

In Jesus' parable we hear how it was the son who did the right thing and chose to help his father in the vineyard after all, who actually did his father's will. It is no good saying the right things, promising that we will do something and then not bother after all. We need to be careful to make sure that we put our words into actions – and this is something that we can challenge ourselves to check up on.

It is easy to say that we are going to do something, that we will support a certain cause, raise money for a charity, sign a petition or take part in a campaign, get to know our neighbours, reduce our environmental impact etc. It is sometimes harder to actually get around to doing these things. Perhaps if we think of a specific action that we can take, and write this down, we can then check that we really are doing what we have said that we are going to do. And then, as these things become a habit, it will become easier to remember to take action.

Discussion Starters

- **How can we help each other in our church community to make good choices and take action with regard to supporting charities, caring for the environment or caring for others?**

Intercessions

Lord, lead us,
may we do your will.

Dear Lord, we bring before you
those things which we meant to do
and the things we meant to change.
Give us the strength and courage
to live and act for your kingdom.

We pray that as a church
we would work together to do your will,
not just in our words
but in our actions, too.
Help us to support each other
with empathy, understanding and kindness
which shines out on and blesses
the community in which we live.
Lord, lead us,
may we do your will.

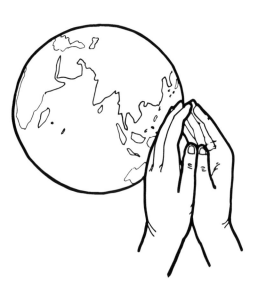

Pour out your love and healing on our world,
so that kind choices flourish
and those who are forgotten and marginalised
are valued as human beings of equal worth.
May we be ready to learn from others
from different backgrounds and cultures from our own,
so that we may all grow closer to you.
Lord, lead us,
may we do your will.

We pray for those affected by illness, pain or disability
of any kind
and ask that your healing and love
would surround them
and bring them peace.
We particularly think of those known to us, who need our prayers, including . . .
Lord, lead us,
may we do your will.

As we remember with love
those who have died,
we thank you for your promise
of a home in heaven
where everyone will be able to know
the joy of being in your presence
and worshipping you.
We particularly think of those who are missed at this time, including . . .
Lord, lead us,
may we do your will.

May our knowledge of your love for us grow,
enabling us to see others as people of worth.
May we also appreciate all you have given us,
so that we are empowered to be generous.
Amen.

Children's Prayer

Lord, you are so kind to us,
help us love others too.
Sharing what you've given,
we know it's all from you.
Amen.

Other Ideas!

Have some charity campaign or action cards for people to fill in, or a computer, phone or tablet already on the right site.

All-age Talk

Cut out some bunches of grapes from paper, and write on them things like 'doing a sponsored event for charity', 'tidying up litter', 'making friends with someone new', 'visiting someone who lives on their own', and other kind actions. You can also have some which are blank. Stick them around the church at a height that children can reach, using Blu Tack or something similar.

Talk about how in the Gospel reading today, Jesus explained how what we do is more important than what we say. The boy who had at first sounded like he was going to help his dad, saying the right things and promising that he would do some work for him, ended up being the one who did not actually do what his father wanted. At first the other boy sounded grumpy and didn't want to help, but he changed his mind and made the choice to do what was right, even though he did not really want to at the beginning.

Sometimes it is like this with us, too. Although, of course, ideally we would be a bit like both of those sons in the story – saying 'yes' to God and then going and doing the right thing straight away, Jesus shows us that it is our actions that are most important of all.

Ask a volunteer to be like that kind son who went and helped his father pick the grapes in the vineyard. Perhaps you have a basket that they can collect their paper grape bunches in.

As they bring them back to you, take out the grapes and read what is written on them. Jesus doesn't necessarily want us to be helpful by harvesting grapes – although sometimes helping with gardening and growing our own fruit and vegetables can be a very kind and useful thing to do. There are lots of things which God would like us to help with.

If people would like to, they can take one of the bunches of grapes to remind them of the actions we can take which make God happy. They might like to have one which has writing on already, or may like to have a blank one, so that they can think of their own ideas.

Children's Corner

Let the children play with child-sized dustpans and brushes, dusters and brooms. Leave a note asking for their help in making their area clean and tidy. They can listen out for two sons who were asked to do a helpful job. Was the son who said 'yes' actually the helpful son in the end? It's their cleaning that has made their space clean today, not whether they said yes or not.

The colouring sheet shows a young man helping in a vineyard, with lots of juicy grapes to colour, and the reference from the Gospel for them to look up and read later, Matthew 21:28-31.

Little Kids' Sunday School

Bring along a hat and some sticky labels. Write clearly, or draw if your children are young, a person or an object on the label, and stick it on the hat, making sure that the hat wearer can't see. They have to ask questions of the rest of the group to find out what is on their hat, but the questions can only have yes or no as an answer.

Tell the Gospel story for today. Once there was a man with two sons. The man called his sons over and asked them, 'Today, can you go and work in the vineyard?' (You can get some children to act this out.) One of the sons said, 'Yes! Of course I will!' The other son said, 'No. I don't want to.' Which of the sons is doing the right thing?

But over the course of the day, the first son just couldn't be bothered to get around to going to the vineyard. He hung around with his friends, he lay in the sun, he drank a nice drink and ate some nice lunch. The end of the day came, and he still hadn't gone to the vineyard after all.

The second son went to enjoy himself but got to thinking about his father's request. He didn't want to go to work in the vineyard that day, but he remembered all the things his father had done for him over the years, and changed his mind. He went to the vineyard, and worked hard, looking after the vines, digging the ground, doing watering. At the end of the day he was tired and dusty.

Which of the sons did as his father had asked? Was it the one who said 'yes' or the one who said 'no'? What mattered more – what they said, or what they did?

The children can use purple and green paint to make fingerprint bunches of grapes on small circles of paper. Give them an A4 piece of paper for them to draw a green vine on. They can take all these home, and whenever they find themselves doing something that God has asked them to do, they can stick one of their bunches of grapes onto the vine. As you fingerprint, you can talk about the kinds of things these might be.

Big Kids' Sunday School

Play the 'Yes/No' game. One child is chosen to be the interviewee, and the other children can take it in turns to ask them questions. The catch is that they can't say yes or no when they answer.

Have they been asked to do something, by their mum or dad, maybe, that they really don't want to do? If your mum says, 'Go and tidy your room!' are you tempted to sometimes say yes, and then go and lie on your bed watching YouTube instead? I think this dynamic isn't new, from what Jesus says in the story for today!

Get them to act out the story, in groups of three. One person is the father, asking his two sons to go and work in the vineyard today. One says, 'Yes of course', the other says, 'No, I don't want to.' Then the son who said 'yes' goes off and hangs out with his friends instead. And the son who said 'no' thinks for a bit and changes his mind. He decides to do as his father asks anyway. He goes off to the vineyard and works there all day, digging and watering and pruning.

Ask the questions: Which of the sons did the will of his father? What was most important, what they said or what they did?

Give each child a box of raisins. Pour out a glass for each of them of clear fizzy drink, but it's not snack time! They need to drop a few raisins into the glass. Make sure they ask the raisins to dance as they drop them in! The raisins are a bit like son number 2. They don't say 'yes' (well, who's ever heard a raisin talk?), and they drop to the bottom, but after a while they think better of it and look! they have decided to dance after all! The children can take home the rest of the raisins to repeat again later. They can look for times when they haven't wanted to do God's will, but have decided to after all, and smile as they remember the dancing raisins doing the same.

MATTHEW 21:28-31

BEARING GOOD FRUIT

Readings

- Isaiah 5:1-7
- Psalm 80:8-16
- Philippians 3:4b-14
- Matthew 21:33-46

Thoughts on the Readings

Both the reading from Isaiah, as well as today's psalm, describe Israel as the vineyard that God had planted. After clearing the land, God made sure that those vines were able to grow well, and flourish, with every opportunity to fruit in abundance. However, in both passages, the vineyard is not cared for or maintained, and is no longer productive or fruitful as it once was.

Jesus, and those who were listening to him, would have been familiar with the reading from Isaiah, as well as the psalm which we have heard. As Jesus described the vineyard which had been planted by the landowner, protected by a fence, and which had a wine press dug out in it ready to process the crop, this would have brought to mind the prophetic warning from Isaiah about the fate that would befall the vineyard which was not looked after properly. Those tenants had either kept the profit for themselves, or had not bothered to care for the grapevines and actually had very little to give the slaves when they came to collect the produce.

Of course, hearing Jesus' story from our perspective in history, we can see the parallel of the landowner sending his son, with God sending Jesus to us and him being rejected. The people who receive the kingdom of God will be those who actually produce its fruit – not those who thought that they were entitled to it because of some existing privilege.

Paul advises in his letter to the Philippians that the best thing to do is to focus on Jesus. This is how we can guard against our own lives falling into a state of disrepair. All the wonderful things which inside we just know instinctively are good, and from God, are nourishing and positive for us in our lives. As we make the effort to do this, everything else will fall into place, and our lives will produce good fruit, blessing others with that which comes from God.

Discussion Starters

- **What fruit can we see around us in unexpected places – places where God is at work?**

Intercessions

All through our lives
may we bear good fruit.

Lord, we come into your presence
knowing that we are in need
of your nourishing and your care.
As we look towards you,
strengthen us, and help us grow.

We give thanks for the church
and all those who help us
in our journey with you.
We pray that you would bless, refresh and guide
all church leaders,
that you would water us all with your Holy Spirit
and nourish us with your love.
All through our lives
may we bear good fruit.

We bring before you in prayer
the needs and challenges of our world.
We particularly pray for those communities
who fear that they have been forgotten,
under-resourced and neglected,
often leading to unrest, insecurity and conflict.
We pray for greater equity
in the sharing of resources and skills,
so that all are blessed.
All through our lives
may we bear good fruit.

We bring to mind those people
who are in need of prayer
and ask that your healing and loving arms
would surround them and reassure them now.
We bring before you anyone known to us,
including . . .
All through our lives
may we bear good fruit.

We remember before you
those who have died
and we thank you for the home in heaven
that is prepared for every one of us.
As they join in worshipping you,
may we be part of that praise.

We remember in your presence today . . .
**All through our lives
may we bear good fruit.**

Lord, we offer you all that we are
and all that we have.
May we bear good fruit
and show your glory.
Amen.

Children's Prayer

Dear Jesus, we are planted
in your garden, like a vine.
You water us with love
and you feed us with sunshine.
And as we grow and
    make good fruit,
we'll always look to you.
You give us everything
    we need
to live our lives for you.
Amen.

Other Ideas!

Bring along some juicy grapes of
different colours and display them
in a basket for people to try.

All-age Talk

Bring along a watering can (without any water
in it), some brown paper of some description
(or newspaper would be fine), a cardboard
box large enough for a small person to stand
inside, some large green leaves cut out from
paper, and a roll of tape.

Ask a small volunteer to come and help you.
They are going to be dressing up as a plant,
like one of the grapevines in our story today!
Can they climb in the box? Lovely!

What does our plant need to grow? We need to make sure that we are looking after it
properly. At the moment it does not have any good soil. Perhaps another volunteer could
crumple up some of the brown paper or newspaper, and place this in the box next to the plant.

The soil is like food for the plant. In our lives, God nourishes us with wise words from the Bible, in hymns and prayers, and from each other.

Next, ask someone to help 'water' the plant. This is like God watering us with his love and care, and the closeness that we feel to him when we spend time in prayer or look at the beautiful world around us.

Point up to the window or a light. The plant needs light to grow, to make it strong and stand up straight. In our lives, as we look towards Jesus and the way that he lived his life on earth, we are shown the way to live with love, kindness and understanding towards others, valuing them for who they are, rather than how rich and important they might be.

As your volunteer starts to grow, they sprout some leaves! Tape the green paper leaves onto their arms. What a great plant!

God has given us lots of wonderful things to help us grow in him. Like this lovely plant, we need to make the most of them, receive them and enjoy them, and that will give us what we need to live for his kingdom.

Children's Corner

Provide green ribbon, green scraps of cloth, and purple scraps of cloth so that the children can tie the green cloth onto the ribbon to be leaves, and the purple cloth onto the ribbon to be grapes, and then display their vine somewhere for everyone in church to see.

The colouring sheet shows a vine with lots of juicy grapes to colour, a watering can sprinkling water, the sun shining, and a fork sticking in the fertile soil. The writing reads, **'God gives us what we need to produce good fruit'**.

Little Kids' Sunday School

Put out a bowl of lengths of green wool, a bowl of pieces of purple fabric, and a bowl of pieces of green fabric. Give each bowl a number between 1-6. The children can pass a dice around, and when they roll a number that corresponds to one of the bowls, they can go and collect the object and tie it on to a group-made vine (the wool is the vine, the purple fabric is the grapes, the green fabric is the leaves). As time goes on, the vine will grow bigger and bigger.

What kinds of things do real vines need to grow? In the Isaiah reading today, we hear of a vineyard that has been made ready to grow grapes. Someone has collected up all the stones so that the soil is easy for the vines to grow in. Someone has dug the soil so that the roots can have plenty of space. Someone has chosen the best kinds of vines to plant and planted them. And yet when they went back to the vineyard to pick their grapes, they only found bad fruit.

God gives us all the good things we need to grow, but we need to use them. We need to make sure that we are producing good fruit in our lives, of love, kindness, patience, and peace.

The children can paint purple paint on bubble wrap in the shape of a bunch of grapes and use this to print grape pictures. They can paint on a green stalk for the grapes to hang off. When they take them home, it will remind them of how the grapes have grown through all the care the farmer gave them, and how we need to make sure we grow in love through all the love God gives us.

320

Big Kids' Sunday School

Pass around a green or purple balloon with a pump attached. The children can take it in turns to add a pump of air to the balloon as they say something that plants need to grow (light, air, not to be trodden on, well-prepared soil, water, nutrients). When the balloon is fully inflated, tie it off and put on another one. Pass it round and say something that animals need to grow, and then something that humans need to grow.

The Isaiah reading today begins by telling us of a vineyard, and all the work that has gone into growing the grapes. The stones have been collected from the soil. The soil had been dug. The very best vines were planted. And yet when it came to picking the grapes, there was only bad fruit. Get a pin and pop the green and purple balloons.

God gives us everything we need to grow. We need to choose to grow well, to live in a loving way, showing God's love to the world. The children can help you blow up lots of green and purple balloons, attaching them together with masking tape to make a giant cluster of grapes. They can write on them (carefully so they don't pop!) with permanent markers, so that the rest of the congregation can be reminded of some of the things God gives us to help us grow.

God gives us what we need to produce good fruit

INVITED TO GOD'S PARTY!

Readings

- Isaiah 25:1-9
- Psalm 23
- Philippians 4:1-9
- Matthew 22:1-14

Thoughts on the Readings

God is a refuge for those people who most need it. He is full of care and compassion. He will provide and bless, and will wipe away our tears. God's blessing and comfort are abundant. We will go through tough times, but God has promised that he will always be with us, accompanying us, guiding us, supporting us and strengthening us. And he has promised that at the end we will be blessed and provided for, more than we could imagine.

In the letter to the Philippians, we hear about some of those early Christians who had worked hard for the gospel. Paul tells us that things had not always been easy or straightforward for them, but the most important thing was that they kept going, standing in God's strength. Throughout our lives, in the tough bits as well as the easy bits, we are to bring everything in prayer to our loving, kind and compassionate God, who is always ready to listen to us. And by turning our thoughts towards the good things that come from God, it will become natural for us to be in the right frame of mind to receive his peace, whatever our circumstances.

Our Gospel reading for today is interesting and also challenging. Those first wedding guests were invited, reminded and encouraged to come, but for some reason were so wrapped up in what they wanted to do that they ended up behaving in a bizarre way, ignoring and laughing at the wonderful invitation from the king. The king then sends messengers out into the streets to gather up everyone there, so that the party is full. Not the great and the good, or those with status. Not those who know the right people, either. Most of them would not have ever attended an event like this before.

When we think about God's style of welcome, this challenges us to think about whether we are also doing this in our church. If God's idea of who is invited to the party is always so much wider than our own, who are we to exclude or judge anyone else?

Finally, we have the question of that wedding guest who was not wearing a robe. At first it might seem unfair that this person is sent out and punished – perhaps they could not afford the right clothes? But thinking about what we know of God, this cannot be the right way to understand the passage. It may be that Jesus was making the point that the invitation from God, to be part of his kingdom, is something wonderful and precious. It is not for us to take it lightly, or think that we can just enjoy the good things without paying any attention to whether we need to change ourselves. That act of taking off the old clothes and putting on a special wedding garment brings to mind the new start that we find through baptism, and whenever we come to God in prayer, asking forgiveness for the things which we know we need to change.

Discussion Starters

- **How can we pass on God's blessings to others in our community, in both practical and spiritual ways?**

Intercessions

**Lord, as we walk through life,
be with us.**

We thank you, dear Lord,
that you are with us,
whatever challenges we are faced with in life.
May we come before you now
and be comforted in your company.

We thank you for all those people
who have been welcomed in by our church
over the years.
We also thank you for all practical acts
of kindness and love
shown by Christian communities.
We pray that you would help us to listen to those
who live near the place where we worship,
so that we can help to provide what is needed
and show your love.
**Lord, as we walk through life,
be with us.**

We pray for our world,
particularly for communities
with little access to healthcare,
transport, communication and sanitation.
We pray that we would work together
and share what we have
to make the world a better place.
**Lord, as we walk through life,
be with us.**

As we bring before you those people
who are in any kind of illness or pain,
we pray that they would know your constant loving presence,

and that they would be encouraged by your love,
which gives the strength to carry on.
We name before you today . . .
**Lord, as we walk through life,
be with us.**

We thank you for the promise
of the abundant blessings and joy
which await us in heaven,
and think of those people
who have now passed from this life
to the next.
We remember before you . . .
**Lord, as we walk through life,
be with us.**

On our journey through life,
may we look to you,
may we follow you
and may we be encouraged
by being with you.
Amen.

Children's Prayer

Lord Jesus,
whether life is like
a grassy field with daisies,
a sharp and rocky slope,
a squelchy, muddy bog
or a forest of prickly bushes,
we know you are
    always with us
and we thank you
    for your love.
Amen.

Other Ideas!

Show a slideshow of paths
through different environments.

All-age Talk

Bring along a few packets of party food – e.g. some crisps, party ring biscuits and grapes. Put these in an ordinary looking box, along with some party poppers, streamers and balloons. If you can get a helium balloon, and fit this into your box, then so much the better!

Tell everyone that you have brought something special along today, in your box. Can they guess what it is? You can let people come up and listen to the box, hold it to see how heavy it is, shake it and smell it to see if they can guess.

Your listeners may or may not have guessed that inside this ordinary box . . . there is a party! Would anyone like to help open it?

As your small helper or helpers undo the box and take the things out, explain that this lovely party box was supposed to be for some really posh people, but for some reason they didn't want it. We don't mind, though, do we?!

Your helpers can share out the biscuits, and some bigger, sensible helpers can let off the party poppers.

This is like the story that Jesus told today. The king had invited lots of important people to his party, but they all said that they were too busy and did not want to come. Instead, he sent messengers out into the streets and they invited all the ordinary people along, to join in the fun and share the food!

It is like this with God's kingdom. He offers it to all of us. His idea of who is invited is always bigger than our own. As a church, we need to remember how kind and generous God has been to us, so that we can share these blessings with everyone around us.

Children's Corner

Set out a table with a tablecloth, decorations for the children to help put up, a toy tea set, and toy cakes and biscuits (or real ones if the children in your church tend to get hungry!). The children can play at being invited to a party, and listen out for the party the king is throwing in the Gospel reading.

The colouring sheet shows a table set out for a party, laden with all kinds of good things. The writing reads, **'Everyone is invited to God's party!'**

Little Kids' Sunday School

Play 'Musical Bumps': put some music on and when it stops you have to sit down on the floor. Whoever is last on the floor is out.

Do you feel like you're having a party yet? Have you ever got an invitation to a party? It's exciting, and something you can really look forward to. In this story from Jesus, a king was throwing a party. That would be really something, wouldn't it? It would make our party game look a little low key. He had prepared his party and sent out the invitations, but all the people he'd invited somehow couldn't be bothered to come. They went off to their field, or off to their business. And when it was the day of the party,

nobody turned up at all. The king didn't want a party with nobody there, so he sent invitations out to everyone in the street. All the common, ordinary people who would never end up at a king's party. And they came and the party room was filled with people having fun.

Show a crown and ask: Who do you think the king is in this story? Show a party invitation. Who do you think the people are who didn't want to come? Show another party invitation. Who do you think the other people are who got invited? Who are you in this story?

The children can make their own party hats by cutting a circle in thin coloured card, cutting up to the centre, and rolling it into a cone. They can tape it along the edge, and staple some elastic to the edge to hold it under their chin. Their hat can be decorated with pompoms and stickers. When they wear their hats, they can remember how they and everyone are invited to God's party.

Big Kids' Sunday School

Count around the circle. Any number that is a multiple of three, you replace with jazz hands and shout PARTY! Any number that is a multiple of five, you replace with dancing hands and shout DISCO! If a number is a multiple of three and five, you have to do both.

Open up a glitzy-looking party invitation. You can read it out to them. It's an invitation from the king inviting you to a party at the palace! Who would be crazy enough to turn that down? Well, Jesus told a story about a king who was throwing a party. He sent invitations all around, but nobody he had invited could be bothered to come. The day of the party came, and his room was empty. So he sent his servants out, to invite in all the ordinary people off the streets, the people who would never normally go to a king's party. And in they all came, to enjoy the food and the party atmosphere.

Who do they think the king is in this story? Who are the people who turned down the invitation? Who are the people who came? Who would you be in this story? Why do they think Jesus told it?

The children can make party blowers that read, 'Everyone is invited!' Use wide straws cut in half, and rectangles cut from a magazine. Fold the rectangle in thirds lengthways, and tape it along where the two sides meet. Fold over one end and tape that too. Make sure it's all well taped down so no air can get out. Write 'Everyone is invited!' in permanent marker along your paper strip. Now, starting from the taped-up end, you need to wrap it round and round a pencil, as tightly as you can. Let it uncoil, then do that again. Now try wrapping it up round and round without the pencil there. You might like to hold it with an elastic band at this point to keep the curl in. Insert the half straw into the open end and tape it all down, again making sure it's all airtight. Then take off the elastic band and blow!

ALL THINGS BELONG TO OUR CREATOR GOD

Readings

- Isaiah 45:1-7
- Psalm 96:1-9 (10-13)
- 1 Thessalonians 1:1-10
- Matthew 22:15-22

Thoughts on the Readings

In the reading from Isaiah, we hear of the power and strength of God. He has made all things on earth and in heaven, and will break down those barriers that are in the way, so that we can live and work for his kingdom. It is not because of anything that we have done, that God helps us like this. It is just because this is his nature, and he loves us.

Today's psalm speaks of the majesty and greatness of God. More powerful than any other king, not only has he established the earth and created all the things on it, but everything, even including the landscape itself, will praise him. Over history, the physical landscape of mountains, trees, rocks and the sea has been seen as something that is just there, to be used and exploited by people, bringing economic growth. However, if we start to see our surroundings in this ancient and biblical way, as part of God's creation, made to praise and worship him, perhaps this will lead us to see things in a different light.

As we think of this, that all the earth is God's, the Gospel reading for today is put in perspective. Coins and money are only a small part of the wonderful wealth of creation, both on earth and in the heavens. If the emperor demanded those pieces of round metal, putting his name and face on them as if he owned them, that was, of course, a way of controlling the people whom he ruled. But taking the long view, it did not matter who held those coins in their hands. The metal itself still belonged to God. We may well have seen Roman coins in a museum, or might be lucky enough to own one. All these years on, those coins are interesting to look at, but we would certainly not consider that they still gave power to the emperor now. Being influential and rich cannot stop someone being mortal.

From the beginning of time, God has been there and his wonderful creativity has resulted in the beautiful world that we can see. When we look up into the sky, the stars which are visible are only a fraction of those which are actually there. All this was made by God, belongs to him, and is loved by him.

Discussion Starters

- Tax, politics and power are important subjects, but can also cause division. Can a long-term view of God's majesty help us to work together better?

Intercessions

**Lord, together with your creation,
we worship you.**

We come into your holy presence
in awe of your wonderful creation
and are thankful for the way
you care for every one of us.

We bring before you our church,
that you would help us
to use the resources we have
in a wise and compassionate way,
always remembering
that everything we have
comes from you.
**Lord, together with your creation,
we worship you.**

We thank you for our beautiful world,
for the sea, the mountains and the sky.
We also thank you for the enormity
of the universe
and the wonder and diversity
of your creation.
We pray that you would help us
to treat it with care and respect.
**Lord, together with your creation,
we worship you.**

As we come into your presence,
we bring before you anyone in need,
including those who do not have access
to essential items which we take for granted.
Help us to share what we have
to bring equity among your people.
We pray for anyone who is in pain
or who is exhausted by illness or disability.
Surround them with your generous love and healing.
We name before you . . .
**Lord, together with your creation,
we worship you.**

We remember with love
those who have died
and think of them worshipping you
in heaven, as part of your creation.

We pray for those people who have lost someone close to them
and name before you those people known to us
who are now with you, including . . .
**Lord, together with your creation,
we worship you.**

Lord, open our eyes
to see the glory and wonder
of your creation,
so that we may be encouraged and inspired
to worship you.
Amen.

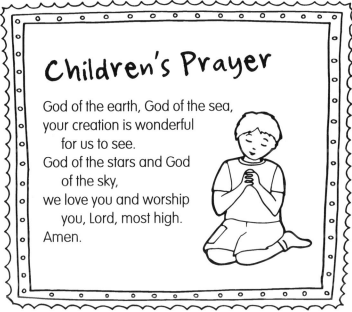

Children's Prayer

God of the earth, God of the sea,
your creation is wonderful
    for us to see.
God of the stars and God
    of the sky,
we love you and worship
    you, Lord, most high.
Amen.

Other Ideas!

Display some old coins (real or replica) for people to look at.

All-age Talk

Bring along a few bags or old wallets with low denomination or foreign coins in them, enough for one for each person in the congregation.

As you pass these around, ask everyone to take a coin, and hold it in their hand. Can anyone remember what the question was that somebody asked Jesus in the reading today? Yes – and Jesus answered it by bringing out a coin.

Ask people what they can see on their coin – has anyone got a picture of a king or queen? Are there any other interesting things on the coins? What about the colour and the metal?

Most of the time, the value of the metal in the coins is less that what the coin is worth itself. This is because they are a way of showing how money moves from one place to another, rather than actually being worth a lot themselves. They show trust in a financial system, and in the people who are in charge of the country. Without that, the coins would not be worth anything.

Jesus told his listeners to give to the emperor what belongs to the emperor, and give to God the things that are God's. Those coins which we are holding are useful for making transactions at the time we are living in. But the metal which they are made from is part of a much more ancient earth, and will go back to being part of that long after we have gone.

This ancient earth, and the beautiful sky and stars around us, are what belong to God. Everything he has made, the sea, the mountains, the rocky cliffs and the grassy plains, all belong to him. We too, are part of his creation. We can offer ourselves to God – our skills and talents, our experiences, the things we don't think we are good at and the things we are proud of – because all these things come from him.

Children's Corner

Allow the children to handle a variety of old or foreign coins. Don't bring precious ones that you'll worry they'll lose, but most people seem to have a handful or two of coins they'll never spend, lurking in the back of a drawer somewhere. Tape a picture of the world to the top of the table or the floor, using masking tape. The children can lay the coins out over this, listening for what Jesus has to say about money in the Gospel.

The colouring sheet has 'coins' drawn on it, with pictures of things that are valuable on them: the stars, the sun, flowers and mountains, people's faces, animals, rain and a rainbow. The writing reads, **'Give to God what belongs to God'**.

Little Kids' Sunday School

Play 'Queenie, Queenie, Who's Got the Ball?' The children stand in a line facing one child at the front who has their back to them. The child at the front throws a ball backwards over their shoulder, and one child picks it up. All the children put their hands behind their backs as if they are holding the ball, and Queenie has to guess who it is.

In the time of Jesus, the country was ruled not by Queenie here, but by the Roman emperor. The Romans had invaded and now they said the country belonged to them. And not just the country, but lots of things in it. Some people trying to make Jesus sound silly thought they would ask him a tricky question in public. A question he couldn't answer without getting in trouble with half of the listeners. 'Tell us,' they said, 'should we pay the tax to the emperor or not?'

Jesus asked someone to bring him a coin. Pull a coin out of your pocket. He asked them, 'Whose head is on this coin?' Have a look at your coin. It's the Queen's head on there, isn't it? They would have had the Roman emperor's head on theirs. 'So, give to the emperor what belongs to the emperor', said Jesus. 'But give to God what belongs to God!'

Can the children think of some things that belong to God? We could keep going all day! It would be a very long list. Even the coin in your hand is made out of metal, mined from deep inside the earth, part of God's creation.

The children can draw round their two hands and cut them out. They can stick them on another piece of thin card, by the wrists, so that they stick out of the page. On one they can draw a coin with a king's head on it. On the other they can draw all the things that God has given them. On the thin cardboard base, they can write, 'Give to God what belongs to God'. As they draw, they can imagine offering all these things to God.

Big Kids' Sunday School

Give the children stickers to be price labels, and send them off outside to put a price label on whatever they like. They might choose to make some natural models of mountains/seas and label them, too. Walk around your 'shop' and price up your purchases.

Well, that's all a bit silly, isn't it? You can't buy the daisies, or the leaves, or the sky. In the time of Jesus, the country was occupied by the Roman army. They had invaded and now claimed it as belonging to them. The land. A share of the crops on the land. A share of the money anyone made. Some people decided to try to show Jesus up by asking him a trick question. 'Should we pay taxes to the emperor or not?' Jesus asked someone to pass him a coin. 'Whose face is this?' he asked. 'The emperor's', they answered. 'Then, give to the emperor what belongs to the emperor, but give to God what belongs to God!'

What does Jesus mean by this? Does our shop activity at the start give you any clues? It's not just the occupying Roman army that wanted to own and control things that weren't theirs. We all do this, to some extent. Because at the end of the day, everything belongs to God. The planet is not ours to plunder as we wish, but to cherish and care for as a gift that God has given us, not just to live on, but to live as part of.

Make cake-pops by squidging up old cake leftovers (cake shops will often let you have these for free or for a small fee) with icing, moulding them into balls, and sticking them on cut-up skewers. Dip these in melted white chocolate with blue food colouring and stand to set. A fridge will speed things up. Roll out green icing and cut out the shapes of continents. Stick these to the blue cake-pops so that they look like our planet. Give these out after church to remind everyone that if we want to follow Jesus, and give to God what belongs to God, that means caring for the world we live in, and not exploiting it for a quick profit.

GIVE TO GOD
WHAT BELONGS TO GOD

LOVE GOD, LOVE YOUR NEIGHBOUR

Readings

- Leviticus 19:1-2, 15-18
- Psalm 1
- 1 Thessalonians 2:1-8
- Matthew 22:34-46

Thoughts on the Readings

Leviticus is really fascinating. In the middle of ancient laws relating to a society very different to our own, we find this key message of kindness, forgiveness and compassion – 'Love your neighbour as yourself.' This is something that has stood the test of time, through different periods of history, times of hardship and plenty, times of peace and of conflict.

Psalm 1 also reminds us of the groundedness which comes from obeying God's law of love. If we use this as the basis for our decisions, our relationships and our actions, we will be supported by God's strength and nourished by him in all that we do. We can live our lives in a way which is tuned in with his kingdom and his values.

Jesus knew the Scriptures well, and when he was asked which was the greatest law of all, he knew the one that stood out above all the others. This was not a rule about family or personal relationships, health and safety or food hygiene, cleanliness or trading regulations. (These are described in detail in the surrounding passage of Scripture in our Old Testament reading.) Straight away, Jesus identified the law which underpins all others – to love God, and to love our neighbour.

God has given us enough intelligence to work out what this means for us in our own circumstances, our own society and community, and in our own church. Within this law, we can agree the rules which we need to make this work.

The reading from 1 Thessalonians describes how the early Christians were putting this love into practice. Caring for each other, with gentleness, like a mother cares for her own children. As a church family, we have this opportunity to love and care for each other, and be open and welcoming to all those around us.

Loving God helps us to love our neighbour, and in loving our neighbour, we draw close to God.

Discussion Starters

- **Which rules in our church show love towards God and our neighbour?**

Intercessions

**Lord, may we love each other
as you have loved us.**

As we come into your presence,
knowing that you love us,
may this guide and inspire us
in all that we do.

We give thanks for our church
and for those worshipping communities
who are our neighbours.
We pray that as we speak to others
and work together,
your law of love would unite us
in our aim to work towards
the common good.
**Lord, may we love each other
as you have loved us.**

We pray for our world
and particularly bring before you
any situations where rules have caused
exclusion, division and suffering.
We pray that those in power
would focus on your law of love.
**Lord, may we love each other
as you have loved us.**

We bring to mind anyone
who is finding life tough,
those who feel that they do not fit in
and anyone who is discriminated against or excluded
from participating fully in the society in which they live.
We also pray for anyone
who is weary with suffering or pain,
and those who feel alone.
We bring into your loving care . . .
**Lord, may we love each other
as you have loved us.**

We remember before you
those who have died
and are now at peace with you
in heaven, where your love reigns
for eternity.
We name before you today . . .
**Lord, may we love each other
as you have loved us.**

Fill us so much with your love, dear Lord,
that those people we speak to
will see something of you.
Help us to make choices based on
kindness and compassion,
as we treasure your law in our hearts.
Amen.

Children's Prayer

Lord, we love you,
help us to show love.
Lord, you are kind to us,
help us to be kind.
Lord, you care for us,
help us to be caring too.
Amen.

Other Ideas!

Place some tea lights (real
or the LED version) in a heart
shape. In the middle, put
a heart-shaped card with
the words 'Love God with
all your heart, and love your
neighbour as yourself.'

All-age Talk

Cover a large book (such as a dictionary) with brown paper, so that the cover is plain. Write the words 'All the Rules' on the front. Fold a piece of pink or red paper into eight, and cut out a heart shape from this. On each of the hearts, write the words 'Love God with all your heart, and love your neighbour as yourself', and place these inside the book.

Show everyone the book. Big, isn't it? Looks like there are a lot of rules in there.

Open the book (carefully, so that the hearts do not fall out) and pretend to read some of the rules out. 'Say please and thank you', 'Don't slam the door', 'Don't drop litter', 'Don't push or thump people', 'Wipe your feet if they are muddy', 'Put the rubbish in the right bin' etc.

Hmmm, there are a lot of rules that we are supposed to follow. It's hard to remember them all, isn't it? And all the time, there are new things invented which need new rules to go with them. 'Don't hide the charger', 'Don't spend too much money online', 'Don't say nasty things on social media'.

But thankfully, God has given us one good law which covers everything!

Ask a volunteer to come and hold the book up high and shake out the hearts. What do they say? 'Love God with all your heart, and love your neighbour as yourself.' This sums it all up. If we are always thinking about the kind way to act and speak, about how we can care for others, we will be showing love to them as well as to God. And if we love God with all our heart, this will mean that we want to look after and care for the beautiful world that he has made for us to live in as well.

Children's Corner

Cut two large overlapping hearts out of paper, and give the children pink and red chalks and crayons to scribble over them with. Their parents and carers can draw on ways they love God and love their neighbour, and the children can 'draw' what they talk about, too.

The colouring sheet has two overlapping hearts, one filled with ways in which we show our love to God, and one filled with ways in which we show our love to our neighbour. The writing reads, **'Love God, love your neighbour'**.

Little Kids' Sunday School

Play 'In and out the dusty bluebells' but sing, 'Love God and love your neighbour' as the words instead.

There are a lot of rules in the Bible, in the Old Testament. Hundreds of rules. There were people whose job it was to know all the rules and make sure people followed them correctly. They tried to trick Jesus by asking him, 'What is the most important rule?'

Jesus answered them by quoting the Scriptures back at them, 'Love the Lord your God with all your heart, and with all your soul, and with all your mind, and love your neighbour as yourself. All the other rules hang off these.'

The children can make mobiles using a coat hanger. Tie a piece of thread to each end, and attach a cardboard square to each, reading 'Love God' and 'Love your neighbour'. The children can write some of the other rules we have, like say grace before meals, don't say mean things, pick up litter, be gentle. They can hang these off one or other of those two most important laws.

Big Kids' Sunday School

Write out some rules – rules from the Bible, rules from the Green Cross Code, rules from Sunday school, rules from parliament. Get the children to put them in order from most to least important.

What a job! And there are so many rules and laws out there. However can we put them all in order?

The Pharisees, the teachers of the law, had a tricky question to put to Jesus. They wanted to ask a question that would show him up. 'Teacher, which is the greatest commandment in the law?' they asked. How could Jesus answer without missing out something important?

What might you answer?

Jesus quoted the Scriptures back at them. 'Love the Lord your God with all your heart, and with all your soul, and with all your mind, and love your neighbour as yourself. All the other rules hang off these.'

Have a look at some of these rules from earlier. Is that true? Can we trace all good rules back to these two rules?

Give each child two pieces of origami paper, and follow instructions online to fold an origami heart. They can write 'Love God' on one, and 'Love your neighbour' on the other.

GOD'S SAINTS

Readings

- Revelation 7:9-17
- Psalm 34:1-10
- 1 John 3:1-3
- Matthew 5:1-12

Thoughts on the Readings

The reading from Revelation and the psalm for today both give a wonderful picture of the rescuing goodness of God for those who follow him. Although life might not always be easy or straightforward for those who set their hearts on doing God's will, he will never leave them and will protect them and look after them.

Jesus' famous sermon tells us of the blessings that God has in store for those whose lives reflect him – the peace makers, those who hunger and thirst for righteousness, the pure in heart, the merciful, those who mourn, the meek, and those who are 'poor in spirit'. There is certainly no guarantee that they will escape problems and suffering – in fact it is the opposite. But God will be with them through all of this, providing his grace, strength and joy in abundance, and preparing a reward in heaven for them.

This should make us think twice when we hear religious teaching promising that our problems will be taken away, that blessings will come in the form of material wealth, or that we will never face hardship or opposition. Jesus promised nothing of the sort.

In the reading from 1 John, we also hear those comforting words about how we are children of God, part of his family. The rest of the world might not understand, or might be hostile towards our values and actions, but the message that Jesus gave to the world was one that was challenging and radical to many people too.

This is the example that was shown to us by the saints, both the 'official' ones and those Christians who have inspired us with their faith, their words and their actions. Their priority was to serve God, far more than their own fame, wealth, success or popularity. As we remember and honour these saints today, we look to God to guide us, lead us and teach us as we travel through our own lives, too.

Discussion Starters

- **If you could nominate someone to be a saint, who would it be?**

Intercessions

**As we look towards you,
may we reflect your love.**

Inspired by the example of the saints who came before us
we come into your presence in prayer,
opening our hearts to your will.

We thank you for those saints and holy people
throughout history
who have helped the church to grow
in faith, understanding and in numbers
and for those whose steadfastness
is an inspiration to us all.
We also thank you for all those people
within the church across the world
whose faith shines out,
showing your love.
**As we look towards you,
may we reflect your love.**

We thank you for the world in which we live
and for all the things which have changed for the better
because of people who have been brave enough
to make a difference.
We pray that you would give us strength, too,
to stand up for justice and peace
and to speak out for the care of the world
and all who live in it.
**As we look towards you,
may we reflect your love.**

We bring into your healing presence
all those who live with long-term physical or mental illness
and those who daily face the challenges
of disability or limited mobility.
We pray that you would surround them
with the strength that you have promised to all of us.
We name before you in prayer today . . .
**As we look towards you,
may we reflect your love.**

We give thanks for those
whose shining and saintly lives of love have inspired us
and for those whose ordinary acts of simple kindness
have made a difference to ourselves and to others.

We remember before you
those known to us who have died, including . . .
**As we look towards you,
may we reflect your love.**

As we look towards you,
nourish us with your presence,
comfort us with your peace
and fill us with your love.
Amen.

Children's Prayer

Lord, to live for you like the saints,
we don't need to be clever,
    talented or famous.
In fact, you just want us
    to be ourselves,
blessing others
    with kindness.
Amen.

Other Ideas!

Print and cut out some pictures of
saints, and other people who have
inspired us with the way their faith
has shaped their lives. Provide
some larger squares of card, and
some glue sticks, so that people
can choose a picture of a person
who inspires them, and 'frame' it
to take home.

All-age Talk

Bring along some dressing-up costumes
or accessories, and ask some children to
come and try them on or hold them. These
might be things like a crown, a princess
outfit, a first-aid kit, a pad of paper and
pens, and a bowl or saucepan with a
wooden spoon.

Ask the children to line up and say what
they think their job might be.

But all these people have got something
in common! It might be that they all like chocolate, or playing games (is that right?) but there is
something else as well.

Today we think about all the people who have given their lives to God, to serve him
and to show his love to others. Some of them were kings, some princesses. Some were
doctors or helped care for people who were ill. Some were writers, and others cooked and

made food for people who were in need. Other saints did all sorts of other interesting and different things.

Whatever we are able to offer, whatever skills we have, God can use.

We don't need to be famous, we don't need to be clever, and we don't need to be in charge of things. All we need to do to live godly lives like those saints is to humbly listen to God, to treat others with kindness and gentleness, and to speak out for what is right. And God will help us with all of this.

Children's Corner

Provide a light box (sometimes people have these with letters to put on them to use as a sign in their house) and some coloured plastic shapes, or those glass nuggets people use in flower arranging. The children can enjoy arranging these over the glowing light box, and seeing how the light shines through them.

The colouring sheet shows framed pictures of some famous saints, alongside 'St Margaret who helps her neighbours', 'St Osama who encourages people', and 'St Tyreece who tries his best'.

Little Kids' Sunday School

Thread ring doughnuts on a string to be halos, and get the children to eat them with their hands behind their back.

Today we are remembering all those people we see in pictures with halos behind their heads. The people who look like they have a doughnut balanced on their head. It's just the way that the artist tried to show that they were holy. Not holey like our doughnuts with a hole in the middle, but shining with God's love and light.

Share pictures of some saints with the children, giving some of their story and why we remember them so many years later. You can share some photos of old members of your church, too, maybe even some that the older children will remember. Make sure that they know that these people too were shining with God's love and light, even if we can't see the halo.

Have one headband per child and a pack of gold and silver pipe cleaners. Help the children to twist a pipe cleaner at the top of the headband, and attach another pipe cleaner, until you've got enough to bend it into a halo. They can wear their halos into church to remind the rest of the congregation that we are all called to be saints.

Big Kids' Sunday School

Cut a large orange pumpkin out of paper, and two eyes and a grin out of bright yellow paper. Put sticky tack on the back of these, and blindfold one child at a time to come and pin the face on the pumpkin.

Today we're remembering all those people who shone with God's love and light in our world through all the years past. Can the children think of any saints they know about? How long a list can you come up with? Do they know any stories of why these saints are remembered? What about people who we don't call saints, but have shone brightly in their lives? You may have a story about someone whose faith was inspiring to you, someone who is now dead, but alive in heavenly glory with Jesus. It's good for the children to hear stories of ordinary people and the effect they can have on the world, as well as the extraordinary famous people.

Under careful supervision, allow the children to carve some pumpkins. They'll be fine with one between several of them as there's plenty to do. Cut off the top, and scoop out all the seeds. Scoop out some flesh and save this for pumpkin soup when you get home! They can work together to design a pumpkin that shines in the darkness, like the saints did, shining in the darkness of our world.

GOD'S TRUTH

Readings

- Micah 3:5-12
- Psalm 43
- 1 Thessalonians 2:9-13
- Matthew 24:1-14

Thoughts on the Readings

Micah the prophet speaks out against those who only say what people want to hear. This must have been something that was quite common then, as now – bringing short-term popularity but nothing but trouble in the long term, as it distracts people's focus from looking towards God, and what is true and right. This may be a more difficult message to receive, but through listening and changing in response to God's words and wisdom, a whole heaven's worth of blessing is open to us.

In today's psalm, too, the sadness caused by injustice and lies is acknowledged. The words in the psalm call out to God for his truth, light and protection – the most precious gift of all.

If we hear God's words, receive his truth and light, this will lead us to want to live in the right way – with kindness, integrity, honesty, faithfulness, respectfulness and transparency. Our lives give credibility to the Gospel message. We may not always get everything right, but if we recognise this and live with God's values, then others will know that we do mean what we say. The reading from 1 Thessalonians describes how Paul and his friends are confident that they have done their best to act with integrity.

In today's Gospel reading Jesus also warns about false prophets, claiming all sorts of things for themselves. This leads us to wonder what are those messages around us which lead people away from God. Messages which claim greatness or authority; messages telling of an easier or more prosperous life, without thought for others; messages which excuse selfish or damaging lifestyles. These are the things which we need to watch out for. By focusing on Jesus, his message and the actions in his life, we will be more and more able to assess and understand when there are other ways of thinking which are just not right. His strength and comfort will get us through the most difficult times and in the end, God's kingdom will prevail.

Discussion Starters

- **What messages around us – in advertising, in the media – can distract us from God's truth?**

Intercessions

**Holy God,
lead us in your truth.**

Lord, as we come into your holy presence,
may we open our eyes to your holiness
and be ready to hear the words
that you have to say to us.

We give thanks for our church
and the worldwide community of people of faith,
of which we are a part.
We pray for all those who lead us in worship,
for those who study and write about faith
and for those who enable and encourage others
in their ministry.
We pray that your truth and integrity
would be a hallmark of all that we do as a church,
underpinned by love.
**Holy God,
lead us in your truth.**

We pray for the world in which we live,
that you would shed your light on those situations
where honesty and accountability are in short supply
and those who have the least power
are the ones who pay the price.
We pray that all political and economic leaders
would act according to your values
for the common good.
**Holy God,
lead us in your truth.**

We bring into your loving care
anyone who is suffering in any way;
those who are waiting for results of tests and screening,
those who are waiting for medical appointments,
those who are waiting for a cure.
We pray that you would strengthen and encourage them
with your hope and love.
We bring before you today . . .
**Holy God,
lead us in your truth.**

Surround with your love
anyone who is nearing the end of their life's journey,
whether this is long or short,
and comfort those who love them.

We also remember those who have died
and now know the fullness of your promise of heaven.
We particularly remember today . . .
Holy God,
lead us in your truth.

We give thanks that you have promised
to be with us, whatever happens in life.
We put our trust in you.
Amen.

Children's Prayer

Jesus, we want to know your truth,
Jesus, we want to know your love,
Jesus, we want to live your way.
Amen.

Other Ideas!

Collect together some of the messages which bombard us through advertising – perhaps cut out of magazines. Arrange these on one side of a noticeboard, poster or table. On the other side, on some attractive paper, write God's values on them – truthfulness, integrity, honesty, compassion, care, peace-making etc.

All-age Talk

Prepare beforehand some advertising posters on large pieces of paper. These don't have to be complicated – just writing with thick black pen or crayon would be fine:

'Lilies and Roses Shower Gel – use this and all your day will be beautiful!'

'Long Lash Mascara – wear this and you will be glamorous all day long!'

'Super juice – to be super healthy'

'Buy our special Yorkshire Puddings and all your family will want to spend time together'

'If you buy this new car then you will be really popular'

Also prepare some cards with those qualities which are God's values on them. Decorate these with some gold stars or stickers:

Trustworthiness

Resilience

Patience

Truth

Integrity

Honesty

Love

Kindness

Honesty

Ask a volunteer to hold up your adverts, one by one, and someone else to read them out. Would anyone like to buy any of these things? We are surrounded by advertisements like this every day (ok, with a slightly larger budget behind them than these ones!) and we become so used to them that they seem normal.

But when we think about what they are offering along with the product, we realise that these are treasures that money actually can't buy. Having good relationships with your family won't be achieved by buying Yorkshire puddings, and good friends are not dependent on having this or that car – they will want to spend time with you anyway.

Our readings today talk about the false prophets who only told people the messages that they wanted to hear, a bit like the adverts that we see today.

God says that we don't need to listen to them. Those messages might make us feel better for a little while, but they won't help us in the long run.

Now put away the paper adverts and ask someone to hold the cards with God's values on them. Explain that God has a message for us that is much deeper, will last longer, is real and makes a difference to us. These are the things which God tells us are important, the things which are part of his character, and the things which he can give us in our lives.

Children's Corner

Tape black paper over a table, and splodge a few blobs of bright yellow paint on top of them. Lay out some paintbrushes, so that the children can spread this all over the dark paper. They can listen out for people holding on to hope in dark places throughout the Bible readings this Sunday as they paint.

The colouring sheet shows a weary traveller on a path leading to a mountain. They are coming from a dark forest, and light beams are shining down the path onto them as they climb. The writing reads, **'Send me your light and your faithful care, let them lead me; let them bring me to your holy mountain, to the place where you dwell. Psalm 43:3'**.

Little Kids' Sunday School

One of the leaders crouches down into a small ball on the floor. The children can take it in turns to come up to them and tap them on the shoulder. Eventually, sometimes sooner, sometimes later, the leader jumps up and roars like a bear, and chases all the children. Then you can do it again!

That was a scary game to play first thing today! When that bear jumped up and roared it made us jump too! Playing at being scared can be fun. But being scared for real isn't fun at all. Have a dark-coloured bag and pull some things out of it that people might be scared of: maybe a plastic spider, a cuddly dog, a compass for people who are scared of getting lost, a pair of ear defenders for people who are scared of loud noises, a toy gun for people who are scared of wars. And sometimes we're right to be scared. Some of those things are pretty horrible. In our Gospel reading today Jesus said that bad things will happen. They always do. But we mustn't be frightened because he has promised that he will be with us and save us.

The children can make nightlights from those old polystyrene cups you've had hanging around since someone bought them for a church function, and you couldn't bear to throw them out and add to the plastic bobbing around in the sea, so you washed them up and now they're a bit icky to drink from. Give the children a toothpick each and let them poke holes in their cups. Pop the cups upside down over a battery-powered tea light, and the comforting glow of the nightlight will remind them that God has promised to keep us safe, no matter how scary life seems.

Big Kids' Sunday School

Give the children some real news headlines and some fake news headlines. Can they sort them into real and fake news? What makes this difficult? How can we be sure about the stuff we read and hear?

Fake news isn't new. Jesus' friends were worried about the future. They asked him if all the bad things happening meant that it was nearly the end of the world. Jesus told them that lots of bad things will happen, but they don't need to be afraid because God will keep them safe. Jesus also told them that when times are hard, people appear saying things that aren't true. Sometimes it can be hard to pick out the things that are true from the things that are fake news. Sometimes the fake news can feel like a more comforting or a more hopeful truth.

What kinds of 'false prophets' do we hear in our lives? Adverts telling us that if we look this way, if we buy this thing, then we'll be happy? Politicians telling us that the reason our life feels hard is the fault of these people, or those people, and that if we can get rid of them, our lives will suddenly be easier? Social media telling us that everyone else is happy all the time and that their family lives are perfect? The news telling us that one thing is important, when there are other pressing and important issues of the day that just aren't being covered?

What can we use to judge if things are true or not?

Make some red cabbage litmus water, by grating red cabbage and adding a little water. Squish it about with a wooden spoon, and then sieve it to get the purple liquid out. Decant this into several cups, and give the children some liquids to experiment with. They'll find that an acidic liquid like lemon juice or vinegar turns the purple litmus water pink. If they add soap solution or bicarbonate of soda, it will turn the liquid blue. This litmus water is a bit like how we use the Bible, our community of Christians, and the Holy Spirit in our lives to test whether something is good and from God, or not. As soon as we measure it against God's rule of love, we can see if it matches up or not, just as some substances caused the litmus water to change colour.

SHINING GOD'S LIGHT IN THE WORLD

Readings

- Amos 5:18-24
- Psalm 70
- 1 Thessalonians 4:13-18
- Matthew 25:1-13

Thoughts on the Readings

It's not about the quality of the music, how well maintained the building is, how well read and clear the prayers are. It's not about how much money comes in through donations, either. It's not about having a carefully constructed sermon, based on well-respected arguments from sensible-looking books. God makes it absolutely clear in our reading from Amos this morning. What is much more important is that we work for justice and fairness for everyone. The worship will then follow on from this, but if our attitude is not right then there is no point going through the motions of religious activity. We need to be ready for the day of God's judgement in every way, so that these good things become a habit.

Our New Testament readings also remind us of this. As Jesus tells the story of the ten bridesmaids to warn us always to be ready, this makes us wonder about what this means for us. Of course, we want to be like the sensible bridesmaids, with their spare oil, just in case. Perhaps for us, that spare oil is the good habits we get into, so that they become a part of normal life. The habit of spending time in prayer with God – not just to ask for things but really to listen and be ready to offer up all the things in our lives, ready to change those things which we come to realise are not holy. The habit of acting with kindness, honesty, generosity and integrity. The habit of making choices which help bring about justice and fairness for other people and for the planet we live on.

And this makes sense, too. If we really want to live as part of God's kingdom, and let his love transform our lives through and through, this will be shown in our words and actions. Then those around us will see what God can do.

Discussion Starters

- How can we, as a church, work for justice both locally and globally?

Intercessions

God of righteousness and justice,
we offer our lives to you.

We come into your presence,
wanting to be with you
and to grow closer to you.
We pray that you would help us
to align our lives and our values
with your own.

We give thanks for our own community
in which we worship
and pray that you would help us,
guide us and strengthen us
as we take action to fight poverty,
injustice and inequality
and try to live respectfully and responsibly
on our beautiful earth.
God of righteousness and justice,
we offer our lives to you.

We pray for our world,
that you would bring justice and peace
where there is violence, poverty and conflict,
and that you would show us
where we can make a difference.
We also pray that your love and generosity
would bring freedom from materialism and greed,
offering an alternative, real and satisfying way of living.
God of righteousness and justice,
we offer our lives to you.

We bring before you
those who are not able
to be as active or mobile as they would like
and who would love to help others in practical ways.
We pray that you would show them their value
and worth in your eyes,
so that they can be refreshed and strengthened
in your loving presence.
We pray too, that your healing love would surround those
who are in need today, and bring before you now . . .
God of righteousness and justice,
we offer our lives to you.

We remember before you
those who now dwell in heaven,
having completed their journey through life,
and pray that you would bring peace and comfort
to their families and friends.
We remember in your presence today . . .
God of righteousness and justice,
we offer our lives to you.

Be with us, dear Lord,
all through our lives.
We pray that you would lead us
in your good way of righteousness.
Amen.

Children's Prayer

Dear God,
we will be ready
with our lamps burning bright,
full of joyfulness and
        kindness,
so that we can do
        what's right.
Amen.

Other Ideas!

Make an arrangement of tea
lights in jam-jars (or LED tea lights)
with a Bible open at today's
Gospel reading.

All-age Talk

Bring along two large jam-jars and two
LED tea lights (alternatively a packet of
glowsticks will work).

Also bring along some yellow tissue
paper and some thick black paper or card.

Ask a couple of volunteers to come and
hold the jars, and either put an LED candle
in each, or a few, lit, glowsticks. Explain
that these are their lamps, and they need
to look after them like the bridesmaids in
the story today.

But you have got a few things to add into the jars. Tear off a piece of yellow tissue paper –
this is some kindness. Ask one of your volunteers to pop this into their jar.

Next, tear off a piece of black card. This is some unfriendly words. Ask your other volunteer to add this into their jar.

Keep doing this with more yellow tissue paper going into the yellow jar, and more black card going into the other jar. Name the yellow pieces things like 'generosity', 'patience', 'honesty', 'unselfishness', 'love' and 'friendship'. Name the pieces of card things like 'selfishness', 'greed', 'lies', 'violence', 'hatred', and 'resentment'.

When the jars are filled up with tissue paper or card, have a look at them. Which of them is still glowing? (You might need to place another piece of black card behind each jar so that the light inside them shows up better.)

Explain that this is like us, being ready for Jesus. Those lazy bridesmaids in Jesus' story forgot to bring spare oil with them, and their lamps went out. If we forget to keep topping up the oil in our lamps with the right things, all those good actions which God leads us and strengthens us to do, we will be tempted to take the easier option and get into the habit of covering our light with things which put it out, instead.

Luckily, we can always come before God and bring him our lives, just as they are. If we are ready to change, he will help us to take away those things which stop us shining with his love (take out the pieces of black card from the jar as you explain this). As we pray to him and ask his forgiveness, he will give us a fresh, new start in his strength. We don't need to wait to do this – God is always ready to listen and forgive. Both jars will now be bright and glowing.

Add in a few pieces of yellow tissue paper to the jar which used to have the card inside. God fills us with his love, his strength, his holiness, his joy and his peace. All these things will help us as we choose to live his way.

Children's Corner

The children can enjoy playing with a variety of lamps: camping lanterns, electric tea lights, glowstick lamps, nightlights.

The colouring sheet shows the bridesmaids waiting, ready, with their glowing lamps. **'Matthew 25:1-13'** is written on the sheet for parents and carers to look up later.

Little Kids' Sunday School

With some long matches help the children to take it in turns to light a candle and then blow it out. You'll know your children best, and which of them will need hand-over-hand assistance and which can give it a go alone. Explain to them about how to hold the match with their hand down and the flame up, so they don't burn themselves, and how to move the match away when they blow it out so they don't blow out their just-lit candle.

Use a candle to help tell the story of the wise and foolish bridesmaids. Light the candle and explain that Jesus told a story where there were some bridesmaids waiting in the darkness to welcome home the bridegroom. Their lamps weren't quite like the candle here. They had a wick, just like this candle, but rather than solid wax, the wick was hanging in a pool of oil. When the oil ran out, the lamp would go out. As they waited, their lamps started to run out of oil.

Some of the bridesmaids had been wise. They had brought along a jar of oil to keep filling up their lamp when it ran low. The other bridesmaids asked for some of their oil. But the wise bridesmaids refused. If they shared their oil then nobody would have a lamp still lit when the bridegroom returned! The foolish bridesmaids went off to find more oil, and while they were gone, they missed out on seeing the bridegroom returning.

We need to keep our light shining, God's light of love in our lives. How do we do that? We need to make sure we keep spending time with him, praying and worshipping him, by ourselves and with the rest of the community of faith.

Draw ten little oil lamps for each child on ten small stickers. Stick one on the end of each finger. As they retell the story, they can bend down the five lamps that go out, and keep the other five shining.

Big Kids' Sunday School

Play a game of 'How Long Can You Hum?' First of all, challenge the children to take a deep breath in, and on the count of three all begin to hum. Who can carry on humming longest? Now explain that they're allowed to take in a little breath from time to time as long as they start humming again straight away. How long can they hum now? Basically forever! Or at least until lunchtime.

Have two little pottery containers with two string wicks. Explain that these were the kind of lamps that people used in the time of Jesus, and still used until relatively recently. They were powered by oil. You can pour a tiny dribble of olive oil into both lamps and light the wicks. Jesus told the story of some bridesmaids who were staying up late to welcome home the bridegroom. He was a long time coming, and their lamps were using up all the oil. Have a look in your lamps. Is there much left? They realised that their lamps were going to go out before the bridegroom came back. Some of the bridesmaids had brought more oil with them, so topped up their lamp. You can do this to one of the lamps. But the other bridesmaids hadn't. They asked to borrow some oil, but then there wouldn't have been enough to keep any lamps alight. And look what happened to their lamp, as it ran out of oil. Hopefully by this point your un-topped-up lamp will be guttering and about to go out.

Who are we in this story? What do you think the lamps mean? What do you think the oil is? Why do you think Jesus told this story?

Like our humming game at the beginning, we can't just tank up with worship and prayer, with reading the Bible and spending time in a community of Christians, with time spent in God's company, and then expect that to keep us going forever. The biggest breath in the world couldn't have made us hum until lunchtime. We need to keep breathing in, we need to keep our connection with the God who loves us, so that our light will keep shining in the world.

The children can use clay to shape their own lamp, with a bit of string in to be the wick. They might like to light them in church if you come in during the service, so that the congregation can use them as a reflection to help them think about those things that keep their lamp lit.

Matthew 25:1-13

USING OUR GIFTS WISELY

Readings

- Zephaniah 1:7, 12-18
- Psalm 90:1-8 (9-11), 12
- 1 Thessalonians 5:1-11
- Matthew 25:14-30

Thoughts on the Readings

Don't be apathetic or underestimate God's power – the people who think 'I'm ok', without a concern for their neighbour, will be the ones who will lose out on the wealth and property that they have amassed. Their wealth will be worth nothing in the time of God's judgement. There is no point in trusting money to save us – it is better to use our lives to serve God and help others as best we can.

Today's psalm reminds us that our lives are a small and fleeting part of God's amazing, wonderful and eternal creation. He has the creative power to begin things, to end things, and to bring new life all over again. The Psalmist tells that we have come from dust – which of course, in the long view of things is absolutely true. All the dust and rock that swirled around in space, eventually forming the earth on which we live, provided the basic components from which our own bodies are built. And eventually, when we have died, our bodies will become ash, or will compost down to become part of the earth again.

Jesus' parable about the talents highlights how those things that we are given in our lives are there to be used for good, for God's glory. It doesn't matter whether we are given a little, or a lot, what we do with it is the important thing. And we are not to sit around putting it off, either.

We may think that what we have to offer is not enough to make a difference – our skills and experience may not be as good as someone else's, or we may not be able to commit as much time or money to something as we would like. We don't need to despair. If we offer what we can do, rather than what we can't, God can use this for his glory.

Our lives are short, in the grand scheme of things. Whatever actions we can do, however small or insignificant we may think that they are, are worth getting on with. They are all essential contributions that can make a difference in the important work of building God's kingdom.

Discussion Starters

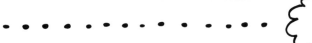

- First of all, what actions to make the world a better place do we feel unable to take because they are too big/difficult/expensive (e.g. replant the rainforest)? Now, what small actions are we actually able to do (e.g. plant a tree, donate to a charity which helps restore the natural environment, choose ethical options in the shops)? Are there ways in which we can support each other within the church with this?

Intercessions

**Generous God, you have blessed us,
use our lives for your glory.**

Lord, when we think
of the enormity of your creation
and your eternal nature,
we feel small in your sight.
May our sense of wonder
lead to worship
as we come to know you more.

We give thanks for the chance
to worship together as a community
and we are grateful for the diversity
of gifts that you have blessed us with.
May we be appreciative and respectful
of others' talents
as we work together for your kingdom.
**Generous God, you have blessed us,
use our lives for your glory.**

In awe of the universe which you have created,
we repent of the times we have thought of the world
as being there for us to exploit.
As part of your creation,
may we care for the earth
and all who live on it,
learning to live in peace
and without greed.
**Generous God, you have blessed us,
use our lives for your glory.**

We bring into your loving presence
those whose lives are a daily struggle,
who carry on within the limitations of their own bodies in spite of pain and disability,
and those who courageously live with anxiety, depression and other conditions.
We pray that you would bring your love and healing
to those known to us who are in need, including . . .
**Generous God, you have blessed us,
use our lives for your glory.**

In wonder at your eternal nature
and in awe at your majesty,
we give thanks that at the end of our brief earthly lives,
your welcome awaits us in heaven.
We pray that you would give peace to those
who are on the last part of that journey,

and we name before you those who have died, including . . .
**Generous God, you have blessed us,
use our lives for your glory.**

May our lives reflect your glory,
may our actions show your love,
may our words be ones of kindness,
may we be one with you.
Amen.

Children's Prayer

Holy God,
the universe you have made
    is amazing,
the billions of stars out there
and all the planets
show that it is bigger
than we can ever imagine.
But you know us,
    you love us,
and we are so thankful.
Amen.

Other Ideas!

Show some pictures on a slideshow of stars and planets, as well as some beautiful and awe-inspiring places on earth.

All-age Talk

First, create two sets of cards of different colours. One set has various needs on it, and the other has things which can help with these needs. These might include things like:

Need to learn to swim / swimming pool

Feeling cold / blanket

Refugee with no home / mansion

Feeling hungry / packet of biscuits

Need a lift to hospital / car

Have to tie hair up for PE or will get detention / hairband

Give out the second set of cards to people, telling them that each of the cards tells them about a really special and important gift. All these gifts are just as valuable as each other.

Ask people to read out what is on their card. A swimming pool – wonderful! A hairband – you must be really excited!

Would anyone prefer a different gift? Does it seem fair?

We are given all sorts of things by God. Sometimes they are things which are seen as important and valuable by the world around us, like the swimming pool, car or mansion. Sometimes we are given things to share which seem very ordinary, and not important at all, like the packet of biscuits, the hairband or the blanket. But in God's eyes, it is what we do with the gifts that is most important.

Now give out the 'needs' cards to some other people, and ask them to read them out. Does anyone have something that can help them? Lovely!

By using the things that we have, we can make a real difference to others, and show them something of God's love and generosity. The slave who hid his one single talent in the ground may have thought that it was too little to make a difference, compared to the amount that other people had. But Jesus' point is that whatever gifts God gives us will be just what is needed to help in his kingdom.

Children's Corner

Provide a treasure chest filled with paper, crayons, and stickers. Should they leave the things inside or use them? If they leave them in the treasure chest, they'll still be here later. But if they use them to make beautiful pictures to share with everyone in church, that would be using them wisely for God's glory.

The colouring sheet shows a child with thought bubbles of all the different things they can do with their talents to spend them wisely and well. The writing reads, **'We use our gifts for your glory'**.

Little Kids' Sunday School

Look up a recipe for a no-bake treat that you think the children in Sunday school would like to make. Buy the ingredients and put them in a box along with a mixing bowl and whatever else you need. Wrap it up, and tie on a label reading, 'Sorry, I can't be here this week. Can you look after these until I get back?'

Help the children to discover the parcel. What could be inside? Read the note together, and open it up. Look at all the things. How very interesting. What should we do? Some children might say 'Let's do baking!' but others might say that the note said we had to look after the things. Sit with this for the moment.

Tell the story we have today, a story Jesus told about a rich man and his servants. The rich man was going away for a long time, so he called his servants to him and gave them some of his money to look after. The first servant was given ten bags of gold. The second was given five bags of gold. And the third was given one bag of gold. The first servant went off and invested his money, spending it on things that would make him more money. He ended up with ten bags of gold more than he'd had in the first place. The second servant did the same. He ended up with five bags of gold more than he'd had in the first place. The third servant was afraid and hid his money in the ground. When the rich man came home, he was overjoyed to see how well the first servant and the second servant had looked after his money. But when the third servant showed that his money was still exactly as he'd left it, he was cross. 'Why didn't you look after my money wisely?' he asked.

Maybe we should look after this parcel wisely. How could we use what's in there to make something better? Something that could be enjoyed by more people?

Enjoy cooking together, and share out what you made after church. As you cook, talk together about the other things we have that we can use to make the world a better place. What are their talents? How could they use them for God's glory?

Big Kids' Sunday School

Set out a stage area, with some curtains if you can manage it. Bling it up to be as glitzy as you like. Tell the children you're going to have a talent show, and give them five minutes to sort out a talent to perform. Everyone's got something! Sit back and enjoy each other's talents.

What a talented bunch you all are! The word talent comes from an old unit of weight, which was used for money as the equivalent of how much gold a cow would weigh. Bit by bit, as language changed, it started to mean a more general idea of measuring something, summing something up. And eventually to the meaning we have, of the things that we are good at.

Jesus told a story that's called 'The Parable of the Talents'. At the time he was speaking, people would have understood the 'talent' to mean the big pile of gold. But Christians have always understood the story to refer to talents as we know them, the things that we are good at.

Once there was a rich man. He was going away for a long while, so he gave some of his money to his servants for safe keeping. To one servant he gave ten talents (give them ten coins), to another he gave five talents (give them five coins), and to a third servant he gave one talent (give them one coin). The first servant took the money and used it to make more money. Soon he had twenty talents (give them ten more coins). The second servant took the money and used it to make more money too. Soon he had ten talents (give them five more coins). The third servant was afraid to risk his money, so he buried it. When the rich man came back, he summoned the servants to him, and asked to see his money. The first servant showed him how much money he had made (hold out the twenty coins). The second servant showed him how much money he had made (hold out the ten coins). The rich man was very pleased. The third servant showed him the money he had dug up from its hiding place in the ground. The rich man was cross. 'Why did you not use the money wisely?' he said.

Do you think the rich man was fair? Why do you think the third servant hid the money? What do you think Jesus meant by this story? Does 'talents' mean money, or skills, or something else?

Find instructions for folding an origami purse online. The children can write on the 'inside' side of their origami paper the things that God has given to them that they want to try to use wisely. When the origami purse is folded, it will be filled with these 'talents'.

WE USE OUR GIFTS FOR YOUR GLORY

JESUS IS OUR SHEPHERD KING

Readings

- Ezekiel 34:11-16, 20-24
- Psalm 95:1-7
- Ephesians 1:15-23
- Matthew 25:31-46

Thoughts on the Readings

God is like a shepherd, looking after his sheep. He particularly cares for those who have been pushed out and excluded by others. God's kind, restorative and gentle care will bring together all those who have been scattered. The 'fat' sheep who have looked after themselves at others' expense will see the consequences of this.

Jesus' teaching in the Gospel reading also reminds us of how our attitude should be towards others. His words are challenging – it is that practical action of caring towards others which shows the real attitude of our heart towards God. And not just caring for those who are the easiest or most appealing. Jesus also says that when we visit those in prison, we are doing it for him. As we pass people in the street who are homeless, addicted to drugs or alcohol, when we see families in need, struggling to cope with their children's behaviour, and when we see elderly people sitting vacantly in their care homes, we can feel a sense of hopelessness and guilt. We may well want to help, we may not be sure how to, and this sometimes results in us choosing to ignore the people in front of us.

Perhaps we can start by acknowledging this. We can't always solve all the problems we come across, but perhaps we can get into some habits of kindness which might help a little. The human contact which comes from a smile or a kind word can make the difference to someone's day. Perhaps if the weather is hot, we might be able to carry a few paper cups with us as well as our own bottle of water, to offer a drink to those we see who are homeless, or share something from our bag of shopping with them. Of course, there are often other organisations who are able to help with the underlying issues, and it is good to support them as well as to help publicise the services which are available too.

In the reading from Ephesians we are given a wonderful picture of the glory of God, his authority and power, his wisdom and greatness. Who are we to think that we are more important than anyone else, more deserving of wealth or comfort than others? Compared to God himself, we are all so small. Through listening to his wisdom and learning from his example as a shepherd King, we can start to take on board this way of loving and caring for others and for the world, treating people as children of God, valuable and of worth.

Discussion Starters

- **What does a shepherd do in their job?
And what does this tell us about God?**

Intercessions

**Shepherd King,
we thank you for your care.**

Lord, we thank you
that you help us, lead us,
care for us and feed us.
As we come before you,
refresh us today.

We give thanks for the church
and for those in leadership.
We pray that you would strengthen and inspire them,
filling them with your wisdom
as they seek to act with care, compassion and good sense.
We also pray for those people
who are prayerfully considering your call to leadership
and ask that you would bless them
and lead them as they seek you.
**Shepherd King,
we thank you for your care.**

We pray for our world
and for those who hold economic, political,
cultural or religious power.
We pray that their actions
would lead to kindness, compassion,
equity and justice.
We also pray for anyone who has felt excluded
by the community to which they had felt that they belonged
and ask that you would bring healing and reconciliation.
**Shepherd King,
we thank you for your care.**

We bring before you those
who have suffered from discrimination
and those whose health conditions
are little understood.

We also pray for those known to us
who are suffering or in need, including . . .
**Shepherd King,
we thank you for your care.**

In your loving, heavenly presence,
we remember those who have died
and pray that you would comfort those
who miss them and were part of their lives.
We name before you those
who are now at rest with you, including . . .
**Shepherd King,
we thank you for your care.**

God of heaven, inspire us to love,
give us courage to act with compassion
in the face of opposition
and misunderstanding
as we look towards you.
Amen.

Children's Prayer

King of heaven,
like a shepherd,
    you feed us,
you help us, you lead us,
with your love, you
    heal us
and you care for
    our needs.
Amen.

Other Ideas!

Show a picture or video clip
of sheep happily grazing in
a field.

All-age Talk

Bring along a toy sheep (a cuddly one if
possible), and ask a volunteer to come and
look after it. Also bring along some sort of
crown (paper is fine) and some sort of robe
(an old curtain or a blanket is fine).

Explain that today we are thinking about how Jesus is our King – but a very different sort of King to what people might imagine.

Put the crown on the head of your volunteer, and the cloak around their shoulders. Jesus is King of earth and heaven, and he was there from the very beginning. He is full of glory, wisdom, and majesty. There aren't any kings on earth to compare to him.

But what about this lovely sheep? As well as being a King, Jesus is like a good, kind shepherd.

What do shepherds do? They give their sheep food, and take them to places they can drink good, clean water. Shepherds find somewhere their sheep can rest for the night, and make sure that they are safe from any predators. Shepherds rescue their sheep when they wander off and get lost, or if they get stuck in a hedge. They help them get the prickles and sticks out of their wool and care for their injuries if they are hurt.

Your volunteer can pretend to feed/ stroke / look after the sheep if they would like to.

God is like this with us. He leads us through life, he cares for us and feeds us, he looks after us and loves us. And as we come to know him more and more, he will give us his love to share with others, too. As we choose to care for others, to give people a drink when they are thirsty, something to eat when they are hungry, and a smile or kind word if they are sad, we will become more like Jesus.

Children's Corner

Provide a basket of crowns and tiaras for the children to try on, so they can dress up as kings and queens, as we celebrate Jesus being our King.

The colouring sheet shows Jesus, as a shepherd King, wearing a crown on his head, leading his flock of sheep towards the grass, beside the water. The writing reads, **'Jesus our King is like a shepherd, looking after his sheep'**.

Little Kids' Sunday School

Stick a picture of a king on one side of the room, and a shepherd on the other side of the room. Call out different things that one might do, and the children have to run to the right side of the room. These might include: sit on a throne, sleep in a field, eat posh food, check their animals for diseases, drink champagne, look after newborn lambs.

It isn't too hard to see the differences between kings and shepherds. They live quite a different life. But today in church we are thinking of how Jesus is our King, and yet our Bible reading talks of how God is like a shepherd. The children can all turn into sheep as you look after them. God says he will look for his sheep when they are lost (you can do this as they baaah in hidden places). God says he will find them good grass to eat (you can find them a 'grassy' patch and they can nibble it). God says he will help his sheep find a safe place to sleep (herd them somewhere safe so they can lie down). God says he will bandage up his injured sheep and heal them (pretend to do some sheep first-aid).

So Jesus is our King, but he is not a King like we sometimes think of kings. He is a shepherd King. The children can make cardboard crowns but decorate them with tufts of cotton wool, to remember the special way that Jesus is our King.

Big Kids' Sunday School

Provide some leaflets for charities and groups that help others, locally, nationally, and internationally. Make sure some of the charities are Christian ones, but try to ensure that at least some of them are non-faith based. Have a look through the kinds of things they do. Maybe you'd like to sort them into groups based on the kind of work they're involved with. Have any of the children heard of some of these before? Can they think of some other charities or organisations that help people?

Read Matthew 25:31-46. How does it fit in with those leaflets we looked at earlier? What about the charities that aren't Christian charities? What do you think God feels about what they're doing? Does this Bible passage give you a clue? Can people who are not part of the church be part of God's mission in the world?

Give the children a chance to put some of this in practice. Maybe you could use the time to collect some ideas from them about what they'd like to do in the light of the Gospel reading today. Maybe you could bring along some ideas for things they could do today? Perhaps they could sort out the Foodbank box? Maybe they could write letters to send to a missionary partner your church supports? What about sorting through and folding clothes to send to refugees?

Jesus our King is like a shepherd, looking after his sheep

LECTIONARY HEADINGS